I0754700

A GUIDE

TO THE

SCIENTIFIC KNOWLEDGE

OF THINGS FAMILIAR;

BY

REV. DR. BREWER,

TRINITY HALL, CAMBRIDGE,

Head Master of King's College School, Norwich—in union with King's College, London.

Carefully Revised, and adapted for use in Families and Schools of the United States.

NEW YORK:

JAMES MILLER, 522 BROADWAY,

(SUCCESSOR TO C. S. FRANCIS & CO.)

1864.

PREFACE.

No science is more generally interesting than that which explains the common phenomena of life. We see that salt and snow are both white, a rose red, leaves green, and the violet a deep purple; but how few persons ever ask the reason why! We know that a flute produces a musical sound, and a cracked bell a discordant one—that fire is hot, ice cold, and a candle luminous—that water boils when subjected to heat, and freezes from cold; but when a child looks up into our face and asks us "why"—how many times is it silenced with a frown, or called "very foolish for asking such silly questions!" The object of the present book is to explain about 2000 of these questions (which are often more easily asked than answered) in language so simple that a child may understand it, yet not so childish as to offend the scientific. In order to secure the strictest accuracy in the answers, the most approved modern authors have been consulted, and each edition has been submitted to the revision of gentlemen of acknowledged reputation for scientific attainments. Sincere thanks are due to the REV. A. BATH POWER, M. A., and to ROBERT JAMES MANN, ESQ., M. R. C. S., of Buxton, for their most careful revisions of the whole book, for many excellent hints and useful additions. In conclusion, the almost unparalleled success of this little volume, of which 25,000 copies have been printed, since the year 1848, is an incontrovertible proof of its acceptability; and has induced the author to spare neither labor nor expense to render his "Guide to the Scientific Knowledge of Things Familiar" instructive and amusing to the young, as well as to those of maturer life.

To teachers of schools it may be advisable to state, that, as every question has been again and again submitted to a most rigid investigation, no material alterations will be made in future editions.

A remarkable instance came before the author a few months since of the statement made in the early part of this preface. The conversation was about smoke—why it was black, and not white like the fine dust of lime. A little child who was present, asked, "Why is the kettle so black with smoke?" Her papa answered, "Because it has been on the fire;" "But" (urged the child) "what is the good of its being black?" The gentleman replied, "Silly child—you ask very foolish questions—sit down and hold your tongue." He might have read pp. 185, and 186, and answered the child more discreetly.

THE AMERICAN PUBLISHERS offer their revised edition of this useful book, in full confidence that it will meet with an equal and universal acceptance both in families and schools, throughout this country. They believe it will be found to contain an amount of useful information never before collected in a shape so convenient for study, and so easy for reference.

SUBJECTS OF THE CHAPTERS.

PART I.—HEAT.

PART II.—AIR.

PART III.—MISCELLANEOUS.

PART I.

HEAT.

INTRODUCTION.

Q. *What is* HEAT?

A. The sensation of warmth.

Q. *How is this sensation produced?*

A. When we touch a substance hotter than ourselves, *a subtile invisible stream* flows from the *hotter substance*, and produces on our nerves the "sensation of warmth."

Q. *What is that "subtile invisible stream"* CALLED, *which flows from the hotter substance?*

A. CALO RIC. *Caloric*, therefore, is the *agent*, which produces the *sensation of warmth*; but HEAT is the *sensation itself*.

Q. *What are the four principal* SOURCES *of heat?*

A. 1.—The Sun. 2.—Electricity. 3.—Chemical Action; and 4.—Mechanical Action.

Q. *What are the principal* EFFECTS *of heat?*

A. Expansion, Liquefaction, Vaporization, and Ignition.

CHAPTER I.

THE SUN.

Q. *What is the* PRINCIPAL *source of heat?*

A. The SUN.

Q. *Why do* BURNING GLASSES *set fire to substances submitted to their power?*

A. Because, when the rays of the Sun pass *through* the burning glass, they are bent toward *one point*, called the "focus;" in consequence of which, the light and heat at *this point* are very greatly increased.

Q. *Why is there a* DARK RIM *round this focus?*

A. Because the rays of light are bent *from the rim* into the *focus;* and, as the rim is *deprived of these rays*, it is darkened.

Q. *Are* ALL *the rays bent into one point?*

A. Not quite all: and, therefore, the rim round the focus is *not quite* black, but only dim.

CHAPTER II.

ELECTRICITY.

Q. *What is the* SECOND *chief source of heat?*

A. ELECTRICITY.

Q. *What is* LIGHTNING?

A. Lightning is *accumulated electricity* discharged *from the clouds.*

Like that from a "Leyden jar."

Q. *What* CAUSES *the discharge of an electric cloud?*

A. When a cloud, *overcharged* with electric fluid, approaches another which is *undercharged,* the fluid rushes from the former into the latter, till both contain the same quantity.

N. B. It is generally supposed that there are two different sorts of Electricity—one Vitreous, and the other Resinous.

Q. *Is there any* OTHER *cause of lightning, besides the one just mentioned?*

A. Yes; sometimes mountains, trees, and steeples, will discharge the lightning *from* a cloud floating near; and sometimes electric fluid rushes *out of the earth* into the clouds.

Q. *What produces* ELECTRICITY *in the* CLOUDS?

A. 1st—The *evaporation* from the earth's surface;

2dly—The *chemical changes*, which take place on the earth's surface; and

3dly—Currents of air of unequal temperature, which excite electricity by *friction*, as they pass by each other.

Q. *How* HIGH *are the* LIGHTNING CLOUDS *from the earth?*

A. Sometimes they are elevated 4 or 5 miles high; and sometimes actually *touch the earth* with one of their edges: but they are rarely *discharged* in a thunder storm, when they are more than 700 yards above the surface of the earth.

Q. *How high are the clouds* GENERALLY?

A. In a *fine day*, the clouds are often 4 or 5 miles above our heads; but the *average* height of the clouds is from 1½ to 2 miles.

Q. *Why is lightning sometimes* FORKED?

A. Because the lightning-cloud is a *long way off;* and the *resistance of the air* is so great, that the electrical current is diverted into a zig-zag course.

Q. *How does the resistance of the air make the lightning zig-zag?*

A. As the lightning *condenses* the air in the immediate advance of its path, it flies from side to side, in order to pass where there is the *least resistance.*

Q. *Why are there sometimes* TWO *flashes of forked lightning at the same moment?*

A. Because (in very severe storms) the flash will divide *into two or more parts;* each of which will assume the zig-zag form.

Q. *Why is the* FLASH *sometimes quite* STRAIGHT?

A. Because the lightning-cloud is *near the earth;* and, as the flash meets with very little resistance, it is *not diverted;* (in other words) the flash is straight.

Q. *What is* SHEET LIGHTNING?

A. Either the *reflection of distant flashes* not distinctly visible; or else several flashes intermingled.

Q. *What* OTHER *form does lightning occasionally assume?*

A. Sometimes the flash is *globular;* which is the most *dangerous* form of lightning.

Q. *What are those* BALLS *of* FIRE, *which sometimes fall to the earth in a thunder-storm?*

A. Masses of explosive gas, formed in the air: they generally move more slowly than lightning.

Q. *Why are* BALLS *of* FIRE *so very* DANGEROUS?

A. Because, when they fall, they

explode like a cannon; and occasion much mischief.

Q. *Do these* BALLS *of* FIRE *ever run along the ground?*

A. Yes; sometimes they run a considerable way along the ground, and explode *in a mass*:

At other times they *split* into numerous *smaller balls*, each of which explodes in a similar manner.

Q. *What* MISCHIEF *will these balls of fire produce?*

A. They will set houses and barns on fire; and kill all cattle and human beings, which happen to be in their course.

Q. *Why does* LIGHTNING *sometimes* KILL *men and beasts?*

A. Because (when the electric current passes through a man or beast) it produces so *violent an action upon the nerves*, that it destroys life.

Q. WHEN *is a person struck* DEAD *by lightning?*

A. Only when his body forms a part of the *lightning's path;* i. e. when the electric fluid (in its way to the earth) actually passes *through his body.*

Q. *Why are* MEN *sometimes* MAIMED *by lightning?*

A. Because the electric fluid produces an *action upon the nerves sufficient to injure* them, but not to *destroy life.*

Q. *What is* THUNDER?

A. The noise made by the concussion of the air when it *closes* again, after it has been parted by the lightning flash.

A part of the noise is owing to certain *physical and chemical changes* produced in the air by the electric fluid.

Q. *Why does* LIGHTNING *part the air through which it passes? it does not part a rod of iron.*

A. As iron is a *conductor*, it allows the fluid to pass *freely over it;* but air (being a *non-conductor*) *resists* its passage.

Q. *Why is* THUNDER *sometimes* ONE VAST CRASH?

A. Because the lightning-cloud is *near the earth;* and as all the vibrations of the air (on which sound depends) reach the ear at *the same moment*, they seem like *one vast sound.*

Q. *Why is the* PEAL *sometimes an* IRREGULAR, *broken* ROAR?

A. Because the lightning-cloud is a long way off; and as *some* of the vibrations of the air have much further to travel than *others*, they reach the ear at *different times*, and produce a *continuous sound.*

Q. *Which vibrations will be soonest heard?*

A. Those produced in the *lowest* portions of the air.

Q. *Why will those vibrations be heard* FIRST, *which are made* LAST?

A. Because the flash (which produces the sound) is almost *instantaneous*, but sound takes a whole *second of time* to travel 380 yards.

Q. *If a thunder-cloud were* 1900 *yards off, how long would the peal last?*

A. *Five seconds:* we should *first* hear the vibrations produced in those portions of the air *contiguous to the earth;* then those *more remote;* and it would be 5 seconds before those vibrations reached us, which were made in the immediate *vicinity of the cloud.*

$$380 \times 5 = 1900.$$

A popular method of telling how far the storm is off is this—Immediately you see the flash, put your hand upon your pulse, and count how many times it beats before you hear the thunder: if it beats 6 pulsations, the storm is 1 mile off; if 12 pulsations, it is 2 miles off, and so on.

Q. *Why is the* THUNDER *sometimes like a deep* GROWL?

A. Because the storm is *far distant*, and the sound of the thunder indistinct.

Q. *Is not the sound of thunder affected by* LOCAL *circumstances?*

A. Yes; the *flatter* the country, the more unbroken the peal. *Mountain* scenery *breaks* the peal, and makes it harsh and irregular.

Q. *What is the cause of* ROLLING THUNDER?

A. The vibrations of air (having *different lengths* to travel) reach the ear at *successive intervals.*

The reverberation (or echo) amongst the massive clouds contributes in some measure to this effect.

Q. *Why is a flash of lightning generally followed by* POURING RAIN?

A. The flash produces a change in the *physical condition of the air*, rendering it unable to hold so much water in solution as it could before; in consequence of which, a part is given off in heavy *rain.*

Q. *Why is a flash of lightning generally followed by a* GUST OF WIND?

A. Because the *physical condition of the air* is disturbed by the passage of the lightning, and wind is the result of this disturbance.

Q. *Why is there* NO THUNDER *to what is called* SUMMER LIGHTNING?

A. Because the lightning-clouds are *so far distant*, that the sound of the thunder is *lost*, before it reaches the ear.

Q. *Do* THUNDER-BOLTS *ever drop from the clouds?*

A. No; the notion of *thunder-bolts*

arises, either from the *globular* form which lightning sometimes assumes; or else from the gaseous *fire-balls*, which sometimes fall from the clouds.

See page 13.

Q. *Why is the* THUNDER *often several moments* AFTER *the* FLASH?

A. Because it has a long way to come. Lightning travels nearly *a million* times faster than thunder; if, therefore, the thunder has *a long way to come*, it will not reach the earth, till a considerable time *after the flash.*

Q. *Can we not tell the* DISTANCE *of a thunder-cloud, by observing the interval which elapses between the flash and the peal?*

A. Yes; the flash is *instantaneous*,* but thunder will take a whole *second of time* to travel 380 yards: hence, if the flash be 5 seconds before the thunder, the cloud is 1900 yards off. (*See note, p.* 16.)

i. e. $380 \times 5 = 1900$ yards.

Q. *What* PLACES *are most* DANGEROUS *during a* STORM?

A. It is very dangerous to be near a tree, or lofty building; and also to be near a river, or any running water.

* The speed of lightning is so great, that it would go 480 times round the earth in one minute: whereas thunder would go scarcely 13 miles in the same space of time.

Q. *Why is it* DANGEROUS *to be* NEAR *a* TREE, *or lofty building, during a thunder-storm?*

A. Because a tall pointed object (like a tree or spire) will frequently *discharge* a lightning-cloud; and if any one were standing near, the lightning might diverge from the tree, and pass through the fluids of the human body.

Q. *How can a* TREE *or* SPIRE DISCHARGE *a lightning-cloud?*

A. A lightning-cloud (floating over a *plain*) may be *too far off* to be discharged by it; but, as a tree or spire would *shorten* this distance, it might no longer be too far off to be discharged.

For example. If a lightning-cloud were 700 yards above the earth, it would be *too far off* to be discharged: but a tree or spire 50 yards high would make the cloud only 650 yards off a conductor; in consequence of which, the cloud would be instantly *discharged*.

Q. *Is not* AIR *a* CONDUCTOR *of lightning?*

A. No; dry air is *not* a conductor of lightning.

Q. *Why would lightning fly from a tree or spire, into a* MAN *standing near?*

A. Because the electric fluid (called lightning) always chooses for its path the *best conductors;* and, if the human fluids proved the better conductor, would pass through the man standing near the tree rather than down the tree itself.

There would be no danger if the tree or spire were made of *metal;* because metal is a better conductor than the human fluids.

Q. *Does lightning go through the inside, or down the* OUTSIDE *of a tree?*

A. It runs down the *outside* of a *tree;* but passes through the *inside* of a *man.*

Q. *Why does lightning pass down the* OUTSIDE *of a tree?*

A. Because it always makes choice of the *best conductors;* and the *outside* of a tree is a better conductor than the inside.

Q. *Why does lightning pass through the* INSIDE *of a man?*

A. Because the *fluids* of the human body make a better conductor than the *skin;* therefore, lightning passes *through* a man, and not down his skin.

Q. *Why is it* DANGEROUS *to be near a deep* RIVER, *or any other running water, during a thunder-storm?*

A. Because running water is a good conductor; and lightning always takes in its course the *best conductors.*

Q. *Why is it dangerous for a man to be* NEAR WATER *in a thunder-storm?*

A. Because the *height of a man* may be sufficient to discharge a cloud and (if there were no *taller* object nigh) the lightning might make the *man* its conductor to the water.

See note on p. 19.

Q. *Why is it* DANGEROUS *to* RING CHURCH BELLS *during a thunder-storm?*

A. For two reasons: 1st—Because the steeple may *discharge* the lightning-cloud, merely from its *height;* and

2dly—As the swinging of the bells puts the *air in motion*, it diminishes its *resistance* to the electric fluid.

Q. *Why is it unsafe to* RUN *or* DRIVE FAST *during a thunder-storm?*

A. Because it produces a *current of air;* and, as air in motion affords *less resistance* to the flash, it is a better conductor than *air in a state of rest.*

Q. *What* PARTS *of a* DWELLING *are most* DANGEROUS *during a thunder-storm?*

A. The fire-place, especially if the fire be *lighted;* the attics and cellar. It is also imprudent to sit close by the walls, to ring the bell, or to bar the shutters, during a thunder-storm.

Q. *Why is it* DANGEROUS *to sit* BEFORE A FIRE *during a thunder-storm?*

A. Because the heated air and soot are *conductors* of lightning; especially when connected with such excellent conductors as the stove, fender and fire-irons.

Q. *Why are* ATTICS *and* CELLARS *more* DANGEROUS *in a thunder-storm, than the middle story of a house?*

A. Because lightning sometimes passes *from the clouds* to the earth, and sometimes *from the earth* to the clouds; in either cases the *middle story* would be the safer place.

Q. *When does lightning pass* FROM THE EARTH *to the* CLOUDS?

A. When the clouds are in a "negative" state of electricity.

Q. *When does lightning pass* FROM THE CLOUDS *to the* EARTH?

A. When the clouds are in a "positive" state of electricity.

Q. *What is meant by the clouds being in a "positive state of electricity?"*

A. When the clouds contain *more* electric fluid than they *generally* do, they are said to be in a "*positive* state of electricity."

Q. *What is meant by the clouds being in a "negative state of electricity?"*

A. When the clouds contain *less* electric fluid than they ought to do, they are said to be in a "*negative* state of electricity."

Q. *Does the flash proceed from a negative or* POSITIVE *body?*

A. Always from a *positive* body; that is, from one *over*-charged with electric fluid.

It is generally thought that there are two *sorts* of electricity, one called VITREOUS, corresponding to *positive* electricity; and the other called RESINOUS, corresponding to *negative* electricity.

Q. *When lightning flashes from the earth to the clouds, what is the flash called?*

A. It is popularly called the "returning stroke;" because the earth (being over-charged with electric fluid) *returns* the surplus quantity to the clouds.

Q. *Why is it* DANGEROUS *to lean* AGAINST A WALL *during a thunder-storm?*

A. Because the electric fluid will sometimes run down a *wall;* and (as a man is a better conductor than a *wall*) would leave the *wall*, and run down the man.

Q. *Why is it dangerous to* RING *a* BELL *during a thunder-storm?*

A. Bell-wire is an *excellent conductor;* and (if a person were to touch the bell-handle) the electric fluid, passing down the wire, might run through his hand and injure it.

Q. *Why would the lightning run through a man touching a bell-handle?*

A. Because the human body is a better conductor than the *wall* (between the bell-handle and the floor); and as lightning always chooses the *best* conductor for its path, it would (in this case) pass through the *man*, and injure him.

Q *Why is it* DANGEROUS *to* BAR *a* SHUTTER *during a thunder-storm?*

A. Because the iron shutter-bar is an *excellent conductor*; and the electric fluid might run from the bar *through the person touching it*, and injure him.

Q. *Why is it dangerous to be in a* CROWD *during a thunder-storm?*

A. For two reasons: 1st—Because a *mass* of people forms a *better conductor* than an individual; and

2dly—Because the *vapor* arising from a crowd *increases* its conducting power.

Q. *Why is a* MASS *of bodies a better conductor than a single body?*

A. *Each* living body is a *conductor of electricity;* and a connected *mass* of such conductors is more likely to be struck, than a *single individual.*

Q. *Why is the danger increased by the* VAPOR *which rises from a crowd?*

A. Because *vapor* is a conductor; and the more *conductors* there are, the greater the danger will be.

Q. *Why is a* THEATRE *dangerous during a thunder-storm?*

A. Because the *crowd*, and *great vapor* arising from so many living bodies, render it an *excellent conductor of lightning*.

Q. *Why is a* FLOCK *of sheep in greater danger than a smaller number?*

A. 1st—Because *each* sheep is a *conductor* of lightning, and the conducting power of the *flock* is increased by its *numbers:* and

2dly—The very *vapor* arising from a flock of sheep *increases its conducting power*, and its danger.

Q. *Why is a* HERD *of cattle in danger during a storm?*

A. 1st—Because the *number* of living bodies increases the conducting power of their *animal fluids:* and

2dly—The very *vapor* arising from a herd increases its conducting power.

Q. *If a person be* ABROAD *in a thunder-storm, what place is the* SAFEST?

A. Any place about 20 or 30 feet from some tall tree or building; except it be near to running water.

Q. *Why would it be safe to stand* 20 *or* 30 *feet from some tall tree, in a thunder-storm?*

A. Because the lightning would always choose the *tall tree* as a conductor; and we should not be sufficiently *near* the tree, for the lightning to diverge from it to *us*.

Q. *If a person be in* A CARRIAGE *in a thunder-storm, in what way can he travel most* SAFELY?

A. He should not lean *against* the carriage; but sit upright, without touching any of the four sides.

Q. *Why should not a person lean* AGAINST *the carriage in a storm?*

A. Because the electric fluid might run down the sides of the carriage; and (if a person were leaning against them) would make choice of *him* for a conductor, and perhaps destroy life.

Q. *If a person be in* A HOUSE *during a thunder-storm, what place is* SAFEST?

A. Any room in the *middle story*. The middle of the room is best; especially if you place yourself on a mattress, bed, or hearth-rug.

Q. *Why is the* MIDDLE STORY *of a house* SAFEST *in a thunder-storm?*

A. Because the fluid (if it struck the house at all) would be diffused among the several conductors of the *upper* part of the house, before it reached the *middle* story; in consequence of which, its force would be weakened.

Q. *Why is the* MIDDLE *of the* ROOM *more* SAFE *than any other part of it, in a thunder-storm?*

A. Because the lightning (if it struck the room at all) would come down the *chimney*, or *walls* of the room; and, therefore, the further distant from these, the better.

Q. *Why is a* MATTRESS, BED, *or* HEARTH-RUG *a good security against injury from lightning?*

A. Because they are all *non-conductors;* and, as lightning always makes choice of the *best* conductors, it would not choose for its path such things as these.

Q. *Is it better to be* WET *or dry during a storm?*

A. To be *wet:* if a person be in the open field, the best thing he can do, is to stand about 20 feet from some tree, and get *completely drenched to the skin.*

Q. *Why is it better to be* WET *than dry?*

A. Because *wet clothes* form a *better conductor* than the *fluids of our body;* and, therefore, lightning would pass down our wet clothes, *without touching our body at all.*

Q. *What is the* SAFEST *thing a person can do, to avoid injury from lightning?*

A He should draw his bedstead into the middle of the room, commit himself to the care of God, and go to bed; remembering that our Lord has said, "The very hairs of your head are all numbered."

N. B. No great danger needs really to be apprehended from lightning, if you avoid taking your position near tall trees, spires, or other elevated objects.

Q. *What is a* LIGHTNING-CONDUCTOR?

A. A metal rod fixed in the earth, running up the whole height of a building, and rising in a point above it.

Q. *What metal is the best for this purpose?*

A. Copper makes the best conductor.

Q. *Why is* COPPER *better than iron?*

A. 1st—Because copper is a better conductor than iron:

2dly—It is not so easily fused or melted: and

3dly—It is not so much injured by weather.

Q. *What is the* USE *of a lightning-conductor?*

A. As metal is a most excellent conductor, lightning (which makes choice of the *best conductors*) will run down a *metal rod*, rather than the walls of the building.

Q. *How* FAR *will the beneficial influence of a lightning-conductor extend?*

A. It will protect a space all round,

4 times the length of that part of the rod which *rises above the building*.

Q. *Give me an example.*

A. If the rod rise 2 feet above the house, it will protect the building for (at least) 8 feet all round.

Q. *Why are not lightning-conductors more generally used?*

A. Because many accidents have arisen from conductors of defective construction.

Q. *How can lightning-conductors be productive of* HARM?

A. If the rod be *broken* by weather or accident, the electric fluid (being obstructed in its path) will damage the building.

Q. *Is there any other evil to be apprehended from a lightning-rod?*

A. Yes; if the rod be not big enough to conduct the *whole* current to the earth, the lightning will *fuse* the metal, and injure the building.

The conducting rod should be (at least) *one inch* in diameter.

Q. *How does* LIGHTNING *sometimes* KNOCK DOWN HOUSES *and churches?*

A. The steeple or chimney is first struck; the lightning then darts to the iron bars and cramps, employed in the building; and (as it darts from bar to bar) shatters to atoms the bricks and stones which oppose its progress.

Q. *Can you tell me how St. Bride's Church (London) was nearly destroyed by lightning, about* 100 *years ago?*

A. The lightning first struck the metal vane, and ran down the rod; it then darted to the iron cramps, employed to support the building; and (as it flew from bar to bar) smashed the stones of the church which lay between.

Q. *Why did the lightning fly about from place to place, and not pass down in a straight course?*

A. Because it always takes in its course the *best conductors;* and will fly both right and left, in order to reach them.

Q. *Why does* LIGHTNING *turn milk* SOUR?

A. Lightning causes the gases of the air (through which it passes) to *combine,* and thus produces a poison, called *nitric acid;* some small portion of which, mixing with the milk, turns it sour.*

---

* The air is composed of two gases, called oxygen and nitrogen, *mixed* together, but *not combined.* Oxygen *combined* with nitrogen, produces five deadly poisons, viz.—nitrous oxide, nitric oxide, hyponitrous acid, nitrous acid, and nitric acid, according to the proportion of each gas in the combination.

N. B. Sometimes the mere *heat* of the air, during the storm, turns milk sour.

Q. *What is the difference between* COMBINING *and* MIXING?

A. When different ingredients are mingled together *without undergoing any chemical change*, they are said to be *mixed;* but when the natural properties of each are *altered by the union*, then those ingredients are said to be *combined.*

Q. *Give me an example.*

A. Different colored sands (shaken together in a bottle) will *mix* together, but ot combine: but water poured on quicklime, will *combine* with the lime, and not mix with it.

Q. *Why are different grains of sand said to be* MIXED, *when they are shaken together?*

A. Because (though mingled together) the property of each grain remains the *same as it was before.*

Q. *Why is water, poured on lime, said to* COMBINE *with it?*

A. Because the properties of each are *altered* by the mixture; the lime alters the character of the water, and the water that of the lime.

Q. *Do oxygen and nitrogen* COMBINE, *or only* MIX *together, in common atmospheric air?*

A. They only *mix* together, as grains

of sand would do when shaken in a bottle. When oxygen and nitrogen *combine*, they do not constitute *air*, but acid *poisons*. (*See note on p.* 30.)

Q. *Why does* LIGHTNING *turn* BEER SOUR, *although contained in a close cask?*

A. Because, if beer be *new* and the process of fermentation incomplete, lightning will so *accelerate* the process, as to turn the sugar into *acetic acid* at once, without passing through the intermediate state of *al'cohol.*

Q. *Why is* NOT OLD *beer and strong* PORTER *made* SOUR *by lightning?*

A. Because the *fermentation is more complete;* and, therefore, is less affected by electrical influence.

Q. *Why is* METAL *sometimes* FUSED *by lightning?*

A. Because the dimension of the metal is *too small* to afford a path for the electric current.

Q. *Why does* LIGHTNING PURIFY *the* AIR?

A. For two reasons: 1st—Because the electric fluid produces "nitric acid" in its passage through the air:

2dly—Because the agitation of the storm *stirs up the air.*

The "nitric acid" is produced by the *combination* of some portions of the oxygen and nitrogen of the air.*

Q. *How does the production of nitric acid* PURIFY *the air?*

A. Nitric acid acts very powerfully in *destroying the exhalations*, which arise from putrid vegetable and animal matters.

Q. *Why is* LIGHTNING *more common in* SUMMER *and in* AUTUMN, *than in spring and winter?*

A. Because the heat of summer and autumn produces *great evaporation;* and the conversion of *water into vapor* always developes *electricity*.

Q. *Why does a* THUNDER-STORM *generally follow very dry weather?*

A. Because *dry air* (being a non-conductor) will not relieve the clouds of their electricity; so the fluid accumulates, till the clouds are discharged in a storm.

Q. *Why does a* THUNDER-STORM *rarely succeed* WET *weather?*

A. Because moist air or falling rain (being a conductor) carries down the electric fluid gradually and silently to the earth.

Q. *What is the general* DIRECTION *of a* THUNDER-STORM?

---

* The oxygen and nitrogen are not *combined*, but simply *mixed*, in the ordinary air; but lightning causes some portions of the mixed elements to *combine*. See note, p. 30.

A. Either from east to west; or from north to south.

Q. *Why is* ELECTRICITY *excited by* FRICTION?

A. Electricity, like heat, exists in *all* matter; but is often in a *latent state:* friction *disturbs* it, and brings it into active operation.

"Latent," see p. 37.

Q. *Why is a* TREE *sometimes* SCORCHED *by lightning, as if it had been set on fire?*

A. Lightning scorches by its own *positive heat,* just the same as fire would.

Q. *Why is the* BARK *of a* TREE *often ripped quite off by a flash of lightning?*

A. Because the latent heat of the tree (being very rapidly developed by the electric fluid) forces away the bark in its impetuosity to escape.

Some part of this is probably due to the simple *mechanical force* of the lightning.

Q. *Why are* BOUGHS *of* TREES *broken off by lightning?*

A. Because the *mechanical force* of lightning is very great; and, as the boughs of a tree are imperfect conductors, they will often be broken off by this force.

Q. *Why is an electric shock felt* MOST *at the* ELBOW JOINT?

A. Because the path of the fluid is

obstructed by the joint; and the shock (felt at the elbow) is caused by the fluid *leaping from one bone to another.*

Q. *Is electricity accompanied with any* ODOR?

A. Yes; near a large electrical machine in good action, there is always a peculiar odor, resembling *sulphur* and *phosphorus;* this odor is called "OZONE."

Pronounce O-ZONE, in two syllables.

Q. *Has this peculiar odor, called* "OZONE," *been observed in thunder-storms?*

A. Yes; sometimes the *sulphurous* odor prevails, and sometimes the *phosphoric.*

If the gaseous body disengaged by lightning, reaches us in a *concentrated* form, the odor is SULPHUROUS; if in a *diluted* form, it is PHOSPHORIC.

Q. *What are* FUL'GURITES?

A. Hollow tubes produced in sandy soils by the action of lightning.

Q. *How does lightning produce fulgurites?*

A. When it enters the earth, it fuses the flinty matter of the soil into a vitreous (or glassy) substance, called a fulgurite.

Q. *Does not lightning sometimes affect the character of* IRON *and* STEEL?

A. Yes; bars of iron and steel are sometimes rendered *magnetic* by lightning.

Q. *Give me an instance of the magnetic effects of lightning.*

A. Sometimes it will *reverse* the magnetic needles of the electric telegraph, and sometimes *destroy* their magnetism altogether.

Q. *What is meant by the magnetic needles being* REVERSED?

A. That part of the needle which ought to point toward the *north*, is made to point toward the *south*; and that part which ought to point south, is made to point toward the north.

Q. *How does lightning act upon the magnetic needles of the electric telegraph?*

A. The electric fluid is conveyed along the *conducting wires* to the telegraphic needles.

CHEMICAL ACTION.

CHAPTER III.

Q. *What is the* THIRD *chief source of heat?*

A. CHEMICAL ACTION.

Q. *What is meant by chemical action being the source of heat?*

A. Many things, when their chemical constitution is changed (either by the abstraction of some of their gases, or by the combination of others not before united) evolve *heat*, while the change is going on.

Q. *Explain by illustration what you mean.*

A. Water is cold, and sulphuric acid is cold; but if these two *cold* liquids be mixed together, they will produce *intense heat.*

Q. *Why does* COLD WATER, *poured on* LIME, *make it intensely* HOT?

A. Because heat is evolved by the *chemical action* which takes place, when the cold water combines with the lime.

N. B. Heat is always *evolved*, when a fluid is converted into a *solid* form. Heat is always *absorbed*, when a solid is changed into a *liquid* state. As the water is changed from its liquid form when it is taken up by the lime, therefore, heat is given off.

Q. *Where does the heat come from?*

A. It was in the water and lime before; but was in a *latent state.*

Q. *Was there heat in the cold water and lime, before they were mixed together?*

A. Yes. *All* bodies contain heat; the coldest ice, as well as the hottest fire.

Q. *Is there* HEAT *even in* ICE?

A. Yes; but it is *latent* (i. e., not perceptible to our senses.)

Latent, from the Latin word Lateo, (to lie hid.)

Q. *How do you* KNOW *there is heat, if you cannot* PERCEIVE *it?*

A. Thus:—Ice is 32° by the thermometer; but if ice be melted over a fire, (though 140° of heat are absorbed by the process,) it will feel no *hotter* than before.

i. e., it will be only 32°, and not 172°.*

Q. *What becomes of the* 140° *which went into the ice to melt it?*

A. It is hidden in the water; or (to speak more scientifically) it is stored up in a *latent state.*

Q. *How* MUCH *heat may be thus secreted or made latent?*

A. *All* things contain a vast quantity of latent heat; but as much as 1140° of heat may remain latent in *water.*

Q. *How can* 1140° *of heat be added to water, without being perceptible to our feelings?*

A. 1st—140° of heat are hidden in water, when *ice is melted* by the sun or fire.

2dly—1000° more of heat are secreted, when water is converted into *steam.* Thus, before *ice* is converted into steam, 1140° of heat become *latent.*

One pint of boiling water, (212° according to the thermometer,) will make 1800 pints of steam; but the steam is no hotter to the touch than boiling water—both are 212°; therefore, when water is converted into steam, 1000°

* 32°, i. e., 32 degrees; 140°, i. e., 140 degrees, &c.

of heat become latent. Hence, before ice is converted into steam, it must contain 1140° of latent heat.

Q. *Can we be made to* FEEL *the heat of* ICE *or snow?*

A. Yes. Into a pint of snow put half as much *salt;* then plunge your hands into the liquid; and it will feel so intensely cold, that the snow itself will seem *warm* in comparison to it.

Q. *Is* SALT *and* SNOW *really* COLDER *than snow?*

A. Yes, many degrees; and by dipping your hand into the mixture *first,* and into snow *afterward,* the snow will seem to be comparatively warm.

CHAPTER IV.

COMBUSTION.

Q. *What is* FIRE?

A. Heat and light, produced by the combustion of inflammable substances.

Q. *How is* HEAT *evolved by combustion?*

A. By *chemical action.* As latent heat is liberated, when water is poured upon lime, by chemical action; so latent heat is liberated in *combustion,* by chemical action also.

Q. *What* CHEMICAL ACTION *takes place* IN *combustion?*

A. The *elements of the fuel* combine with the *oxygen of the air.*

Q. *What is meant by the* "ELEMENTS OF FUEL?"

A. As bread is a compound of flour, yeast, and salt; so fuel is a compound of hydrogen and carbon.

Q. *What are the* ELEMENTS *of atmospheric* AIR?

A. Oxygen and nitrogen, *mixed* together in the following proportions; 4 gallons of nitrogen and one of oxygen will make 5 gallons of common air.

Q. *What is* CARBON?

A. The solid part of fuel. Carbon abounds in all animal bodies, earths, and even in some minerals.

Q. *Mention some different species of* CARBON.

A. Common charcoal, lamp-black, coke, and the diamond.

Q. *What is* HYDROGEN?

A. An inflammable gas. The gas used in our streets is hydrogen *driven out of coals by heat.*

Coal gas (more correctly speaking) is carburetted hydrogen, i. e., carbon and hydrogen. See p. 262.

Q. *What are the peculiar characteristics of hydrogen gas?*

A. 1st—It is the *lightest* of all known substances:

2dly—It will burn immediately it is ignited: and

3dly—A lighted candle (immersed in this gas) will be instantly extinguished.*

Q. *What is* OXYGEN?

A. A gas, much heavier than hydrogen; it gives brilliancy to flame, and is essential to animal life.†

---

* Hydrogen gas may be made thus:—Put some pieces of zinc or iron filings into a glass: pour over them a little sulphuric acid (vitriol) diluted with twice the quantity of water; then cover the glass over for a few minutes and hydrogen gas will be given off.

EXPERIMENTS.

If a flame be put into the glass, an EXPLOSION will be made.

If the experiment be tried in a phial, which has a piece of tobacco-pipe run through the cork, and a light held a few moments to the top of a pipe, a FLAME will be made.

If a balloon be held over the phial, (so that the gas can inflate it,) the balloon will ascend in a very few minutes.

† Oxygen gas is much more troublesome to make than hydrogen. The *cheapest* plan is to put a few ounce of manganese (called the black oxide of manganese) into an iron bottle, furnished with a bent tube; set the bottle on a fire till it becomes red hot, and put the end of the tube into a pan of water. In a few minutes, bubbles will rise through the water; these bubbles are oxygen gas.

These bubbles may be collected thus:—Fill a common bottle with water; hold it inverted over the bubbles which rise through the pan, but be sure the mouth of the bottle be held *in the water.* As the bubbles rise into the bottle the water will run out; and when all the water has run out, the bottle is full of gas. Cork the bottle while the *mouth remains under water;* set the bottle on its base; cover the cork with lard or wax, and the gas will keep till it be wanted.

N. B. The *quickest* way of making oxygen gas, is to rub together in a mortar half an ounce of oxide of copper

Q. *What is* NITROGEN ?

A. An invisible gas, which abounds in animal and vegetable substances. The following are its peculiar characteristics :

1. It will not burn ;
2. An animal cannot live in it ;
3. It is the principal ingredient in common air.*

Nearly 4 gallons out of every 5 being nitrogen gas.

---

and half an ounce of chlorate of potassa. Put the mixture into a common oil flask, furnished with a cork which has a bent tube thrust through it. Heat the bottom of the flask over a candle or lamp; and when the mixture is red hot, oxygen gas will be given off. Note—the tube must be immersed in a pan of water, and the gas collected as before.

(Chloride of potassa may be bought at any chemist's; and oxide of copper may be procured by heating a sheet of copper red hot, and when cool, striking it with a hammer; the scales that peel off, are oxide of copper.)

Exp. Put a piece of red hot charcoal (fixed to a bit of wire) into your bottle of oxygen gas; and it will throw out most dazzling sparks of light.

Blow a candle out; and while the wick is still red, hold the candle (by a piece of wire) in the bottle of oxygen gas; the wick will instantly ignite, and burn brilliantly.

(Burning sulphur emits a *blue* flame, when immersed in oxygen gas.)

* Nitrogen gas may easily be obtained thus:—Put a piece of burning phosphorus on a little stand, in a plate of water; and cover a bell glass over it. (Be sure the edge of the glass stands *in the water*.) In a few minutes the *oxygen* of the air will be taken up by the burning phosphorus; and nitrogen alone will be left in the bell glass.

(N. B. The white fume, which will arise and be absorbed by the water in this experiment, is phosphoric acid; i. e. phosphorus combined with oxygen of the air.)

Q. *Why is there so* MUCH *nitrogen in the air?*

A. In order to *dilute* the oxygen. If the oxygen were not thus diluted, fires would burn out too quickly, and life would be too rapidly exhausted.

Q. *What three elements are necessary to produce* COMBUSTION?

A. Hydrogen gas, carbon, and oxygen gas: The two former in the *fuel;* and the last in the *air*, which surrounds the fuel.

Q. *What causes the combustion of the fuel?*

A. The hydrogen gas of the fuel (being set free, and excited by a match), *unites* with the *oxygen of the air*, and makes a yellow flame; this flame heats the *carbon of the fuel*, which (also uniting with oxygen of the air) produces *carbonic acid gas.*

Q. *What is* CARBONIC ACID GAS?

A. Only carbon (or charcoal) combined with oxygen gas.

Q. *Why does* FIRE *produce* HEAT?

A. Because it liberates *latent heat* from the air and fuel.

Q. *What* CHEMICAL CHANGES *in air and fuel are produced by* COMBUSTION?

A. 1st—*Some* of the oxygen of the air, combining with the *hydrogen* of the fuel, condenses into *water:* and

2dly—Some of the oxygen of the air combining with the *carbon* of the fuel, forms *carbonic acid gas.*

Q. *Why is a* FIRE *(after it has been long burning)* RED HOT?

A. Because the whole surface of the coals is so thoroughly heated, that every part of it is undergoing a rapid union with the oxygen of the air.

Q. *In a* BLAZING *fire, why is the* UPPER *surface of the* COALS BLACK, *and the* LOWER *surface* RED?

A. Because carbon (being solid) requires a great degree of heat to make it unite with the oxygen of the air. In consequence of which, the hot *under* surface of coals is frequently *red* from its union with oxygen, while the cold *upper* surface remains *black.*

Q. *Which burns the more quickly, a* BLAZING *fire, or a* RED HOT *one?*

A. Fuel burns quickest in a *blazing* fire.

Q. *Why do* BLAZING COALS BURN QUICKER *than red hot ones?*

A. Because the inflammable *gases* of the fuel (which are then *escaping*) greatly assist the process of combustion.

Q. *Why do the coals of a* CLEAR BRIGHT *fire burn out more slowly than blazing coals?*

A. Because most of the *inflammable*

gases, and much of the *solid fuel*, have been consumed already; so that there is less food for combustion.

Q. *What is* SMOKE?

A. *Unconsumed* parts of fuel (principally carbon) separated from the solid mass, and carried up the chimney by currents of hot air.

Q. *Why is there* MORE SMOKE *when* COALS *are* FRESH *added, than when they are red hot?*

A. Because carbon (being solid) requires a great degree of heat to make it unite with oxygen, (or, in other words, to bring it into a state of perfect combustion:) when coals are fresh laid on, *more carbon is separated* than can be *reduced to combustion*, and the surplus flies off in smoke.

Q. *Why is there so* LITTLE SMOKE *with a* RED HOT FIRE?

A. Because the *entire surface* of the coals is in a *state of combustion;* and, as very little carbon remains unconsumed, there is but little smoke.

Q. *Why are there* DARK *and* BRIGHT SPOTS *in a* CLEAR *cinder* FIRE?

A. Because the *intensity* of the combustion is *greater in some parts* of the fire, than it is in *others*.

Q. *Why is the intensity of the combustion so* UNEQUAL?

A. Because the air flies to the fire in various and unequal currents.

Q. *Why do we see all sorts of* GROTESQUE FIGURES *in hot* COALS?

A. Because the *intensity* of combustion is *unequal*, (owing to the gusty manner in which the air flies to the fuel:) and the various shades of red, yellow, and white heat (mingling with the black of the unburnt coal), produce strange and fanciful resemblances.

Q. *Why does* PAPER BURN *more readily than wood?*

A. Because it is of a *more fragile texture;* and, therefore, its component parts are more easily heated.

Q. *Why does* WOOD BURN *more readily than coal?*

A. Because it is not so *solid;* and, therefore, its elemental parts are more easily separated, and made hot.

Q. *When a* FIRE *is* LIGHTED, *hy is* PAPER *laid at the* BOTTOM, *against the grate?*

A. Because paper (in consequence of its fragile texture) very readily catches fire.

Q. *Why is* WOOD *laid on the top of the paper?*

A. Because wood (being more *substantial*) *burns longer* than paper; and, therefore, affords a *longer contact of flame* to heat the coals.

Q. *Why would not paper do* WITHOUT *wood?*

A. Because paper burns out so *rapidly*, that it would not afford sufficient *contact of flame* to heat the coals to combustion.

Q. *Why will not wood do* WITHOUT *shavings, straw, or paper?*

A. Because wood is too *substantial* to be heated into combustion by the feeble flame issuing from a *match*.

Q. *Why would not the paper do as well, if placed on the* TOP *of the coals?*

A. Because every blaze *tends upward;* if, therefore, the paper were placed on the *top* of the coals its blaze would afford *no contact of flame* to the fuel lying *below*.

Q. *Why should* COAL *be placed* ABOVE *the wood?*

A. Because otherwise, the *flame* of the fuel would not rise *through the coal*, to heat it.

Q. *Why is a* FIRE KINDLED *at the* LOWEST BAR *of a grate?*

A. That the flame may *ascend through the fuel*, to heat it. If the fire were kindled from the *top*, the flame would *not come in contact* with the fue placed below.

Q. *Why does* COAL *make such* EXCELLENT FUEL?

A. Because it contains a large amount of *carbon* and *hydrogen gas*, in a very compact and convenient form.

Q. *Why will* CINDERS *become* RED HOT *more quickly than* COALS?

A. Because they are sooner reduced to a state of combustion, as they are *more porous* and *less solid.*

Q. *Why will not* IRON CINDERS *burn?*

A. Because they contain *impurities*, which are not so ready to combine with oxygen, as *carbon* and *hydrogen* are.

Q. *Why are* CINDERS *lighter than* COALS?

A. Because they are full of little holes; from which vapor, gases, and other volatile parts, have been driven off by *previous combustion.*

Q. *Why will not* STONES *do for fuel as well as* COALS?

A. Because they contain no *hydrogen*, and little or no *carbon.*

Q. *Why will not* WET KINDLING *light a fire?*

A. 1st—Because the moisture of the wet kindling prevents the *oxygen of the air from getting to the fuel;* and

2dly—The heat of the fire is perpetually *drawn off*, by the conversion of *water* into *steam.*

Q. *Why does* DRY *wood burn* BETTER *than* GREEN?

A. 1st—Because none of its heat is *carried away* by the conversion of *water into steam;* and

2dly—The pores of dry wood (being *filled with air*) supply the fire with oxygen.

Q. *Why do* TWO *pieces of* WOOD *burn* BETTER *than* ONE?

A. 1st—Because they help to entangle the *heat of the passing smoke,* and *throw it on the fuel;* and

2dly—The air, impinging against the pieces of wood, is thrown upon the fire in a kind of *eddy* or draught.

Q. *Why does* SALT CRACKLE, *when thrown into a* FIRE?

A. Salt contains *water;* and the *crackling* of the salt is owing to the sudden *conversion of this water into steam.*

Q. *Why will not wood or paper burn if steepea in a solution of* POTASH, *phosphate of* LIME, *or* AMMONIA (*hartshorn*)?

A. Because any "al'kali" (such as potash) will *arrest the hydrogen* which escapes from the fuel, and prevent its *combination* with the *oxygen of air.*

Q. *What is an al'kali?*

A. The con'verse of an *acid:* as

bitter is the con verse of *sweet*, or *insipid* the con'verse of *pungent.*

Q. *Why does a* JET *of* FLAME *sometimes burst into the room* THROUGH THE BARS OF A STOVE ?

A. Because the iron bars conduct heat to the *interior of some lump of coal;* and its volatile gas (bursting through the weakest part) is kindled by the glowing coals over which it passes.

Q. *Why is this* JET *sometimes of a* GREENISH YELLOW *color?*

A. Either because some lump of coal lies *over the hot bars;* or else the coals below it are not *red hot:* in consequence of which, some of the gas *escapes unburnt,* and is of a greenish color.

Q. *Why does the gas escape* UNBURNT ?

A. Because neither the *bars,* nor *coals* over which it passes, are *red hot.*

Q. *Why does a* BLUISH FLAME *sometimes flicker on the surface of hot cinders?*

A. Because the gas from the hot coals *at the bottom of the grate,* mixing with the *carbon of the coals above,* produces an inflammable gas (called carbonic oxide), which burns with a blue flame.

Q. *Why is the* FLAME *of a good fire* YELLOW ?

A. Because both the hydrogen and carbon of the fuel are in a state of *perfect combustion.* It is the *white heat of the carbon*, which gives the pale yellow tinge to the flaming hydrogen.

Q. *What is* LIGHT?

A. Rapid *undulations* of a fluid called *ether*, striking on the eye.

Q. *How does* COMBUSTION *make these undulations of* LIGHT?

A. The atoms of matter (set in motion by heat) *striking against* this ether, produce *undulations* in it; as a *stone* thrown into a stream, produces undulations in the *water*.

Q. *How can* UNDULATIONS *of ether produce* LIGHT?

A. As *sound* is produced by *undulations of air* striking on the *ear*; so *light* is produced by undulations of *ether* striking on the *eye*.

Q. *What is* ETHER?

A. A very subtle fluid, which pervades and surrounds *everything we see.*

N. B. This theory of LIGHT is not altogether satisfactory; but has been retained, as the most plausible hitherto projected.

Q. *Does* HEAT ALWAYS *produce* LIGHT?

A. No; the heat of a stack of hay, or reeking dunghill, though very *great*, is not sufficient to produce *light.*

Q. *Why is a* YELLOW FLAME *brighter than a* RED HOT COAL?

A. Because *yellow rays* produce the greatest amount of *light*, though *red rays* produce the greatest amount of *heat.*

Q. *Why is the* LIGHT *of a fire* MORE INTENSE *sometimes than it is at others?*

A. The *intensity* of fire-light depends upon the *whiteness* to which the carbon is reduced by combustion. If carbon be *white hot*, its *combustion is perfect*, and the light intense; if not, the light is obscured by *smoke.*

Q. *Why will not* CINDERS BLAZE, *as well as* FRESH *coals?*

A. The *flame* of coals is made chiefly by *hydrogen gas.* As soon as this gas has been consumed, the hot cinders produce only a gas, called carbonic acid, which is neither luminous nor visible.

Q. *Where does the hydrogen gas of a fire come from?*

A. All fuel is *composed* of carbon and hydrogen gas, which are separated from each other by the process of combustion. (See p. 40.)

Q. *Why does not a* FIRE BLAZE *on a* FROSTY NIGHT, *so long as it does upon another night?*

A. 1st—Because air *condensed* by the cold contains more *oxygen* than the same quantity of warmer air; and

2dly—Air condensed by the cold is *heavier*. In consequence of which, it falls more quickly on the fire, to supply the place of the hot ascending air.

Q. *Why does a* FIRE *burn* CLEAREST *on a* FROSTY *night?*

A. Because the volatile gases are more quickly consumed; and the solid carbon is *plentifully supplied with oxygen* from the air, to make it burn brightly and intensely.

Q. *Why does a* FIRE *burn more intensely in* WINTER *than in* SUMMER?

A. Because the air is *colder* in winter, than it is in summer.

Q. *Why does the* COLDNESS *of the air increase the* HEAT *of a fire?*

A. 1st—Because air condensed by the cold, supplies more *oxygen* than a similar volume of warmer air; and

2dly—Condensed air, being *heavy*, falls more rapidly into the place of the hot ascending air, to supply the fire with nourishment.

Q. *Why does the* SUN, *shining on a* FIRE *make it* DULL; *and often put it out?*

A. 1st—Because the air (being rarefied by the sunshine) *flows more slowly to the fire;* and

2dly—Even that which *reaches* the fire, affords *less nourishment.*

Sunshine produces also some *chemical effect* upon the air or fuel detrimental to combustion.

Q. *Why does the air flow to the fire more* TARDILY *for being* RAREFIED?

A. Because the greater the *contrast* (between the *external air* and that *which has been heated by the fire*), the more *rapid* will be the current of air toward that fire.

Q. *Why does rarefied air afford* LESS NOURISHMENT *to fire than cold air?*

A. Because rarefied air contains less *oxygen* than the same quantity of condensed air.

Inasmuch as the same quantity of oxygen is diffused over a larger volume of air.

Q. *Why does a* FIRE *burn more fiercely in the* OPEN AIR?

A. 1st—Because the *air out-of-doors* is more *dense* than the air in-doors; and

2dly—It has freer *access* to the fire.

Q. *Why is the air out-of-doors more* DENSE *than that in-doors?*

A. Because it has freer circulation; and, as soon as any portion has been *rarefied*, it instantly escapes, and is supplied by *colder currents.*

Q. *Why does not a* FIRE *burn so freely in a* THAW *as in a* FROST?

A. Because the air is laden with *vapor;* in consequence of which, it both *moves too slowly*, and is too much *rarefied* to nourish the fire.

Q. *Why does a* FIRE *burn so fiercely in* WINDY *weather?*

A. Because *the air is so rapidly changed*, and affords plentiful nourishment to the fire.

Q. *Why does a pair of* BELLOWS *get a fire up?*

A. Because it *drives the air more rapidly to the fire;* and the plentiful supply of oxygen soon makes the fire burn intensely.

Q. *Why is the flame of a* CANDLE EXTINGUISHED *when blown by the breath; and not made more intense like a fire?*

A. Because the flame of a candle is confined to a *very small wick*, from which it is *severed* by the breath; and (being unsupported) *must go out.*

Q. *Why is a* SMOULDERING WICK *sometimes* RE-KINDLED *by blowing it?*

A. Because air is carried to it by the breath with *great rapidity;* and the oxygen of the air kindles the *red hot wick*, as it would kindle charred wood.

Q. *Why is not the red hot wick kindled by the air* AROUND *it, without* BLOWING?

A. Because oxygen is not supplied

with sufficient freedom, unless air be *blown* to the wick.

Q. *When is this experiment most likely to succeed?*

A. In *frosty* weather; because the air contains more oxygen when it is *condensed by the cold.*

Q. *Why does a* POKER LAID ACROSS *a dull* FIRE *revive it?*

A. For two reasons; 1st—Because the poker *concentrates the heat*, and therefore increases it; and

2dly—Air is arrested in the narrow aperture between the poker and the coals, and a *draught* created.

See p. 49.

Q. *Why are* STOVES *fixed on the* FLOOR *of a room?*

A. In order that the air *on the lower part of the room* may be heated by the fire.

Q. *Would not the air of the lower part of a room be heated equally well, if the stoves were fixed higher up?*

A. No; the heat of a fire has a very little effect upon the air *below the level of the grate;* and, therefore, every grate should be as *near to the floor* as possible.

Q. *Our* FEET *are very frequently* COLD *when we sit close by a good fire. Explain the reason of this.*

A. As the fire consumes the air which passes over it, *cold air* rushes through the crevices of the doors and windows *along the bottom of the room* to supply the deficiency; and these currents of cold air, *rushing constantly over our feet*, deprive them of their warmth.

Q. *If a piece of* PAPER *be laid* FLAT *on a clear fire, it will* NOT BLAZE *but* CHAR. *Why so?*

A. Because the carbon of a clear fire, being sufficiently hot to unite with the oxygen of the air, *produces carbonic acid gas*, which soon envelops the paper laid flat upon the cinders: but carbonic acid gas will not *blaze*.

Q. *If you* BLOW *the paper, it will* BLAZE *immediately. Why so?*

A. Because by blowing or opening a door suddenly, *the carbonic acid is dissipated*, and the paper fanned into flame.

Q. *Why does* WATER EXTINGUISH *a* FIRE?

A. 1st—Because the water *forms a coating* over the fuel, which keeps it from the air; and

2dly—The conversion of *water into steam*, draws off the *heat* of the burning fuel.

Q. *A* LITTLE WATER *makes a fire* FIERCER, *while a* LARGER *quantity of water puts it* OUT. *Explain how this is.*

A. Water is composed of *oxygen* and *hydrogen;* when, therefore, the fire can decompose the water into its simple elements, it serves for *fuel* to the flame.

Q. *How can* WATER *serve for* FUEL *to fire?*

A. Because the *hydrogen* of the water burns with a *flame;* and the *oxygen* of the water increases the *intensity* of that flame.

Q. *When a house is on fire, is too* LITTLE *water worse than* NONE?

A. Certainly. Unless water be supplied so plentifully as *to quench the fire*, it will increase its *intensity*, like fuel.

Q. *When will water* EXTINGUISH FIRE?

A. When the supply is so rapid and abundant that the fire cannot decompose it.

Q. *Does not a very* LITTLE *water* SLACKEN *the heat of fire?*

A. Yes, *till it is decomposed;* it then increases the *intensity* of fire, and acts like fuel.

Q. *Why does the* WICK *of a candle (when the flame has been blown out) very readily* CATCH FIRE?

A. Because the wick is already *hot*, and a very little *extra* heat will throw it into flame.

Q. *Why does the* EXTRA *heat revive the flame?*

A. Because it again liberates the *hydrogen* of the tallow, and ignites it.

Q. *Cannot* WOOD *be made to* BLAZE *without actual contact with fire?*

A. Yes; if a piece of wood be held *near* the fire for a little time, it will blaze, even though it does not *touch* the fire.

Q. *Why will* WOOD BLAZE, *even if it does not touch the fire?*

A. Because the heat of the fire *drives out the hydrogen gas* of the wood; which gas is inflamed by contact with the red hot coals.

Q. *Why will a* NEIGHBOR'S HOUSE *sometimes* CATCH FIRE, *though no flame of the burning house ever touches it?*

A. Because the heat of the burning house sets at liberty *the hydrogen gas* of the neighboring wood-work; and this gas is ignited by the flames or red hot bricks of the house or fire.

Q. *What is* COKE?

A. Coal freed from its volatile gases by the action of artificial heat.

Q. *Why do* STOVES *sometimes* SMELL *very strongly of* SULPHUR?

A. Because coal and coke contain sulphur; and whenever the draught is not rapid enough *to drive the sulphur up the flue*, it is emitted into the room.

Q. *What is meant by* SPONTANEOUS COMBUSTION?

A. Combustion produced without the application of *flame.*

Q. *Give an example of spontaneous combustion.*

A. Coals stowed in the hold of a vessel, and goods packed in a warehouse, will often catch fire of *themselves*—especially such goods as cotton, flax, hemp, rags, &c.

Q. *Why do such* GOODS *sometimes* CATCH FIRE *of themselves?*

A. Because they are piled together in very *large masses* in a *damp* state or place.

Q. *Why does this produce spontaneous combustion?*

A. The damp produces *decay*, or the decomposition of the goods; and the great heat of the piled-up mass makes the decaying goods *ferment.*

Q. *How does this* FERMENTATION *produce* COMBUSTION?

A. During fermentation, *carbonic acid gas* is given off by the goods—a slow combustion ensues—till at length the *whole pile* bursts into *flame.*

Q. *Why is the* HEAT *of a* LARGE MASS *of goods* GREATER *than that of a smaller quantity?*

A. Because the carbonic acid cannot

escape through the massive pile; and the products of decomposition being *confined*, hasten further changes.

Q. *Why do* HAY-STACKS *sometimes* CATCH FIRE *of themselves?*

A. Either because the hay was got up *damp;* or else because *rain* has penetrated the stack.

Q. *Why will a* HAY-STACK CATCH FIRE *if the hay be damp?*

A. Because damp hay soon *decays*, and undergoes a *state of fermentation;* during which, *carbonic acid gas* is given off, and the stack catches *fire.*

Q. *Roasted* COFFEE *sometimes* CATCHES *fire spontaneously. Explain the reason of this.*

A. The *heat* of coffee is greatly increased by being *roasted;* and the *carbon of the coffee*, uniting with the *oxygen of the air*, produces *carbonic acid gas*, and bursts into *flame.*

Q. *Why do old* RAGS, *used for* CLEANING LAMPS *and* CANDLESTICKS, *sometimes set a* HOUSE *on fire?*

A. Because they very readily *ferment*, and (during fermentation) throw off exceedingly inflammable gases.

N. B. Lamp-black mixed with linseed oil is more liable to spontaneous combustion than anything that servants handle.

CHAPTER V.

SMOKE.

Q. *Why does* SMOKE ASCEND *the chimney?*

A. Because the air of the room (when it passes over the fire) becomes lighter for being *heated;* and (being thus made *lighter*) ascends the chimney, carrying the smoke with it.

Q. *What is* SMOKE?

A. Small particles of carbon, separated by combustion from the fuel, but not *consumed.*

Q. *Why do* SMOKE *and steam* CURL *as they ascend?*

A. Because they are pushed round and round by the ascending and descending currents of air.

Q. *Why does a* CLOSE STOVE DRAW *up more fiercely than an* OPEN GRATE?

A. Because the air which supplies the stove must pass *through the fire,* and, as it becomes exceedingly *heated,* rushes up the flue with great violence.

Q. *What produces the* ROARING *noise made by the fire in a close stove?*

A. Air rushing rapidly through the crevices of the *iron door,* and up the *chimney flue.*

Q. *Why is the* ROAR LESS *if the stove* DOOR *be thrown* OPEN?

A. Because *fresh air* gets access to the fire *more easily;* and, as the air is not so intensely heated, its motion is not so *violent.*

Q. *Why do some* CHIMNEYS SMOKE?

A. Because fresh air is not admitted into a room *so fast as it is consumed by the fire;* in consequence of which, a current of air *rushes down the chimney* to *supply the deficiency,* driving the smoke along with it.

Q. *Explain this by an illustration.*

A. If water be taken with a pail out of a river, *other* water will rush toward the hole as soon as the pail is lifted out; and, if air be taken from a room (as it is, when some of it goes up the chimney), *other air* will rush toward the void to fill it up.

Q. *What prevents air being supplied so fast as it is consumed by the fire?*

A. Leather and curtains round the doors: sand-bags at the threshold and on the window-frames; and other contrivances to keep out the draught.

Q. *Why will the air come down the* CHIMNEY?

A. Because it can get into the room

n no *other* way, if the doors and windows are all made *air-tight.*

Q. *What is the best* REMEDY *in such a case?*

A. The *speediest* remedy is to open the door or window: but by far the *best* remedy is to carry a small tube from the hearth into the external air.

Q. *Why is that the* BEST *remedy?*

A. Because the fire will be plentifully supplied with air by the tube: the doors and windows may all remain air-tight; and we may enjoy a warm fireside, without the inconvenience of draughts and cold feet.

Q. *Why is a* CHIMNEY *raised so high above the* ROOF?

A. That it may not smoke; as all funnels do which are too short.

Q. *What is meant by the* FUNNEL *or* FLUE *of a chimney?*

A. That part of a chimney through which *the smoke passes.*

Q. *Why does a* CHIMNEY SMOKE, *if the funnel be very short?*

A. Because the *draught* of a short flue is *too slack* to carry the smoke up the chimney.

Q. *Why is the* DRAUGHT *of a* SHORT FLUE *more* SLACK *than that of a long one?*

A. 1st—Because *the fire is always dull and sluggish*, if the chimney be too short:

2dly—Because the smoke rolls *out* of the chimney, before it has acquired its *full velocity;* and

3dly—Because the wind, rain, and air, have more influence over a *short* funnel, than over a *long* one.

Q. *Why is the* FIRE *always* DULL *and* SLUGGISH, *if the* CHIMNEY-FLUE *be very* SHORT?

A. Because the draught is bad; and, as the rarefied air *passes very tardily up the chimney—fresh air* flows as tardily *toward the fire*, to supply it with *oxygen*.

Q. *On what does the* INTENSITY *of fire depend?*

A. The *intensity* of fire is always in proportion to the *quantity of oxygen* with which it is supplied.

Q. *Why does not* SMOKE *acquire its full* VELOCITY *in a* SHORT *funnel?*

A. Because the *higher* smoke ascends, (provided the flue be clear and hot,) the *faster* it goes: if, therefore, a *funnel be very short*, the smoke never acquires its full velocity.

Q. *Does the* DRAUGHT *of a chimney depend on the* SPEED *of the* SMOKE *through the flue?*

A. Yes. The more quickly *hot* air flies *up the chimney*, the more quickly *cold* air will rush *toward the fire* to supply the place; and, therefore, the *longer the flue*, the *greater the draught.*

Q. *Why are the* CHIMNEYS *of* MANUFACTORIES *made so very* LONG?

A. To increase the intensity of the fire.

Q. *Why is the* INTENSITY *of a fire increased by* LENGTHENING *the* FLUE?

A. Because the draught being greater, more fuel is consumed in the same time; and, of course, the intensity of the heat is proportionally greater.

Q. *If a* SHORT CHIMNEY *cannot be lengthened, what is the best* REMEDY *to prevent smoking?*

A. To *contract the opening of the chimney* contiguous to the stove.

Q. *Why will a* SMALLER OPENING *against the stove* PREVENT *the chimney's* SMOKING?

A. Because the air will be compelled to pass *nearer the fire;* and (being more *heated*) will rise through the chimney more rapidly. This *increase of heat* will therefore compensate for the *shortness* of the *flue.*

Q. *Why will a* ROOM SMOKE *if there be* TWO FIRES *in it?*

A. Because the *fiercer* fire will exhaust the most air, and draw from the *smaller* one, to supply its demand.

Q. *Why will a chimney* SMOKE *if there be a* FIRE *in* TWO ROOMS *communicating with each other?*

A. Because (whenever the *door* between the two rooms is *opened*) air will rush from the chimney of the *inferior* fire to supply the *other;* and *both* rooms will be filled with smoke.

Q. *What is the best* REMEDY *in this case?*

A. Let a tube be carried from the hearth of each stove into the external air; and then *each* fire will be so well supplied, that neither will need to borrow from the other.

Q. *Why does a* HOUSE *in a* VALLEY *or by the side of higher buildings very often* SMOKE?

A. Because the wind (striking against the surrounding hills or buildings) *bounds back again upon the chimney*, and destroys its draught.

Q. *What is the* REMEDY *in these cases?*

A. To fix a *cowl* on the chimney-top, to turn like a weather-cock, and present its back to the wind.

Q. *Why will not a* COWL *always* PREVENT *a chimney* SMOKING?

A. Because if the wind be *strong*, it will keep the *opening* of the cowl *toward the higher building or hill;* and then the reflected wind will blow *into the cowl*, and *down the chimney*.

Q. *As a cowl is such a poor remedy, can any* OTHER *be suggested?*

A. Yes. If the chimney-flue can be carried *higher* than the other buildings or hills, no wind can enter the flue.

Q. *If a chimney-flue be carried up* HIGHER *than the buildings or hill, why cannot the wind enter it?*

A. Because the reflected wind would strike against the *sides* of the chimney-flue, and not pass over the *opening* at all.

Q. *In what* OTHER *cases will a* CHIMNEY SMOKE?

A. If the door and stove are both placed on *the same side of a room*, the chimney will often smoke.

Q. *Why will a* CHIMNEY SMOKE, *if the* DOOR *and* STOVE *are both on the* SAME SIDE?

A. Because (whenever the door is opened) a current of air will *blow obliquely into the chimney-place*, and drive the smoke into the room.

Q. *What* REMEDY *can be applied to this evil?*

A. The door must be set *opposite* to the chimney-place, or nearly so; and then the draught from the door *will blow the smoke up the chimney*, and not into the room.

Q. *Why will a* CHIMNEY SMOKE *if it* NEEDS SWEEPING?

A. Because loose soot obstructs the

free passage of the smoke, *delays its current*, and prevents the draught.

Q. *Why will a* CHIMNEY SMOKE *if it be* OUT OF REPAIR?

A. 1st—Because the *loose mortar and bricks* obstruct the smoke; and

2dly—*Cold air* (oozing through the chinks) *chills the air in the chimney*, and prevents its ascent.

Q. *Why will a* STOVE SMOKE, *if the joints of the flue do not fit air-tight?*

A. Because *cold air* (oozing through the joints) *chills the air in the flue*, and prevents its ascent.

Q. *Why does an old-fashioned* FARM CHIMNEY-PLACE *generally smoke?*

A. Because the opening is so *very large*, that much of the air which goes up the chimney, *has never passed near the fire;* and this *cold* air (mixing with the hot) so *reduces its temperature* that it ascends very slowly, and the draught is destroyed.

Q. *Why does a chimney smoke if the* DRAUGHT *be* SLACK?

A. Because the current of air up the chimney is not powerful enough to *buoy up the smoke* through the flue.

Q. *If the opening of a chimney be* TOO LARGE, *what* REMEDY *can be applied?*

A. The chimney-place must be contracted.

Q. *Why will* CONTRACTING *the chimney-place* PREVENT *its* SMOKING ?

A. Because the air will then pass *nearer the fire;* and (being *more heated*) fly faster up the chimney.

Q. *Why do almost all* CHIMNEYS SMOKE *in* GUSTY *weather?*

A. Because the column of smoke is suddenly chilled by the wind, and (being unable to ascend) rushes back into the room.

Q. *What is the use of a* CHIMNEY-POT ?

A. It serves to increase the draught, when the opening of a chimney is too *large.*

Q. *How does a* CHIMNEY-POT INCREASE *the* DRAUGHT *of a chimney?*

A. As the *same quantity* of hot air has to escape through a *smaller opening*, it must pass through more quickly.

Q. *Why do* BLOWERS *help to get a fire up?*

A. Because they compel the air to go *through* the fire, and not *over* it; in consequence of which, the fire is well supplied with oxygen, and the draught greatly increased.

Q. *Why does a* BLOWER INCREASE *the* DRAUGHT ?

A. Because the air (by passing *through* the fire) is made much hotter, and ascends the chimney more rapidly.

Q. *Why is a fire better supplied with oxygen while the blower hangs before it?*

A. Because the blower increases the draught; and the faster the *hot* air flies *up the chimney*, the faster will *cold* air rush *toward the fire*, to supply it with oxygen.

Q. *Why does a parlor often* SMELL *disagreeably of* SOOT *in* SUMMER-TIME?

A. Because the air in the *chimney* (being *colder* than the air in the *parlor*) *descends into the room*, and leaves a disagreeable smell of soot behind.

Q. *Why are the* CEILINGS *of* PUBLIC OFFICES *generally* BLACK *and filthy?*

A. Because the heated air of the office buoys up the dust and fine soot; which (being unable to escape through the plaster) is deposited on the ceiling.

Q. *Why are* SOME *parts of the ceiling* BLACKER *and more filthy than others?*

A. Because the air, being unable to penetrate the thick *joists* of the ceiling *passes by those parts*, and deposits its soot and dust on others more penetrable.

N. B. The site of this deposit of soot and dust is frequently determined by draughts and currents of air.

Q. *What is* CHARCOAL?

A. Wood which has been exposed to a red heat, till it has been deprived of all its gases and volatile parts.

Q. *Why is a* CHARCOAL FIRE *hotter than a wood fire?*

A. Because charcoal is very *pure* carbon; and, as it is the *carbon* of fuel which produces the glowing heat of combustion, therefore, the *purer* the carbon, the more intense will the heat of the fire be.

Q. *Why does charcoal* REMOVE *the* TAINT *of meat?*

A. Because it absorbs all putrescent effluvia, whether they arise from animal or vegetable matter.

Q. *Why is* WATER PURIFIED *by being filtered through charcoal?*

A. Because charcoal absorbs the *impurities* of the water, and removes all disagreeable tastes and smells, whether they arise from animal or vegetable matter.

Q. *Why are water and wine* CASKS CHARRED *inside?*

A. Because *charring* the inside of a cask reduces it to a *kind of charcoal;* and charcoal (by absorbing animal and vegetable impurities) keeps the liquor sweet and good.

Q. *Why does a piece of* BURNT BREAD *make impure* WATER *fit to drink?*

A. Because the surface of the bread (which has been reduced to *charcoal* by being burnt) absorbs *the impurities of the water*, and makes it palatable.

Q. *Why should* TOAST *and* WATER, *placed by the side of the sick, be made of* BURNT BREAD?

A. Because the charcoal surface of burnt bread prevents the water from being affected by the impurities of the sick room.

Q. *Why should sick persons eat* DRY TOAST *rather than bread and butter?*

A. Because the charcoal surface of the dry toast helps to absorb the acids and impurities of a sick stomach.

There are other reasons which belong to the science of medicine.

Q. *Why are* TIMBERS *which are to be exposed to damp* CHARRED?

A. Because *charcoal undergoes no change* by exposure to air and water; in consequence of which, timber will resist weather *much longer* after it has been charred.

CHAPTER VI.

LAMPS AND CANDLES.

Q. *Of what are* OIL, TALLOW, *and* WAX *composed?*

A. Principally of carbon and hydrogen gas. The *solid* part is carbon, the *volatile* part is hydrogen gas.

Q. *What is* CARBON?

A. A solid substance, generally of a black color; well known under the forms of charcoal, lamp-black, coke, &c.

Q. *What is* HYDROGEN GAS?

A. The principal ingredient of water. It burns so readily that it used to be called "inflammable air."*

Common coal gas is a mixture of carbon and hydrogen, called "carburetted hydrogen." See p. 262.

Q. *A* CANDLE BURNS *when lighted. Explain how this is.*

A. The heat of the lighted wick *decomposes the tallow* into its elementary parts of carbon and hydrogen; and the *hydrogen of the tallow*, combining with the *oxygen of the air*, produces *flame.*

Q. WHERE *is the tallow or wax of a candle decomposed?*

A. In the *wick.* The melted tallow

* To make hydrogen gas, see p. 41.

or wax, *rises up the wick* by capillary attraction, and is rapidly decomposed by the heat of the flame.

Q. *What is capillary attraction?*

A. The power which very minute tubes possess of causing a liquid to rise in them above its level.

"Capillary," from the Latin word "capillaris" (*like a hair*); the tubes referred to are almost as fine and delicate as a hair.

Water ascends through a lump of sugar, or piece of sponge, by capillary attraction. N. B.—The smaller a tube, the higher will a liquid be attracted by it.

Q. *Why is the* FLAME *of a candle* HOT?

A. Because the flame liberates *latent heat* from the air and tallow.

Q. *How is* LATENT HEAT *liberated by the flame of a* CANDLE?

A. When the elements of the tallow combine with the *oxygen* of the air, latent heat is liberated by the chemical changes.

Q. *Why does the flame of a* CANDLE *produce* LIGHT?

A. Because the chemical changes made by combustion excite *undulations of ether*, which (striking the eye) produce light.

See p. 51.

Q. *Why is the flame of a* CANDLE YELLOW?

A. It is *not* so altogether; only the *outer* coat of the flame is yellow—the *lower* part is *violet;* and the *inside* of the flame *hollow.*

Q. *Why is the outside of the flame* YELLOW?

A. Because the *carbon of the tallow* (being in a state of *perfect combustion*) is made white hot.

See p. 50.

Q. *Why is the* BOTTOM *part of the flame purple?*

A. Because it is *overladen with hydrogen,* raised from the tallow by the burning wick; and this *gas* (which burns with a *blue flame*) gives the dark tinge to the bottom of the candle-flame.

Q. *Why is the* INSIDE *of the flame* HOLLOW?

A. Because it is *filled with vapor,* raised from the candle by the *heat of the wick,* and not yet reduced to a state of combustion.

Q. *Describe the different parts of the* FLAME *of a common* CANDLE.

A. The flame consists of *three cones.* The innermost cone is hollow; the intermediate one of a dingy purple hue; and the outside cone is yellow.

Q. *Why is the intermediate cone of a flame* PURPLE *as well as the* BOTTOM *of the flame?*

A. Because the gases are not in a state of *perfect combustion;* but contain an *excess of hydrogen*, which gives the flame a purple tinge.

Q. *Why is not the* MIDDLE *cone in a state of perfect combustion as well as the outer one?*

A. Because the outer cone *prevents the oxygen of the air* from getting to the middle of the flame; and without the free access of oxygen gas, there is no such thing as complete combustion.

Q. *Why does the* FLAME *of a candle point* UPWARDS?

A. Because it *heats the surrounding air*, which (being hot) *rapidly ascends*, driving the flame upwards at the same time.

Q. *Why is the* FLAME *of a candle* POINTED *at the top like a cone?*

A. Because the *upper* part of a flame is more *volatile* than the lower; and, as it affords *less resistance to the air*, is reduced to a mere point.

Q. *Why are the* LOWER *parts of a flame less* VOLATILE *than the upper?*

A. Because they are laden with unconsumed gas and watery vapor, which present considerable resistance to the air.

Q. *Why is the* FLAME *of a candle* BLOWN OUT *by a puff of breath?*

A. Because it is *severed from the wick*, and goes out for want of support.

Q. *Why does the* FLAME *of a candle make a* GLASS (*which is held over it*) DAMP?

A. Because a "watery vapor" is made by the combination of the *hydrogen of the tallow* with the *oxygen of the air;* and this "vapor" is condensed by the *cold glass* held above the flame.

Q. *Why does our hand, held* ABOVE *a candle, suffer more from heat than when it is placed* BELOW *the flame, or on* ONE SIDE *of it?*

A. Because the hot gases and air (in their ascent) *come in contact* with the hand placed *above* the flame; but when the hand is placed *below* the flame, or on *one side*, it only feels heat from *radiation.*

Radiation: i. e., emission of rays. The candle-flame throws out rays of light and heat in all directions; but when the hand is held *above* the flame, it not only feels the heat of the *rays*, but also of the ascending current of *hot air*, &c.

Q. *Why is a* RUSH LIGHT *extinguished more quickly than a cotton-wick candle?*

A. Because a hard rush imbibes the melted fat or wax much more slowly than porous cotton; as it imbibes less fat, it supplies a smaller volume of *combustible gases;* and, of course, the light is more easily extinguished.

Q. *Why is it more difficult to blow out a* COTTON *wick than a rush light?*

A. Because porous cotton imbibes

the melted fat, or wax, much more quickly than hard rush; as it imbibes more fat, it supplies the flame with a larger volume of *combustible gases;* and, of course, the light is with more difficulty extinguished.

Q. *Why is a* GAS FLAME *more easily extinguished when the jet is very slightly turned on, than when it is in full stream?*

A. Because there is less volume of combustible gases in the small flame than in the full blaze.

Q. *Why does an* EXTINGUISHER *put a candle out?*

A. Because the air in the extinguisher *is soon exhausted of its oxygen* by the flame: and when there is *no oxygen*, flame goes out.

Q. *Why does not a candle set fire to a* PIECE *of* PAPER *twisted into an extinguisher, and used as such?*

A. 1st—Because the flame very soon *exhausts the oxygen* contained in the paper extinguisher: and

2dly—The flame invests the *inside of the paper extinguisher* with *carbonic acid gas*, which prevents it from blazing.

Q. *Why is a* LONG WICK *never upright?*

A. Because it is bent by its own weight.

Q. *A* LONG WICK *is covered with an* EFFLORESCENCE *at the top. What does this arise from?*

A. The knotty or flowery appearance of the top of a wick arises from an accumulation of particles *partly separated* but still loosely hanging to the wick.

Q. *Why is not the* END *of a long wick* BURNT OFF *as it hangs over the flame?*

A. Because the length of the wick diminishes *the heat of the flame;* so that it is no longer *hot* enough to *consume* the wick.

Q. *Why do* PALMER'S METALLIC WICKS *never need* SNUFFING?

A. Because the wick is divided into two parts, each of which bends toward the outside of the flame, where the *end is intensely heated*, and *separated* from the wick by the current of air up the candle.

N. B. The small wire twisted in the wick greatly assists the process.

Q. *Why do common* CANDLES *require to be* SNUFFED?

A. Because the heat of the flame is *not sufficient to consume the wick;* and the *longer* the wick grows, the *less heat* the flame produces.

Q. *Why do* WAX CANDLES NEVER *need* SNUFFING?

A. Because the wick of *wax* candles

is made of *very fine thread*, which the heat of the flame is sufficient to consume. The wick of *tallow* candles (on the other hand) is made of *coarse cotton*, which is too substantial to be consumed by the heat of the flame, and must be cut off by *snuffers*.

Q. *Why does a* PIN *stuck in a* RUSH LIGHT EXTINGUISH *it?*

A. Because a *pin* (being a good conductor) *carries away the heat of the flame from the wick*, and prevents the combustion of the tallow.

Q. *What is the* SMOKE *of a* CANDLE?

A. Solid particles of carbon, separated from the wick and tallow, but not consumed.

Q. *Why are* SOME *particles consumed and not* OTHERS?

A. The *combustion of the carbon* depends upon its *combining with the oxygen of the air:* now, as the outer surface of the flame *prevents the access of air to the interior parts*, much of the carbon of those parts passes off in smoke.

Q. *Why do* LAMPS SMOKE?

A. Either because the *wick is cut unevenly*, or else because *it is turned up too high.*

4*

Q. *Why does a* LAMP SMOKE *when the* WICK *is cut* UNEVENLY?

A. 1st—Because the *points of the jagged edge* (being very easily separated from the wick) *load the flame with more carbon than it can consume;* and

2dly—As the heat of the flame is *greatly diminished by these bits of wick,* it is unable to consume *even the usual quantity of smoke.*

Q. *Why does a* LAMP SMOKE *when the* WICK *is turned up too* HIGH?

A. Because more carbon is separated from the wick *than can be consumed by the flame.*

Q. *Why do not* "ARGAND BURNERS" *smoke?*

A. Because a current of air passes through the *middle of the flame;* in consequence of which, the carbon of the *interior* is consumed, as well as that *in the outer coating of the flame.*

Q. *Why does a* LAMP-GLASS DIMINISH *the* SMOKE *of a lamp?*

A. 1st—Because it increases the supply of *oxygen* to the flame, by producing a draught; and

2dly—It *concentrates* and *reflects* the *heat* of the flame; in consequence of which, the combustion of the carbon is more *perfect*, and very little escapes unconsumed.

CHAPTER VII.

ANIMAL HEAT.

Q. *What is the cause of* ANIMAL HEAT?

A. Animal heat is produced *by the combustion of hydrogen and carbon* in the capillary vessels.

Q. *What are* CAPILLARY VESSELS?

A. Vessels *as small as hairs* running *all over the body;* they are called capillary from the Latin word "capilla'ris" (*like a hair*).

Q. *Do these* CAPILLARY VESSELS *run all over the human body?*

A. Yes. Whenever *blood flows from a wound*, some vein or vessel must be divided; and as you can bring blood from any part of the body by a very slight wound, these little vessels must run through every part of the human frame.

Q. *How do* HYDROGEN *gas and* CARBON *get into these very little vessels?*

A The food we eat is *converted into*

blood; and blood contains both *hydrogen* and *carbon.*

Q. *How does* COMBUSTION *take place in the capillary vessels?*

A. The *carbon of the blood* combines with *oxygen of the air we breathe*, and forms into *carbonic acid gas.*

Q. *What* BECOMES *of this* CARBONIC ACID GAS *formed in the human blood?*

A. The lungs throw off almost all of it into the air, by the act of respiration.

Q. *What* GAS *is generated in a common* FIRE *by* COMBUSTION?

A. *Carbonic acid gas*—formed by the union of the *carbon of fuel* with the *oxygen of the air.*

Q. *What* GAS *is generated by a lighted* CANDLE *or* LAMP?

A. *Carbonic acid gas*—formed by the union of the *carbon* of the *oil* or *tallow* with the *oxygen of the air.*

Q. *What is the cause of* SPONTANEOUS COMBUSTION?

A. The piled-up goods *ferment* from *heat and damp;* and (during fermentation) *carbonic acid gas is formed*, which is attended with combustion.

Q. *Does the* HEAT *of the* HUMAN BODY *arise from the* SAME CAUSE *as the heat of* FIRE?

A. Yes, precisely. The *carbon of*

the blood combines with the *oxygen of the air inhaled*, and produces *carbonic acid gas*, which is attended with combustion.

Q. *If animal heat is produced by* COMBUSTION, *why does not the human body* BURN UP *like a coal or candle?*

A. It actually does so. Every muscle, nerve, and organ of the body, actually *wastes away* like a *burning candle;* and (being reduced to air and ashes) is rejected from the system as useless.

Q. *If every bone, muscle, nerve, and organ, is thus consumed by combustion, why is not the* BODY *entirely* CONSUMED?

A. It would be so, unless the parts destroyed *were perpetually renewed:* but as a lamp will not go out, so long as it is *supplied with fresh oil*—neither will the *body* be consumed, so long as it is *supplied with sufficient food.*

Q. *What is the principal* DIFFERENCE *between the combustion of a* FIRE *or* LAMP *and that of the* HUMAN BODY?

A. In the human body, the combustion is effected at a much *lower temperature;* and is carried on more *slowly*, than it is in a lamp or fire.

Q. *How is it that carbon can be made to burn at so* LOW *a temperature in the human body?*

A. Because the carbon in the blood

is reduced to very *minute particles ;* and these particles are ready to undergo a rapid change as soon as oxygen is supplied.

Q. *When a man is* STARVED, *what parts of the body go first ?*

A. First the *fat*, because it is the most combustible ; then the *muscles ;* last of all the *brain ;* and then the man dies, like a *candle which is burnt out.*

Q. *Why does* WANT *of sufficient* NOURISHMENT *often produce* MADNESS ?

A. Because after the *fat and muscles* of the body have been consumed by animal combustion, the *brain* is next attacked; and (unless the patient dies) *madness ensues.*

Q. *Why does a man* SHRINK *when* STARVED ?

A. Because the capillary fires feed upon the human *body* when they are not supplied with food-fuel. A starved man shrinks *just as a fire does*, when it is not supplied with fuel.

Q. *What is the* FUEL *of the* BODY ?

A. *Food* is the *fuel* of the *body.* The *carbon of the food* mixing with the *oxygen of the air*, evolves heat in the same way that a fire or candle does.

Q. *Why is* EVERY *part of the* BODY WARM ?

A. Because the capillary vessels run through every part of the human body, and the combustion of blood *takes place in the capillary vessels.*

See p. 84.

Q. *Why does* RUNNING *make us* WARM?

A. Because we *inhale air more rapidly* when we run, and cause the blood to pass more rapidly through the *lungs* in contact with it. *Running* acts upon the capillary vessels as a pair of *bellows* on a common *fire.*

Q. *Why does* INHALING AIR RAPIDLY *make the body feel* WARM?

A. Because *more oxygen* is introduced into the body. In consequence of which, the combustion of the blood is *more rapid*—the blood itself *more heated*—and every part of the body is made warmer.

Q. *Why does* HARD WORK *produce* HUNGER?

A. Because it produces *quicker respiration;* by which means, a *larger amount of oxygen is introduced into the lungs,* and the *capillary combustion increased.* Hunger is the *notice* (given by our body) to remind us *that our food-fuel must be replenished.*

Q. *Why does* SINGING *make us* HUNGRY?

A. Because it *increases respiration;* and, as *more oxygen* is introduced into the lungs, *our food-fuel is more rapidly consumed.*

Q. *Why does* READING ALOUD *make us feel* HUNGRY?

A. Because it *increases respiration;* and, as *more oxygen* is introduced into the lungs, *our food-fuel is more rapidly consumed.*

Q. *Why do we feel less* HUNGRY *in the night than in the* DAY?

A. Because we *breathe more slowly during sleep;* therefore, less *oxygen* is introduced into the lungs, to *consume our food-fuel.*

Q. *Why do we need* WARMER CLOTHING *by* NIGHT *than by* DAY?

A. 1st—Because the *night is generally colder* than the day; and

2dly—Our *bodies* are *colder* also; because we breathe more *slowly*, and our animal combustion is retarded.

Q. *Why do we* PERSPIRE *when very hot?*

A. The pores of the body are *like the safety valves of a steam-engine;* when the heat of the body is very great, some of the combustible matter of the blood is thrown off in *perspiration;* and the heat of the body kept more temperate.

Q. *Why do persons feel* LAZY *and averse to exercise when they are* HALF-STARVED *or* ILL-FED?

A. *Animal food* contains great nourishment, and produces a desire for *active occupations;* but, when the body is not supplied with strong food, this desire for muscular action *ceases*, and the person grows slothful.

Q. *Why have persons who follow* HARD, OUT-OF-DOORS OCCUPATIONS *more* APPETITE *than those who are engaged in* SEDENTARY *pursuits?*

A. Hard bodily labor in the open air *causes much oxygen* to be conveyed into the *lungs by inspiration;* the combustion of the food is carried on quickly; *animal heat increased;* and need for nutritious food more quickly indicated by *craving hunger*.

Q. *Why have persons who follow* SEDENTARY PURSUITS *less* APPETITE *than ploughmen and masons?*

A. 1st—Because the air they inhale *is less pure*, being deprived of some of its oxygen: and

A. 2dly—Their respiration is neither *so quick, nor so strong;* and, therefore, the combustion of their food is carried on more slowly.

Q. *Why do we like strong* MEAT *and* GREASY *food when the* WEATHER *is very* COLD?

A. Because strong meat and grease

contain large portions of *carbon* and *hydrogen;* which (when burned in the blood) produce a larger amount of heat, than any other kind of food.

Q. *Why do persons* EAT MORE *food in* COLD *weather than in hot?*

A. Because the body requires more fuel in *cold weather, to keep up the same amount of animal heat;* and as we put more *coals* on a fire on a cold day, to keep our *room* warm; so we eat more *food* on a cold day, to keep our *body* warm.

Q. *Why does* COLD *produce* HUNGER?

A. 1st — Because the air contains more *oxygen* in cold weather; and, therefore, *fires burn more fiercely,* and *animal combustion is more rapid:* and

2dly—As we are more *active* in cold weather, our increased respiration acts *like a pair of bellows* on the capillary combustion.

Q. *Why does rapid* DIGESTION *produce a craving* APPETITE?

A. This is a wise providence to *keep our bodies in health;* they give notice (by hunger) that the *capillary fires need replenishing,* in order that the *body itself* may not be consumed.

Q. *Why do we feel a desire for* ACTIVITY *in cold weather?*

A. 1st—Because activity increases the warmth of the body, *by fanning the combustion of the blood:* and

2dly—The *strong food* we eat creates a desire for muscular exertion.

Q. *Why are the Esquimaux so passionately fond of* TRAIN OIL *and* WHALE BLUBBER?

A. Because oil and blubber contain large quantities of *carbon and hydrogen,* which are exceedingly combustible; and, as these people live in climates of intense cold, the heat of their bodies is increased by the *greasy nature of their food.*

Q. *Why do we feel a* DISLIKE *to strong meat and greasy food in very* HOT *weather?*

A. Because strong meat and grease contain so much *carbon and hydrogen,* that they would make us *intensely hot:* we therefore, instinctively refuse them in hot weather.

Q. *Why do we like* FRUITS *and* VEGETABLES *most in hot weather?*

A. Because they contain *less hydrogen and carbon* than meat; and, therefore, produce both *less blood,* and blood of a *less combustible nature.*

Q. *Why is the blood of a less* COMBUSTIBLE *nature, if we live chiefly upon* FRUITS *and* VEGETABLES?

A. Because fruits and vegetables

supply the blood with a very large amount of *water;* which is not combustible, like the *carbon and hydrogen* of strong meat.

Q. *How do* FRUITS *and* VEGETABLES COOL *the* BLOOD?

A. 1st—They diminish the amount of *carbon and hydrogen* in the blood, which are the chief causes of animal heat: and

2dly—They supply the blood with a large amount of *water*, which exudes *through the skin*, and leaves the body cool.

Q. *Why do we feel* LAZY *and averse to activity in very* HOT WEATHER?

A. 1st—Because muscular activity increases the heat of the body, by *quickening the respiration:* and

2dly—The food we eat in hot weather (not being *greasy*) naturally abates our desire for bodily activity.

Q. *Why do the inhabitants of* TROPICAL *countries live chiefly upon* RICE *and* FRUIT?

A. Because rice and fruit (by digestion) *are mainly converted into water;* and (by *cooling the blood*) prevent the tropical heat from feeling so oppressive.

Q. *Why are the* ILL-FED *instinctively* AVERSE *to* CLEANLINESS?

A. Because *cleanliness increases hunger*, which they cannot allay by food.

Q. *Why are the* ILL-CLAD *also instinctively averse to* CLEANLINESS?

A. Because *dirt is warm*, (thus pigs, who love *warmth*, are fond of *dirt*); to those, therefore, who are very *ill-clad*, the *warmth of dirt* is agreeable.

Q. *Why are very* POOR PEOPLE *instinctively* AVERSE *to* VENTILATION?

A. 1st—Because ventilation *increases the oxygen of the air*—the *combustion of food*—and the *cravings of appetite*: and

2dly—Ventilation *cools the air of our rooms*: to poor people, therefore, who are ill-clad, the *warmth* of an ill-ventilated apartment is agreeable.

Q. *Why does* FLANNEL, *&c., make us* WARM?

A. Flannel and warm clothing do not *make* us warm, but merely *prevent our body from becoming cold.*

Q. *How does* FLANNEL, *&c., prevent our body from becoming cold?*

A. Flannel (being a bad conductor) will neither *carry off the heat of our body* into the *cold air*, nor suffer the cold of the air *to come in contact with our warm body*: and thus it is, that flannel clothing keeps us warm.

Q. *Why are* FROGS *and* FISHES COLD BLOODED *animals?*

A. Because they consume very *little air;* and, without a plentiful supply of air, combustion is too slow to generate much animal heat.

Q. *Why is a* DEAD BODY COLD?

A. Because air is no longer conveyed to the lungs, after respiration has ceased; and, therefore, animal heat *is no longer generated by combustion.*

MECHANICAL ACTION.

CHAPTER VIII.

1.—PERCUSSION.

Q. *How is heat produced by* MECHANICAL ACTION?

A. 1.—By Percussion. 2.—By Friction. And 3.—By Condensation.

Q. *What is meant by* PERCUSSION?

A. *The act of striking;* as when a blacksmith strikes a piece of iron on his anvil with his hammer.

Q. *Why does* STRIKING IRON *make it* RED HOT?

A. Because it *condenses the particles*

of the metal, and makes the latent heat *sensible.*

Q. *Does* COLD *iron contain* HEAT?

A. Yes; *everything* contains heat; but, when a thing *feels cold*, its heat is LATENT.

Q. *What is meant by* LATENT HEAT?

A. Heat *not perceptible to our feelings.* When anything contains heat without *feeling* the hotter for it, that heat is called "*latent heat.*"

See p. 37.

Q. *Does* COLD *iron contain latent* HEAT?

A. Yes; and when a blacksmith *compresses the particles* of iron by his hammer, he brings *out* latent heat; and this makes the iron red hot.

Q. *How used blacksmiths to* LIGHT THEIR MATCHES *before the general use of lucifers?*

A. They used to place a soft iron nail upon their anvil; strike it two or three times with a hammer; and the point became *sufficiently hot to light a brimstone match.*

Q. *How can a* NAIL (*beaten by a hammer*) IGNITE *a brimstone* MATCH?

A. The particles of the nail being *compressed* by the hammer, can no longer contain so much heat in a *latent state,* as they did *before;* some of it, therefore, becomes *sensible*, and increases the temperature of the iron.

Q. *Why does* STRIKING *a* FLINT *against a piece of* STEEL *produce a* SPARK?

A. Because it compresses those parts of the flint and steel which strike *together.* In consequence of which, some of their latent heat is disturbed, and exhibits itself in a spark.

Q. *How does this development of* HEAT *produce a* SPARK *and set* TINDER *on fire?*

A. A very small fragment (either of the steel or flint) *is knocked off red hot*, and sets fire to the tinder on which it falls.

Q. *Why is it needful to keep* BLOWING *the* TINDER *with the breath?*

A. In order that the increased supply of air may furnish the tinder with more *oxygen* to assist combustion.

Q. *Where does the* OXYGEN *of the air* COME FROM, *which is blown to the lighted tinder?*

A. From the air itself, which is composed of two gases (*nitrogen and oxygen*) mixed together.

Every 5 gallons of common air contain nearly 4 gallons of nitrogen, and 1 of oxygen.

Q. *What is the* USE *of* OXYGEN GAS *to lighted tinder?*

A. It *supports the combustion* of the tinder. *Blowing* lighted tinder carries *oxygen* to it and *quickens* it, in the same way as a pair of bellows quickens a dull fire.

Q. *Why do* HORSES *sometimes* STRIKE FIRE *with their* FEET?

A. Because when their iron shoes strike against the flint stones of the road, *very small fragments* (either of the shoe or stones) are *knocked off red hot*, and look like sparks.

Q. *What makes these fragments* RED HOT?

A. The percussion *condenses* the part struck: In consequence of which, some of its *latent heat* is rendered *sensible*, and exhibits itself in these red hot fragments.

CHAPTER IX.

2.—FRICTION.

Q. *What is meant by* FRICTION?

A. The act of *rubbing two things together;* as the Indians rub two pieces of *wood* together to produce fire.

Q. *How do the Indians produce* FIRE *by merely* RUBBING TWO PIECES *of dry* WOOD TOGETHER?

A. They take a piece of dry wood, sharpened to a point, which they rub quickly up and down a *flat piece*, till a *groove* is made; and the *dust* (collected in this groove) *catches fire.*

Q. *Why does the dust of the* WOOD CATCH FIRE *by* RUBBING?

A. Because *latent heat* is developed from the wood *by friction.*

The best woods for this purpose are *boxwood* against *mulberry*, or *laurel* against *poplar* or *ivy.*

Q. *Do not* CARRIAGE WHEELS *sometimes* CATCH FIRE?

A. Yes; when the wheels are *dry*—or *fit too tightly*—or *revolve very rapidly.*

Q. *Why do wheels catch fire in such cases?*

A. Because the *friction* of the wheels against *the axle-tree* disturbs their *latent heat*, and produces ignition.

Q. *What is the use of* GREASING CART WHEELS?

A. Grease *lessens the friction;* and, because there is *less friction*, the latent heat of the wheels is less disturbed.

Q. *Why does* RUBBING *our* HANDS *and* FACES *make them feel* WARM?

A. 1st—Because friction *excites* the *latent heat* of our hands and faces, and makes it sensible to our feeling: and

2dly—The blood is made to *circulate more quickly;* in consequence of which, the quantum of heat (left in its passage) is increased.

Q. *When a man has been almost* DROWNED, *why is suspended animation* RESTORED *by* RUBBING?

A. 1st—Because friction *excites the latent heat* of the half-inanimate body: and

2dly—It makes the *blood circulate more quickly*, which increases the animal heat.

Q. *Why do two pieces of* ICE (*rubbed together*) MELT?

A. Ice contains 140 *degrees of latent heat*, and (when two pieces are *rubbed together*) some of this latent heat is made *sensible*, and melts the ice.

Q. *Are not* FORESTS *sometimes* SET *on* FIRE *by friction?*

A. Yes; when two branches or trunks of trees (blown about by the wind) *rub violently against each other*, their *latent heat is developed*, and sets fire to the forests.

Q. *Why do carpenters'* TOOLS (*such as gimlets, saws, files, &c.*) *become* HOT *when used?*

A. Because the friction of the tools against the wood disturbs its *latent heat*, and makes it *sensible*.

Q. *Give an* ILLUSTRATION *of this.*

A. When cannon is bored, the borers

become so intensely hot from friction, that they would blister the hands, if touched.

Q. *Why do these* BORERS *become so intensely* HOT?

A. Because the friction of the borers against the metal is so great, that it sets free a large quantity of latent heat.

CHAPTER X.

3.—CONDENSATION *or* COMPRESSION.*

Q. *What is meant by* COMPRESSION?

A. The act of *bringing parts nearer together;* as a sponge is *compressed* by being *squeezed in the hand.*

Q. *Cannot* HEAT *be evolved from common air merely by* COMPRESSION?

A. Yes; if a piece of *German tinder* be placed at the *bottom of a glass tube,* and the air in the tube *compressed by a piston,* the tinder will catch fire.

In a common syringe or squirt, the *handle* part (which *contains the sucker,* and is forced up and down) is called "the Piston."

---

* N. B. The reduction of matter into a smaller compass by any *external* or *mechanical* force is called COMPRESSION.

The reduction of matter into a smaller compass by some *internal action* (as by the escape of caloric) is called CONDENSATION.

Q. *Why will the tinder catch fire?*

A. Because the *air is compressed*, and *its latent heat being squeezed out*, sets fire to the tinder at the bottom of the tube.

Q. *When an* AIR-GUN *is discharged in the dark, why is it accompanied with a slight* FLASH?

A. Because the *air* is very rapidly *condensed*, and its latent heat developed in a *flash of light*.

N. B. If a glass lens be fixed in the copper ball, (where the *air* of the gun is *condensed*,) a flash of light may be distinctly discerned at the stroke of the piston.

Q. *Why do* DETONATING *salt and powder* EXPLODE *on being rubbed or struck?*

A. Because the mechanical action of rubbing or striking, produces sufficient heat to ignite the explosive materials of which they are composed.

Q. *Why are* SHOT *and* CANNON-BALLS HEATED *by being discharged from a gun or cannon?*

A. Because the air is so rapidly condensed, when the discharge is made, that sufficient latent heat is developed to make the shot or balls hot.

Q. *Why does the* HOLE *made by a shot or cannon-ball in a wall or timber, look as if it were* BURNT?

A. Because the shot or cannon-balls were so heated by the discharge, as actually to scorch the material into which they penetrated.

EFFECTS OF HEAT.

CHAPTER XI.

1.—Expansion.

Q. *What are the principal* EFFECTS *of* HEAT?

A. 1.—Expansion. 2.—Liquefaction. 3.—Vaporization. 4.—Evaporation; and 5.—Ignition.

Q. *Does* HEAT EXPAND AIR?

A. Yes; if a bladder (partially filled with air) be tied up at the neck, and *laid before the fire*, the air will expand till the bladder *bursts*.

Q. *Why will the* AIR SWELL *if the bladder be laid before the fire?*

A. Because the heat of the fire will drive the particles of air *apart from each other*, and cause them to occupy more room than they did before.

Q. *Why do unslit* CHESTNUTS CRACK *with a loud noise when* ROASTED?

A. Because they contain a great deal of air which is expanded by the heat of the fire; and not being able to escape, *bursts* violently through the thick rind, *slitting it*, and making a great noise.

Q. *What occasions the loud* CRACK *or report which we hear?*

A. 1st—The *sudden bursting of the rind* makes a report; in the same way as a piece of *wood* or *glass* would do, if *snapped in two:* and

2dly—The *escape of hot air* from the chestnut makes a report also; in the same way as *gunpowder*, when it escapes from a *gun.*

Q. *Why does the sudden* BURSTING *of the rind, or* SNAPPING *of a piece of wood, make a* REPORT?

A. Because a *violent jerk* is given to the air, when the attraction of cohesion is thus suddenly overcome. This jerk produces *rapid undulations* in the air, which (striking upon the ear) give the brain a sensation of *sound.*

Q. *Why does the* ESCAPE *of* AIR *from the chestnut, or the* EXPLOSION *of* GUNPOWDER, *produce a* REPORT?

A. Because the sudden expansion of the imprisoned air produces a partial vacuum; the *report* is caused by the *rushing of fresh air* to fill up this vacuum.

See Thunder, p. 15.

Q. *If a* CHESTNUT *be* SLIT, *it will* NOT CRACK; *why is this?*

A. Because the *heated air* of the

chestnut can then *freely escape* through the *slit in the rind.*

Q. *Why does an* APPLE *split and* SPURT *about when roasted?*

A. Because it contains a vast quantity of *air*, which (being expanded by the heat of the fire) *bursts through the peel*, carrying the juice of the apple along with it.

Q. *Does an* APPLE *contain* MORE AIR *in proportion than a* CHESTNUT?

A. Yes, much more. There is as much condensed air in a common apple, as would fill a space 48 *times as large as the apple itself.*

Q. *How can all this* AIR *be stowed in an* APPLE?

A. The *inside* of an apple consists of *little cells* (like a honey-comb), each of which contains a portion of the air.

Q. *When an* APPLE *is* ROASTED, *why is one part made* SOFT, *while all the rest remains hard?*

A. Because the air in those *cells next the fire* is expanded, and flies out; the *cells are broken, and* their juices *mixed together;* so the apple *collapses* (from loss of air and juice), and feels *soft* in those parts.

Q. *What is meant by the "apple* COLLAPSING?"

A. It means that the *plumpness* gives

way, and the apple becomes *flabby* and *shrivelled.*

Q. *Why do* SPARKS *of fire start (with a crackling noise) from pieces of* WOOD *laid upon a* FIRE?

A. Because the *air* (expanded by the heat) *forces its way through the pores of the wood;* and carries along with it the *covering of the pore,* which resisted its passage.

Q. *What is meant by the* "PORES *of the* WOOD?"

A. Very small *holes in the wood,* through which the *sap* circulates.

Q. *What are the* SPARKS OF FIRE *which burst from the* WOOD?

A. Very small pieces of wood made *red hot,* and separated from the log by the *force of the air,* when it bursts from its confinement.

Q. *Why does* DRY PINE *make more snapping than any* OTHER WOOD?

A. Because the pores of pine are *very large,* and contain *more air* than wood of a *closer grain.*

Q *Why does* GREEN WOOD *make* LESS SNAPPING *than* DRY?

A. Because the pores being filled with *sap,* contain *very little air.*

Q. *Why does* DRY WOOD *make* MORE SNAPPING *than green?*

A. Because the sap is *dried up*, and the pores are filled with *air* instead.

Q. *Why does* DRY *wood* BURN *more easily than* GREEN *or wet wood?*

A. Because the pores of dry wood are *filled with air* which supports combustion; but the pores of green or wet wood are filled with *moisture*, which extinguishes flame.

Q. *Why does* MOISTURE EXTINGUISH FLAME?

A. 1st—Because it prevents the *hydrogen* of the fuel from mixing with the *oxygen* of the air, to form *carbonic acid gas;* and

2dly—Because heat is perpetually carried off, by the formation of the sap or moisture *into steam.*

Q. *Why do* STONES SNAP *and fly about when heated in the* FIRE?

A. Because the close texture of the stone prevents the hot air from escaping; in consequence of which, it *bursts forth with great violence*, tearing the stone to atoms, and forcing the fragments into the room.

Probably some part of this effect is due to the setting free of the *water of crystallization.*

Q. *When bottled* ALE *or* PORTER *is set before a* FIRE, *why is the* CORK FORCED OUT *sometimes?*

A. Because the *carbonic acid* of the

liquor *expands* by the heat, and drives out the cork.

Carbonic acid gas is a compound of carbon and oxygen. The *carbon* comes from the *fuel*, and the *oxygen* from the *air*. See p. 40.

Q. *Why does* ALE *or* PORTER FROTH *more after it has been set before the fire?*

A. Because the heat of the fire sets free the *carbonic acid* of the liquor; which is entangled as it rises through the liquor, and produces bubbles or froth.

Q. *When a boy makes a* BALLOON, *and sets fire to the cotton or sponge (which has been steeped in spirits of wine), why is the balloon* INFLATED?

A. Because the *air* of the balloon is *expanded by the flame*, till every crumple is inflated and made smooth.

Q. *Why does the* BALLOON RISE *after it has been inflated by the expanded air?*

A. Because the same quantity of air is *expanded to three or four times its original volume;* and made so much *lighter*, that even when all the paper, wire, and cotton are added, it is still lighter than common air.

Q. *Why does* SMOKE RUSH UP *a* CHIMNEY?

A. Because the heat of the fire *expands the air in the chimney;* which (being thus made *lighter* than the air around) *rises up the chimney*, and carries the smoke in its current.

Q. *Why will a* LONG *chimney* SMOKE, *unless the* FIRE *be pretty* FIERCE?

A. Because the heat of the fire will not be sufficient to *rarefy all the air in the chimney.*

Q. WHY *will the chimney smoke, unless the fire be* FIERCE *enough to heat* ALL *the air in the* CHIMNEY FLUE?

A. Because the *cold air* (condensed in the upper part of the flue) *will sink from its own weight;* and sweep the ascending smoke *back* into the room.

Q. *What is the use of a* COWL *upon a chimney-pot?*

A. It acts as a *screen*, to prevent the wind from blowing into the chimney.

Q. *What* HARM *would the* WIND *do if it were to* BLOW *into a* CHIMNEY?

A. 1st—It would prevent the smoke from getting out; and

2dly—The *cold air* (introduced into the chimney by the wind) *would fall down the flue*, and drive the smoke with it *into the room.*

Q. *Why are some things* SOLID, *others* LIQUID, *and others* GASEOUS?

A. Because the particles which compose some things are nearer together than they are in others. Those in which the particles are *closest* are *solid;* those in which they are *furthest apart* are *gaseous;* and the rest *liquid.*

Q. *Why does heat change a* SOLID *(like ice) first into a* LIQUID, *and then into a* GAS?

A. Because heat drives the component particles further *asunder;* hence a certain quantity of heat changes solid ice into a *liquid*—and a further addition of heat changes the liquid into *steam.*

Q. *Why does* WATER SIMMER *before it boils?*

A. Because the particles of water *near the bottom* of the kettle (being formed into *steam* sooner than the rest) *shoot upwards;* but are *condensed* again (as they rise) *by the colder water*, and produce what is called "simmering."

Q. *What is meant by* SIMMERING?

A. A gentle tremor or *undulation* on the surface of the water. When water *simmers*, the bubbles *collapse beneath the surface*, and the steam is condensed to *water again;* but when water *boils*, the bubbles *rise to the surface*, and the *steam is thrown off.*

Collapse, i. e., burst.

Q. *Why does a* KETTLE SING *when the water simmers?*

A. Because the *air* (entangled in the water) escapes by *fits and starts* through the *spout* of the kettle, which makes a noise like a wind instrument.

Q. *Why does* NOT *a kettle* SING *when the water* BOILS?

A. Because *all* the water is *boiling hot;* so the steam escapes in a *continuous stream*, and not by *fits* and *starts.*

Q. *When does a kettle sing* MOST?

A. When it is set on the *hob* to boil.

Q. *Why does a kettle* SING MORE *when it is set on the* SIDE *of a fire, than when it is set in the* MIDST *of the fire?*

A. Because the heat is applied so *unequally*, that *one side is made hotter than the other;* in consequence of which, the steam is more *entangled.*

Q. *Why does a* KETTLE *sing, when the boiling water begins to* COOL *again?*

A. Because the *upper* surface cools *first;* and the steam (which rises from the lower part of the kettle) is *again entangled*, and escapes by *fits* and *starts.*

Q. *Why does* BOILING WATER SWELL?

A. Because it is *expanded by the heat:* i. e.—The heat of the fire drives the particles of water *further apart* from each other: and (as they are not *packed so closely together*) they take up *more room;* in other words, the water *swells.*

Q. *What is meant when it is said, that "* HEAT *drives the* PARTICLES *of water further* APART *from each other?"*

A. Water is composed of little globules, like very small grains of sand; the heat *drives* these particles away from each other; and (as they then require more *room*) the water *swells.*

Q. *Why does* BOILING WATER BUBBLE?

A. Because the *vapor* (rising through the water) is *entangled,* and forces up bubbles in its effort to escape.

N. B. All the *air* of water is expelled at the commencement of its boiling.

Q. *Why does a* KETTLE *sometimes* BOIL OVER?

A. Because the water is *expanded by heat;* if, therefore, a kettle is *filled with cold water*, some of it must *run over*, as soon as it is *expanded by heat.*

Q. *But I have seen a* KETTLE BOIL OVER, *although it has not been filled* FULL *of* WATER; *how do you account for* THAT?

A. If a fire be *very fierce*, the air and vapor are expelled so *rapidly*, that the *bubbles are very numerous;* and (towering one above another) reach the *top of the kettle*, and *fall over.*

Q. *Why is a pot (which was full to* OVERFLOWING, *while the water was boiling* HOT) NOT FULL, *after it has been taken off the fire for a short time?*

A. Because (while the water is *boiling*) it is *expanded* by the heat, and fills the pot even to overflowing: but, when it becomes cool, it *contracts* again, and occupies a much less space.

Q. *Why does the water of a* KETTLE *run out of the* SPOUT *when it* BOILS?

A. Because the lid fits so tightly, that the steam cannot lift it up and escape: being confined, therefore, in the kettle, it *presses on the water* with great power, and forces it out of the spout.

Q. *What causes the* RATTLING NOISE, *so often made by the* LID *of a saucepan or boiler?*

A. The steam (seeking to escape) *forces up the lid* of the boiler, and the *weight* of the lid carries it *back again:* this being done *frequently*, produces a rattling noise.

Q. *If the steam* COULD NOT LIFT UP THE LID *of the boiler how would it escape?*

A. If the lid fitted so tightly, that the steam could not raise it up, the boiler would *burst into fragments*, and the consequences might be fatal.

Q. *When steam pours out from the spout of a kettle, the* STREAM *begins apparently* HALF AN INCH *off the* SPOUT; *why does it not begin* CLOSE *to the spout?*

A. Steam is really *invisible* · and the

half-inch (between the spout and the "*stream of mist*", is the *real steam*, before it has been condensed by air.

Q. *Why is not* ALL *the steam* INVISIBLE *as well as that half-inch?*

A. Because the invisible particles are *condensed by the cold air;* and, rolling one into another, look like a thick mist.

Q. *What* BECOMES *of the* STEAM? *for it soon vanishes.*

A. After it has been condensed into mist, it is *dissolved by the air*, and dispersed abroad as *invisible vapor.*

Q. *And what* BECOMES *of the* INVISIBLE VAPOR?

A. Being *lighter* than air, it *ascends* to the upper regions of the atmosphere, where (being again *condensed*) it contributes to form *clouds*.

Q. *Why does a* METAL SPOON (*left in a saucepan*) RETARD *the process of* BOILING?

A. Because the metal spoon (being an excellent *conductor*) *carries off the heat from the water;* and (as heat is carried off by the spoon) the water takes a longer time to boil.

Q. *Why will a* POT (*filled with water*) NEVER BOIL, *when immersed in* ANOTHER *vessel full of water also?*

A. Because water can never be heated *above the boiling point;* all the heat.

absorbed by water after it *boils*, is employed in generating *steam.*

Q. *How does the conversion of water into steam, prevent the* INNER POT *from* BOILING?

A. Directly the water in the larger pot is *boiling hot* (or 212°), *steam is formed* and *carries off some of its heat;* therefore, 212° of heat can never *pass through it*, to raise the *inner* vessel to *boiling heat.*

Q. *Why do* SUGAR, SALT, *&c.*, RETARD *the process of* BOILING?

A. Because they increase the *density* of water; and whatever increases the *density* of a fluid, retards its boiling.

Q. *If you want water to boil without* COMING IN CONTACT *with the* SAUCEPAN, *what plan must you adopt?*

A. We must *immerse the pot* (containing the water to be boiled) in a saucepan containing *strong brine*, or sugar.

Q. *Why would the* INNER *vessel boil, if the* OUTER *vessel contained strong* BRINE?

A. Because *brine* will not boil, till it is raised to 218 or 220°. Therefore, 212° of heat may easily pass through it, to *raise the vessel immersed in it to boiling heat.*

Q. *Why will brine impart to another vessel* MORE *than* 212°, *and water* NOT SO MUCH?

A. Because no liquid can impart so high a degree of heat, as its own *boiling* temperature: As water boils at 212° it cannot impart 212° of heat: but, as brine will not boil without 21° of heat, it can impart enough to make water boil.

Q. *Why can liquids impart no* EXTRA *heat, after they boil?*

A. Because all *extra* heat is spent *in making steam.* Hence water will not boil a vessel of *water* immersed in it, because it cannot impart to it 212° of heat; but *brine* will, because it can impart *more* than 212° of heat, before it is *itself* converted into steam.

Ether boils at - -	100 *degs.*	Syrup boils at - -	221 *degs.*
Alcohol - - - - -	173½ "	Oil of turpentine -	314 "
Water - - - - - -	212 "	Sulphuric acid - -	472 "
Water, with one-fifth salt - -	219 "	Linseed oil - - - -	640 "
		Mercury - - - - -	656 "

Any liquid which boils at a *lower* degree can be made to boil, if immersed in a liquid which boils at a *higher* degree. Thus a *cup of ether* can be made to boil in a saucepan of *water.* A *cup of water* in a saucepan of *brine or syrup.* But a *cup of water* will *not* boil, if immersed in *ether;* nor a *cup of syrup* in *water.*

Q. *Why are* CLOUDS HIGHER *on a* FINE DAY?

A. Because they are *lighter*, and *more buoyant.*

Q. *Why are* CLOUDS LIGHTER *on a* FINE DAY?

A. 1st—Because the vapor of the clouds is *less condensed;* and

2dly—The *air itself* (on a fine day) retains much of its vapor in an *invisible* form.

Q. *Why is a* CUP *put* INVERTED *into a* FRUIT-PIE?

A. Its principal use is to *hold the crust up*, and *prevent it from sinking*, when the cooked fruit gives way under it.

Q. *Does not the cup* PREVENT *the* FRUIT *of the pie from* BOILING OVER?

A. No—it will rather tend to *make* it boil over, as there will be *less room* in the dish.

Q. *Explain this.*

A. When the pie is put into the oven the *air* in the cup will *begin* to *expand*, and drive every particle of juice from under it; in consequence of which, the pie-dish will have a cup-full *less room* to hold its fruit in, than if the cup were *taken out*.

Q. *If the juice is driven* OUT *of the cup, why is the* CUP *always* FULL *of* JUICE *when the pie is cut up?*

A. Because immediately the pie is *drawn*, the air in the cup begins to *condense again*, and occupy a *smaller space*; and, as the cup is no longer full of *air*, *juice* rushes in to occupy the void.

Q. *Why does* JUICE *rush into the cup when the cup is* NOT FULL *of* AIR?

A. Because the external air *presses upon the surface of the juice*, which rushes *unobstructed* into the cup; as mercury rises through the tube of a barometer.

N. B. Since the juice of the pie runs into the cup, as soon as it is taken out of the oven; the cup prevents the juice from being *spilt over the crust*, when the pie is carried about from place to place; although it does not prevent the fruit from boiling over.

CHAPTER XII.

Expansion from Heat.

(*Continued.*)

Q. *Does heat expand everything* ELSE *besides air and water?*

A. Yes: *every* thing (that man is acquainted with) is expanded by heat.

Q. *Why does a* COOPER *heat his* HOOPS RED HOT *when he puts them on a tub?*

A. 1st—As *iron expands by heat*, the hoops will be *larger* when they are red hot; in consequence of which, they will fit on the tub *more easily:* and

2dly—As *iron contracts by cold*, the hoops will *shrink* as they cool down, and girt the tub with a *tighter grasp*.

Q. *Why does a* WHEELWRIGHT *make the hoops* RED HOT *which he fixes on the* NAVE *of a* WHEEL?

A. 1st—That they may *fit on more easily:* and

2dly—That they may *girt the nave more tightly.*

Q. *Why will the wheelwright's* HOOP FIT *the nave* MORE EASILY, *for being made* RED HOT?

A. Because it will be *expanded* by the heat; and (being larger) will go on the nave more *easily.*

Q. *Why will the* HOOPS *which have been* PUT ON HOT GIRT *the nave more* FIRMLY?

A. Because they will *shrink* when they cool down; and, therefore, *girt the nave with a tighter grasp.*

Q. *Why does a* STOVE *make a* CRACKLING NOISE *when a fire is very hot?*

A. Because it *expands* from the heat; and the parts of the stove *rubbing* against each other, or driving against the *bricks*, produce a *crackling* noise.

Q. *Why does a* STOVE *make a similar* CRACKLING NOISE *when a large* FIRE *is* TAKEN DOWN?

A. Because it *contracts again*, when the fire is removed; in consequence of which, the parts *rub against* each other again, and the *bricks are again disturbed.*

Q. *Why does the* PLASTER *round a* STOVE CRACK *and fall away?*

A. Because (when the fire is light ed) the *iron-work* expands more than the brick-work and plaster, and *pushes them away;* but (when the fire is put out) the metal *shrinks* again, and leaves the "setting" behind.

The "setting" is a technical word for the plaster, &c., in immediate contact with the stove.

Q. *Why does the* PLASTER FALL AWAY?

A. As a *chink* is left (between the "setting" and the stove), the plaster will frequently fall away from its own weight.

Q. *What* OTHER *cause contributes to* BRING *the* PLASTER DOWN?

A. As the *heat of the fire* varies, the *size of the iron stove* varies also; and this swelling and contracting keep up such a *constant disturbance* about the plaster, that it *cracks and falls off*, leaving the fire-place very unsightly.

Q. *Why does the* MERCURY *of a* THERMOMETER RISE *in hot weather?*

A. Because heat *expands the metal*, which (being increased in bulk) occupies a *larger space;* and, consequently, rises higher in the tube.

Q. *Why is a* GLASS BROKEN *when* HOT WATER *is poured into it?*

A. Because the *inside* of the glass is expanded by the hot water, and *not the outside;* so the *glass snaps*, in consequence of this unequal expansion.

Q. *Why is not the* OUTSIDE *of the* GLASS *expanded by the hot water as well as the* INSIDE?

A. Because glass is a *bad conductor of heat*, and *breaks* before the heat of the *inner* surface is conducted to the *outside.*

Q. *Why does a* GLASS *snap because the* INNER *surface is* HOTTER *than the* OUTER?

A. Because the *inner* surface is expanded and not the *outer:* in consequence of which, an *opposing force* is created, which breaks the glass.

Q. *Why is a* CHINA CUP *broken if* HOT WATER *be poured over it, or into it?*

A. Because it is a *bad conductor;* and, as the *inner* surface expands from the heat, (and *not* the *outer*,) an *opposing force* is created, which breaks the cup.

Q. *If a* GLASS BEAKER *be set on a warm* HOB, *why does the* BOTTOM COME OFF?

A. Because glass is a *bad conductor;* and (as the *bottom* of the glass expands from the warmth of the hot stove, before the *sides* are heated) the two parts *separate* from each other.

CHAPTER XIII.

2.—LIQUEFACTION.

3.—VAPORIZATION.

Q. *What is meant by* LIQUEFACTION ?

A. The *state of being melted;* as ice is melted by the heat of the sun.

Q. *Why is* ICE MELTED *by the* HEAT *of the* SUN ?

A. Because, when the heat of the sun enters the solid ice, it *forces its particles asunder;* till their attraction of cohesion is sufficiently overcome, to *convert the solid ice into a liquid.*

See p. 109.

Q. *Why are* METALS MELTED *by the heat of* FIRE ?

A. Because, when the heat of the fire enters the solid metal, it *forces its particles asunder;* till their attraction of cohesion is sufficiently overcome, to *convert the solid metal into a liquid.*

Q. *Why is* WATER *converted into* STEAM *by the heat of the* FIRE ?

A. Because, when the heat of the fire enters the water, it *separates its globules* into very *minute bubbles;* which (being lighter than air) fly off from the surface in the form of *steam.*

Q. *Why does not* WOOD MELT *like metal?*

A. Because the heat of the fire *decomposes* the wood into *gas*, *smoke*, and *ashes;* and the different parts *separate* from each other.

Q. *What is meant by* VAPORIZATION?

A. The *conversion* of a *solid* or *liquid into vapor:* as snow or water is converted into vapor by the heat of the sun.

Q. *What are* CLOUDS?

A. Moisture *evaporated from the earth*, and again partially *condensed* in the upper regions of the air.

Q. *What is the difference between a* FOG *and a* CLOUD?

A. Clouds and fogs differ only in one respect. *Clouds* are *elevated above our heads:* but *fogs come in contact with the surface of the earth.*

Q. *Why do* CLOUDS FLOAT *so readily in the air?*

A. Because they are composed of *very minute globules* (called ves′icles); which (being lighter than air) float, like *soap bubbles.*

Q. *Why does* VAPOR *sometimes form into* CLOUDS, *and sometimes rest upon the earth as* MIST *or* FOG?

A. This depends on the *temperature* of the air. When the *surface of the earth* is *warmer than the air*, the vapor of the earth (being condensed by the chill air) becomes *mist or fog*. But, when the *air* is *warmer than the earth*, the vapor *rises through the air*, and becomes cloud.

Q. *Are* ALL *clouds* ALIKE?

A. No. They vary greatly in *density*, *height*, and *color*.

Q. *What is the chief* CAUSE *of fog and* CLOUDS?

A. The changes of the wind.

Many *local* circumstances also favor the formation of clouds.

Q. *How can the* CHANGES *of the* WIND *affect the* CLOUDS?

A. If a *cold current of wind* blows suddenly over any region, it *condenses* the invisible vapor of the air into *cloud* or *rain*: but if a *warm current of wind* blows over any region, it *disperses* the clouds, by *absorbing their vapor*.

Q. *What* COUNTRIES *are the* MOST *cloudy?*

A. Those where the winds are *most variable*, as Britain.

Q. *What* COUNTRIES *are the* LEAST *cloudy?*

A. Those where the winds are *least variable*, as Egypt.

Q. *What* DISTANCE *are the* CLOUDS *from the* EARTH?

A. Some *thin*, *light clouds* are elevated above the highest mountain-top;

some *heavy* ones touch the steeples, trees, and even the earth: but the *average* height is between *one and two miles.*

N. B. Streaky, curling clouds, *like hair*, are often 5 or 6 miles high.

Q. WHAT CLOUDS *are the* LOWEST?

A. Those which are *most highly electrified;* lightning clouds are rarely more than about 700 yards above the ground; and often actually *touch the earth with one of their edges.*

Q. *What is the* SIZE *of the* CLOUDS?

A. Some clouds are 20 *square miles in surface,* and above *a mile in thickness;* while others are only a *few yards or inches.*

Q. *How can persons ascertain the* THICKNESS *of a cloud?*

A. As the *tops* of high mountains are generally above the clouds, travellers may pass *quite through* them into a clear blue firmament; when the clouds will be seen *beneath their feet.*

Q. *What produces the great* VARIETY *in the* SHAPE *of the* CLOUDS?

A. Three things: 1st—The cause and manner of their *formation:*

2dly—Their *electrical* condition: and

3dly—Their relations to *currents of wind.*

Q. *How can* ELECTRICITY *affect the* SHAPE *of* CLOUDS?

A. If one cloud be *full of electricity* and another *not*, they will be *attracted* to each other, and either coalesce—diminish in size—or vanish altogether.

Q. WHAT CLOUDS *assume the most* FANTASTIC *shapes?*

A. Those that are the most *highly electrified.*

Q. *What effect have* WINDS *on the* SHAPE *of* CLOUD?

A. They sometimes *absorb them entirely;* sometimes *increase their volume and density;* and sometimes *change the position of their parts.*

Q. *How can* WINDS ABSORB CLOUDS *altogether?*

A. *Warm, dry winds* will convert the substance of clouds into *invisible vapor*, which they will carry away in their own current.

Q. *How can* WINDS INCREASE *the bulk and density of* CLOUDS?

A. *Cold* currents of wind will condense the *invisible vapor* of the air, and *add it to the clouds* with which they come in contact.

Q. *How can winds* CHANGE *the* SHAPE *of* CLOUDS, *by altering the position of their parts?*

A. Clouds are so voluble and light,

that every breath of wind changes the position of their ves'icles or bubbles.

Q. *What are the general* COLORS *of the* CLOUDS?

A. White and grey, when the sun is *above the horizon:* but red, orange, and yellow, at *sun-rise* and *sun-set.*

The *blue sky* is not *cloud* at all.

Q. *Why are the* LAST CLOUDS *of* EVENING *generally of a* RED *tinge?*

A. Because *red* rays (being the *least refrangible* of all) are the *last to disappear.*

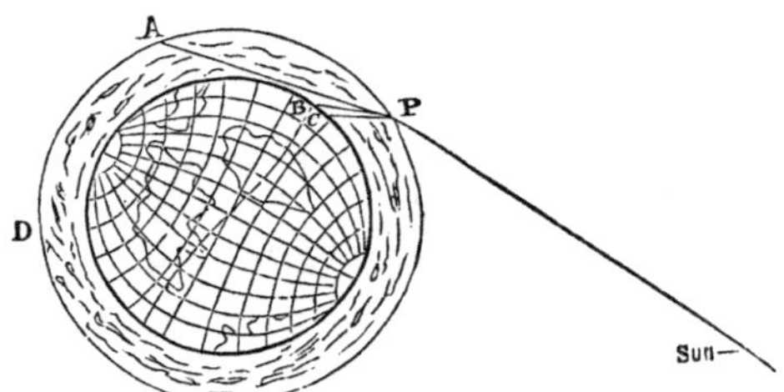

Suppose P A to be the red rays, P B the yellow, P C the blue. If the earth turns in the direction of P A D, it is quite manifest that a spectator will see A, (the red rays,) some time after P C and P B have passed from sight.

Q. *What is meant by being* "LESS REFRANGIBLE"?

A. Being *less able to be bent.* Blue and yellow rays are more easily bent *below the horizon* by the resistance of the air: but red rays are not so much *bent down;* and, therefore, we see them later in the evening.

As at A in the figure on p. 126.

Q. *Why are* MORNING CLOUDS *generally of a* RED *tinge?*

A. Because red rays are the *least refrangible* of all; and not being *bent* so much as blue and yellow rays, we see them sooner of a morning.

Thus (fig. on p. 126) if the earth turned in the direction of D A P, a spectator at D would see A (the red rays) long before he saw P B and P C.

Q. *Why is not the color of clouds always* ALIKE?

A. Because their *size, density,* and *situation* in regard to the sun, are perpetually varying; so that sometimes *one* color is reflected and sometimes *another.*

Q. *What regulates the* MOTION *of the* CLOUDS?

A. Principally the *winds;* but sometimes *electricity* will influence their motion also.

Q. *How do you know that* CLOUDS *move by* OTHER *influences besides* WIND?

A. Because (in calm weather) we often see *small clouds meeting each other* from opposite directions.

Q. *How do you know that* ELECTRICITY *affect the motion of the clouds?*

A. Because clouds often meet from *opposite directions;* and, having discharged their opposite electricities into each other, *vanish altogether.*

Q. *Into how many* CLASSES *are the different sorts of* CLOUDS *generally divided?*

A. Into three classes :—viz. Simple, Intermediate, and Compound.

Q. *How are* SIMPLE CLOUDS *sub-divided?*

A. Into 1.—Cirrus; 2.—Cum'ulus; and 3.—Stra'tus clouds.

Q. *What sort of* CLOUDS *are called* CIRRUS?

A. Clouds like *fibres, loose hair,* or *thin streaks,* are called "cirrus clouds."

Q. *Why are these clouds called* CIRRUS?

A. From the Latin word *cirrus* ("a lock of hair, or curl"). Cirrus clouds are the *most elevated of all.*

Q. *What do* CIRRUS *clouds* PORTEND?

A. When the streamers point *upwards,* the clouds are *falling,* and *rain is at hand:* but when the streamers point *downwards,* westerly winds or drought may be expected.

Q. *What sort of* CLOUDS *are called* CUM'ULUS?

A. Cum'ulus clouds are lumps, like great *sugar-loaves—volumes of smoke—*or *mountains towering over mountains.*

Q. *Why are these monster masses called* CUM'-ULUS CLOUDS?

A. From the Latin word *cum'ulus* ("a mass or pile").

What do CUM'ULUS *clouds* FORESHOW?

A. When these piles of cloud are *fleecy*, and sail *against the wind*, they indicate *rain;* but when their outline is very *hard*, and they come up *with* the wind, they foretell *fine weather*.

Cum'ulus clouds should be *smaller* towards evening than they are at noon. If they *increase* in size at sun-set, a thunder-storm may be expected in the night.

Q. *What sort of* CLOUDS *are called* STRA'TUS?

A. *Creeping mists*, especially prevalent in a summer's evening: these clouds rise at sun-set *in low, damp places;* and are always *nearer the earth* than any *other* sort of cloud.

Q. *Why are these mists called* STRA'TUS *clouds?*

A. From the Latin word *stra'tus* ("laid low," or "that which lies low").

Q. *What produces* CIRRUS CLOUDS?

A. Moisture in a visible form, deposited in the *higher regions* of the atmosphere by *ascending currents* of *heated air.*

Q. *What produces* CUM'ULUS CLOUDS?

A. Masses of visible vapor passing from the places where they were *formed*, to other places where they are about to be either *dissolved*, or deposited as falling *rain.*

Q. *What produces* STRA'TUS CLOUDS?

A. Beds of visible moisture, formed

by some chilling effects, acting along the *direct surface* of the *earth.*

Q. *How are the* INTERMEDIATE CLOUDS *sub-divided?*

A. Into two sorts. 1.—The Cirro-Cum'ulus; and 2.—The Cirro-Stra'tus.

Q. *What are* CIRRO-CUM'ULUS CLOUDS?

A. Cirro-Cum'ulus clouds are cirrus clouds springing from a *massy centre*, or *heavy masses*, edged with *long streaks* generally called "*mares' tails.*"

A system of *small round* clouds may be called cirro cum'ulus.

Q. *What do* CIRRO-CUM'ULUS *clouds generally* FOREBODE?

A. Continued drought, or hot, dry weather.

Q. *What are* CIRRO-STRA'TUS CLOUDS?

A. They compose what is generally called a "*mackarel sky.*" This class of clouds invariably indicates *rain* and *wind*; hence the proverb—

"Mackarel's scales and mares' tails
Make lofty ships to carry low sails."

Q. *What produce* CIRRO-CUM'ULUS *clouds?*

A. *Cum'ulus* clouds dissolving away into *cirrus* produce the intermediate class called CIRRO-CUM'ULUS.

Q. *What produce* CIRRO-STRA'TUS *clouds?*

A *Cirrus* clouds accumulating into

denser masses produce the intermediate class, called CIRRO-STRA'TUS.

Q. *How are* COMPOUND CLOUDS *sub-divided?*

A. Compound clouds are also subdivided into two sorts. 1.—The Cum'u-lo-Stra'tus; and 2.—The Nimbus clouds.

Q. *What is meant by* CUMULO-STRA'TUS *clouds?*

A. Those clouds which assume all sorts of *gigantic forms;* such as vast towers and rocks—huge whales and dragons—scenes of battle—and cloudy giants. This class of clouds is the most romantic and strange of all.

Q. *What do the* CUMULO-STRA'TUS *clouds* FORETELL?

A. A *change of weather;* either from fine to rain, or from rain to fine.

Q. *What are* NIMBUS CLOUDS?

A. All clouds from which *rain falls.* Nimbus is the Latin word for "*clouds which bring a storm.*"

Q. *By what particular character may the* NIMBUS *(or rain-cloud) be at once* DISTINGUISHED?

A. By the want of a *defined outline:* Its edge is gradually shaded off from the *deep grey mass* into *transparency.*

Q. *What* APPEARANCE *takes place in the* CLOUDS *at the approach of* RAIN?

A The *cum'ulus* cloud becomes *sta-*

tionary, and *cirrus streaks settle upon it*, forming cum'ulo-stratus clouds; *black* at first, but afterwards of a *grey* color.

Q. *Why do* CLOUDS *gather* ROUND MOUNTAIN TOPS ?

A. Because the air (being *chilled* by the cold mountain tops) deposits its vapor there in a *visible form* or cloud.

Q. *What are the* USES *of* CLOUDS ?

A. 1st—They act as *screens*, to arrest the radiation of heat from the earth;

2dly—They temper the heat of the *sun's rays ;* and

3dly—They are the great *store-houses of rain.*

"Radiation of heat," i. e., the escape of heat, when no *conductor* carries it away.

Q. *Why is* WIND *said to* BLOW UP *the* CLOUDS ?

A. Because a *dry*, *warm* wind (which has travelled over seas) having absorbed a large quantity of moisture, deposits some of it in the *visible form of clouds*, as soon as it reaches a *colder* region of air.

Q. *Why does* WIND *sometimes* DRIVE AWAY *the* CLOUDS ?

A. Because it has travelled over *dry climes* or *thirsty deserts*, and become so *dry*, that it absorbs vapor from the clouds, and causes them to disappear.

Q. *What is the* CAUSE *of a* RED SUN-SET?

A. The vapor of the air, not being *actually condensed into clouds*, but only on the *point of being condensed.*

Q. *Why is a* RED SUN-SET *an indication of a* FINE DAY *to-morrow?*

A. Because the vapors of the earth are *not condensed into clouds*, by the cold of sunset. Our Lord referred to this prognostic in the following words: "When it is evening ye say it will be fair weather, for the sky is red." (Matt. XVI. 2.)

Q. *What is the cause of a coppery* YELLOW SUN-SET?

A. The vapor of the air being *actually condensed into clouds.*

Q. *Why do vapors* (NOT ACTUALLY CONDENSED) *refract* RED *rays, while condensed vapor refracts yellow?*

A. Because the beams of light meet with very little resistance; in consequence of which, those rays are bent down to the eye, which require the least refraction, such as *red.*

See figure on p. 126, where it is evident that the *red* ray P A, is less bent, than the yellow and blue rays, P B, P C.

Q. *Why do* CONDENSED *vapors refract* YELLOW *rays, whereas vapors not actually condensed refract red?*

A. Because the beams of light meet

with *more resistance* from the condensed vapor; in consequence of which, those rays are bent down to the eye, which are *more refracted* than the red, such as yellow.

See on figure p. 126, where it is evident that the yellow ray, P B, is more bent than the red ray, P A.

Q. *Why is a* YELLOW SUN-SET *an indication of* WET?

A. Because it shows that the vapors of the air *are* already *condensed into clouds;* rain, therefore, may be shortly expected.

Q. *What is the cause of a* RED SUN-RISE?

A. Vapor in the upper region of the air *just on the point of being condensed.*

Q. *Why is a* RED *and* LOWERING *sky at* SUN-RISE *an indication of a* WET DAY?

A. Because the higher regions of the air are *laden with vapor* on the very *point of condensation,* which the rising sun cannot disperse. Hence our Lord's observation, "In the morning ye say, it will be foul weather to-day, for the sky is red and lowering." (Matt. XVI. 3.)

Q. *Why is a* GREY MORNING *an indication of a* FINE DAY?

A. Because only the air *contiguous to the earth* is damp and full of vapor. There are no vapors in the *higher* regions of the air, to bend down to the eye even the red rays of any beam of light.

Q. *What difference (in the state of the air) is required, to make a* GREY *and* RED SUN-RISE ?

A. In a *grey* sun-rise, only that portion of air *contiguous to the earth is filled with vapor;* all the rest is clear and dry. But in a *red* sun-rise the air in the *upper regions* is so full of vapor, that the rising sun cannot disperse it.

Q. *Why is a* GREY SUN-SET *an indication of* WET ?

A. Because it shows that the air on the *surface of the earth* is very *damp* at *sun-set;* which is a plain proof that the air is *saturated with vapor;* in consequence of which wet may be soon expected: hence the proverb—

"Evening red and morning grey
Will set the traveller on his way;
But evening grey and morning red
Will bring down rain upon his head."

Q. *What is meant by an* AURORA BOREA'LIS, *or northern light?*

A. *Luminous clouds* in the *north of the sky* at night-time. Sometimes streaks of blue, purple, green, red, &c., and sometimes flashes of light, are seen.

Q. *What is the cause of the* AURORA BOREA'LIS, *or northern light?*

A. *Electricity* in the higher regions of the atmosphere.

Q. *Why are there* DIFFERENT COLORS *in the Aurora Borea'lis, such as white, yellow, red and purple?*

A. Because the electric fluid passes through *air of different densities.* The most *rarefied air* produces a *white light;* the most *dry air, red;* and the most *damp* produces yellow streaks.

Q. *Does the* AURORA BOREA'LIS *forebode fine weather or* WET?

A. When its *coruscations are very bright,* it is generally followed by unsettled weather.

Q. *Why does a* HAZE *round the* SUN *indicate* RAIN?

A. Because the *haze* is caused by *very fine rain falling in the upper regions of the air:* when this is the case, *a rain* of 5 or 6 *hours' duration* may be expected.

Q. *Why is a* HALO *round the* MOON *a sure indication of* RAIN?

A. Because it is caused by *fine rain, falling in the upper regions of the air.* The *larger* the halo, the *nearer the rain-clouds,* and the sooner may rain be expected.

Q. *What is the cause of a* BLACK MIST: *and why does it bring* WET *weather?*

A. The mist is *black*, because it is *overshadowed by dense clouds;* and *wet* weather may be expected, because the air is saturated with vapor.

Q. *Why is* MIST *sometimes* WHITE: *and why does a white mist indicate* FINE *weather?*

A. The mist is *white*, because no *clouds blacken it with their shadow;* and *fine weather* may be expected, because the sky is cloudless.

Q. *Why do we* FEEL *almost* SUFFOCATED *in a hot cloudy night?*

A. Because the heat of the earth cannot escape into the upper region of the air; but is pent in by the clouds, and confined to *the surface of the earth.*

Q. *Why do we feel* SPRIGHTLY *in a clear, bright night?*

A. Because the heat of the earth can readily escape into the upper regions of the air, and is not confined and pent in *by thick clouds.*

Q. *Why do we* FEEL DEPRESSED *in* SPIRITS *on a* WET, *murky* DAY?

A. 1st—Because the air is laden with vapor, and has (proportionally) *less oxygen.*

2dly—The air being lighter than usual, *does not balance the air in our body;* and

3dly—Moist air has a tendency to depress the nervous system.

Q. *What is meant by the "air balancing the air in our body?"*

A. The human body contains air of a given density; if, therefore, we ascend into *rarer air*, or descend into *denser*, the balance is destroyed, and *we feel oppressed.*

Q. *Why do we feel* OPPRESSED, *if the air around is not of the* SAME DENSITY *as that in our body?*

A. Because if the air be *more* dense than our body, it will produce a feeling of *oppression;* if it be *less* dense, the air in our body will produce a feeling of *distension.*

Q. *Why do* PERSONS, *who* ASCEND *in* BALLOONS, FEEL PAIN *in their eyes, ears, and chest?*

A. Because the air in the upper regions of the atmosphere is more *rare* than the *air in their bodies;* and (till *equilibrium is restored*) pain will be felt in the more sensitive parts of the body.

More especially in the tympanum of the ear.

Q. *Why do* PERSONS, *who* DESCEND *in* DIVING-BELLS, FEEL PAIN *in their eyes, ears, and chest?*

A. Because the air in the diving-bell is *compressed* by the upward pressure of the water; in consequence of which, great pain is felt in the more sensitive parts of the body.

The pressure thus caused is sometimes sufficient to *rupture* the membrane of the tympanum, and produce incurable *deafness.*

Q. *Why are* PEARL DIVERS *very frequently* DEAF ?

A. Because the *pressure of the water* against the tympanum of their ears *ruptures* the membrane; and this rupture produces incurable deafness.

Q. *Why does the* SEA HEAVE *and* SIGH, *just* PREVIOUS *to a* STORM ?

A. Because the density of the air is *very suddenly diminished;* and (as the density of the air is diminished) its power to transmit sound is diminished also; in consequence of which, the *roar* of the sea is less audible, and seems like heavy sighs.

Q. *Why is the* AIR *so universally* QUIET, *just* PREVIOUS *to a* TEMPEST ?

A. Because the air is *suddenly and very greatly rarefied;* and (as the density of the air is diminished) its *power to transmit sound* is *diminished also.*

Q. *How do you* KNOW, *that* RAREFIED *air* CANNOT TRANSMIT SOUND *so well as dense air ?*

A. Because the *sound of a bell,* (in the receiver of an air-pump) *can scarcely be heard*, after the air has been partially exhausted; and the report of a pistol (fired on a high mountain) would be scarcely audible.

Q. *Why do we* FEEL BRACED *and* LIGHT-HEARTED *on a* FINE *spring or* FROSTY *morning?*

A. 1st—Because there is *more oxygen* in the air on a fine frosty morning, than there is on a wet day: and

2dly—A brisk and frosty air has a tendency to *brace* the nervous system.

Q. *Why do* DOGS *and* CATS *(confined to a room) feel* LAZY *and* DROWSY, *at the approach of rain?*

A. 1st—Because the air does not contain *its full proportion of oxygen;* and

2dly—The damp *depresses their nervous system*, and makes them drowsy.

Q. *When* SHEEP *lie under a* HEDGE, *and seem unwilling to go to pasture,* RAIN *is at hand: Explain the reason of this.*

A. 1st—As the air does not contain its full proportion of *oxygen*, they feel uneasy; and

2dly—As the damp air *relaxes their nervous system*, they feel listless and drowsy.

Q. *Why do* HORSES *neigh,* CATTLE *low,* SHEEP *bleat, and* ASSES *bray, at the approach of rain?*

A. 1st—As the air does not contain

its full proportion of *oxygen*, they feel a *difficulty in breathing;* and

2dly—As damp *relaxes their nerves*, they feel languid and uneasy.

Q. *Mention some* OTHER ANIMALS, *which indicate the approach of rain in a similar way.*

A. When pigs squeak, as if in great pain—frogs croak with a loud, hoarse noise—owls screech—woodpeckers cry—peacocks scream—guinea-fowls squall—or ducks and geese are unusually noisy, rain is close at hand.

Q. *Why do* CANDLES *and* FIRES *burn with a* BLUER FLAME *in wet weather?*

A. Because the air contains *less oxygen* in wet weather, and therefore, the heat of fire is *less intense:* The flame is *blue*, because the *fuel is not thoroughly consumed.*

Q. *Why do* HILLS, *&c., appear* LARGER *in* WET *weather?*

A. Because the air is *laden with vapor*, which causes the rays of light to *diverge more;* in consequence of which, they produce on the eye *larger images of objects.*

Q. *Why do* TREES, *&c., in* WET *weather appear* FURTHER OFF *than they really are?*

A. Because the fog or mist *diminishes the light* reflected from the object; and as the object becomes *more dim*, it seems to be *further off*.

Q. *Why do* CATS RUB *their* EARS, *when it is likely to rain?*

A. Either because the *air is full of vapor*, and its humidity (piercing between the hair of the cat) *produces an itching sensation:* or more probably, because the air is *overcharged with electricity*.

Q. *How can the* ELECTRICITY *of air produce a sensation of* ITCHING?

A. If the *air* is overcharged with electricity, the *hair of the cat* is overcharged also; and this makes her feel as if she were *covered with cobwebs*.

Q. *Why does the* CAT *keep* RUBBING *herself?*

A. Because her *hair will not lie smooth*, but has a perpetual tendency to become *turgid* and *ruffled;* so the cat keeps rubbing her coat and ears, to *smooth the hair down*, and brush away the feeling of cobwebs.

Q. *Why do our* HEADS *and* SKIN *itch before rain?*

A. Probably because the *air is overcharged with electricity;* and, therefore, a sensation (like that of cobwebs) *irritates the skin*, and produces an itching.

Q. *When the plants called* TREFOIL, DANDE-

LION, PIMPERNEL, *&c.*, FOLD *up their leaves*, RAIN *is always close at hand: Explain this.*

A. 1st—The cloudy weather diminishes the *light of the sun;* and without the stimulus of sun-light, these flowers never open their leaves.

2dly—The vapor of the damp air, insinuating itself into the air-vessels of these delicate plants, causes them to *expand;* in consequence of which, the leaflets *contract and close.*

All these plants close at sun-set also.

Q. *Why do* DOORS SWELL *in* RAINY *weather?*

A. Because the *air is filled with vapor*, which (penetrating into the pores of the wood) *forces the parts further apart*, and swells the door.

Q. *Why do* DOORS SHRINK *in* DRY *weather?*

A. Because the *moisture is absorbed from the wood;* and, as the particles are *brought closer together*, the size of the door is *lessened*—in other words, the *wood shrinks.*

Q. *Why is the* AIR *filled with offensive* SMELLS, *just previous to a coming* RAIN?

A. Because the volatile parts which rise from dunghills, sewers, &c., are prevented (by the *vapor* of the *air*) from *rising* so readily, as when the sun is shining brightly.

Q. *Why do* FLOWERS *smell* SWEETER *and* STRONGER, *just previous to* RAIN?

A. Because the volatile parts which constitute the *perfume* of flowers, are prevented (by the vapor of the air) from *rising;* in consequence of which, they are confined to the lower regions of the atmosphere.

N. B. Many essential oils and other volatile substances, which produce odors in plants, require the presence of *much moisture* for their perfect development.

Q. *Why do* HORSES *and other animals stretch out their necks, and* SNUFF *up the* AIR, *just previous to a fall of* RAIN?

A. Because they *smell the odor of plants and hay*, and delight to snuff in their fragrance.

Q. *Why does* SMOKE FALL, *when* RAIN *is at hand?*

A. Because the air is *less dense*, and *cannot buoy up the smoke* so readily as *dry and heavy air.*

Q. *Why do* SWALLOWS FLY LOW, *when* RAIN *is at hand?*

A. Because the *insects* (of which they are in pursuit) *have fled from the cold, upper regions of the air*, to the *warm* air near the earth; and, as their *food is low*, the swallows *fly low.*

Q. *Why do these* INSECTS *seek the lower regions*

of the air in WET *weather, more than in* FINE *weather?*

A. Because (in wet weather) the *upper* regions of the air are *colder* than the *lower;* and, as insects enjoy warmth, they seek it near the earth.

Q. *Why does a* DOWNWARD *current of* COLD AIR *bring* RAIN?

A. Because it *condenses the warm vapor;* which (being condensed) descends in rain.

Q. *The proverb says,* "A SINGLE MAGPIE *in spring,* FOUL WEATHER *will bring:" Why is this the case?*

A. Because in cold, stormy weather, *one magpie alone* will leave its warm, snug nest *in search of food,* while the other stays with the *eggs, or young ones;* but in *fine, mild* weather (when their brood will not be injured by cold) *both the magpies fly out together.*

Q. *Why is it* UNLUCKY *for* ANGLERS *to see a* SINGLE MAGPIE *in spring?*

A. Because when *magpies fly abroad singly,* the weather is cold and stormy; but, when *both birds fly out together,* the weather is *warm and mild,* which is *favorable for fishing.*

Q. *Why do* SEA-GULLS *fly about the* SEA *in* FINE *weather?*

A. Because they *live upon the fishes*, which are found *near the surface* of the sea in fine weather.

Q. *Why may we expect* STORMY RAINS, *when* SEA-GULLS *assemble on the land?*

A. Because the fishes (on which they live) leave the *surface* of the sea in stormy weather, and are beyond the reach of the *sea-gulls;* in consequence of which, they are obliged to feed on the *worms and larvæ*, which are driven out of the *ground* at such times.

Larvæ, little grubs and caterpillars.

Q. *Why do* PETRELS *fly to the* SEA *during a storm?*

A. Because they *live upon sea insects*, which are always to be found in abundance *about the spray of swelling waves.*

N. B. Petrels are birds of the duck-kind, which live in the open sea. They run on the top of the waves, and are called Petrels, or rather Peter-els, from "St. Peter," in allusion to his walking on the sea, to go to Jesus.

Q. *Why do* CANDLES *and* LAMPS SPIRT, *when* RAIN *is at hand?*

A. Because the *air is filled with vapor* which *penetrates the wick;* where (being formed into *steam*) it expands suddenly, and produces a little explosion.

Q. *Why does a* DROP *of* WATER *sometimes* ROLL *along a piece of hot iron, without leaving the least trace?*

A. Because the *bottom* of the drop is turned into *vapor*, which *buoys the drop up*, without allowing it to touch the iron.

Q. *Why does it* ROLL?

A. Because the *current of air* (which is always passing over a heated surface) *drives it along*.

Q. *Why does a* LAUNDRESS *put a little* SALIVA *on a* FLAT-IRON, *to know if it be hot enough?*

A. Because when the saliva *sticks* to the box, and is *evaporated*, she knows it is *not* sufficiently hot; but, when it *runs along the iron*, it is.

Q. *Why is the* FLAT-IRON HOTTER *if the saliva* RUNS ALONG *it, than if it adheres till it is evaporated?*

A. Because when the saliva *runs along* the iron, the heat is sufficient to *convert the bottom of the drop into vapor;* but, if the saliva *will not roll*, the iron is *not* sufficiently hot to convert the bottom of the drop into vapor.

CHAPTER XIV.

4.—EVAPORATION.

Q. *What is meant by* EVAPORATION?

A. The dissipation of liquid by its conversion into *vapor*.

Q. *What* EFFECTS *are produced by evaporation?*

A. The liquid vaporized *absorbs heat* from the body whence it issues; and the body *deprived of the liquid* by evaporation, *loses heat.*

Q. *If you* WET *your* FINGER *in your mouth, and hold it up in the air, why does it* FEEL COLD?

A. Because the saliva quickly *evaporates;* and (as it evaporates) *absorbs heat from the finger*, making it feel cold.

Q. *If you* BATHE *your* TEMPLES *with ether, why does it allay* INFLAMMATION *and feverish heat?*

A. Because ether very rapidly *evaporates;* and (as it evaporates) *absorbs heat from the burning head*, producing a sensation of cold.

Q. *Why is* ETHER *better for this purpose than* WATER?

A. Because ether requires *less heat to convert it into vapor;* in consequence of which, it evaporates more *quickly.*

N. B. Ether is converted into vapor with 100° of heat: but water requires 212° of heat to convert it into steam.

Q. *Why does* ETHER *very greatly* RELIEVE *a* SCALD *or* BURN?

A. Because it *evaporates very rapidly;* and (as it evaporates) *carries off the heat of the burn.*

Q. *Why do we* FEEL COLD, *when we have* WET FEET *or* CLOTHES?

A. Because the wet of our shoes or

clothes rapidly *evaporates;* and (as it evaporates) *absorbs heat from our body,* which makes us feel cold.

Q. *Why do* WET FEET *or* CLOTHES *give us* "COLD?"

A. Because the evaporation *absorbs heat* so abundantly from the surface of our body, that its temperature is *lowered below its natural standard;* in consequence of which, health is injured.

Q. *Why is it* DANGEROUS *to* SLEEP *in a* DAMP BED?

A. Because the heat is continually absorbed from the surface of our body, to *convert the damp of the sheets into vapor;* in consequence of which, our animal heat is reduced *below the healthy standard.*

Q. *Why is* HEALTH INJURED, *when the* TEMPERATURE *of the* BODY *is* REDUCED *below its natural standard?*

A. Because the *balance of the circulation* is destroyed. Blood is driven away from the *external surface* by the *chill,* and thrown upon the *internal organs,* which are *oppressed* by this increased *load of blood.*

Q. *Why do we not feel the same sensation of cold, if we throw a* MACINTOSH *over our* WET CLOTHES?

A. Because the macintosh (being air tight) *prevents evaporation;* and (as the *wet cannot evaporate*) no heat is absorbed from our bodies.

Q. *Why do* NOT SAILORS *get* COLD, *who are frequently wet all day with* SEA-WATER?

A. 1st—Because the *salt* of the sea *retards evaporation;* and (as the heat of their body is drawn off *gradually*) the sensation of cold is prevented.

2dly—The *salt* of the sea acts as a stimulant, and keeps the blood circulating in the skin.

Q. *Why does* SPRINKLING *a* HOT ROOM *with water* COOL IT?

A. Because the heat of the room causes a *rapid evaporation of the sprinkled water:* and as the water evaporates, *it absorbs heat from the room,* which cools it.

Q. *Why does* WATERING *the* STREETS *and roads* COOL THEM?

A. Because they part with their heat *to promote the evaporation of the water sprinkled on them.*

Q. *Why does a* SHOWER *of* RAIN COOL *the* AIR *in summer-time?*

A. Because the wet earth *parts with its heat to promote evaporation;* and when the *earth* is cooled, it *cools the air* also.

Q. *Why is* LINEN DRIED *by being exposed to the* WIND?

A. Because the wind *accelerates evaporation*, by removing the vapor from the *surface of the wet linen*, as fast as it is formed.

Q. *Why is* LINEN DRIED *sooner in the open* AIR, *than in a confined room?*

A. Because the particles of vapor are more rapidly removed from the surface of the linen by evaporation.

Q. *Why are* WET SUMMERS *generally* SUCCEEDED *by* COLD WINTERS?

A. Because the great evaporation (carried on through the wet summer) *reduces the temperature of the earth lower than usual*, and produces cold.

Q. *Why is* THIS COUNTRY WARMER *and the winters less severe than formerly?*

A. Because it is *better drained* and *better cultivated.*

Q. *Why does* DRAINING *land promote* WARMTH?

A. Because it *diminishes evaporation*, in consequence of which, *less heat* is abstracted from the earth.

Q. *Why does* CULTIVATION *increase the* WARMTH *of a country?*

A. 1st—Because *hedges* and *belts of trees* are multiplied:

2dly—The land is *better drained:* and

3dly—The vast *forests are cut down.*

Q. *Why do* HEDGES *and* BELTS *of* TREES *promote* WARMTH?

A. Because they *retard evaporation*, by keeping off the *wind.*

Q. *If belts of trees promote* WARMTH, *why do* FORESTS *produce* COLD?

A. 1st—Because they *detain* and *condense the passing clouds;*

2dly—They prevent the access of both *wind* and *sun;*

3dly—The soil of forests is always *covered with long, damp grass, rotting leaves*, and *thick brushwood;* and

4thly—In every forest there are always many hollows *full of stagnant water.*

Q. *Why do* LONG GRASS *and* ROTTING LEAVES *promote* COLD?

A. Because *they are always damp*, and evaporation, which they promote, *is constantly absorbing heat* from the earth beneath.

Q. *Why are* FRANCE *and* GERMANY WARMER *now, than when the vine would not ripen there?*

A. Chiefly because *their vast forests have been cut down;* and the soil is better *drained* and *cultivated.*

Q. *What becomes of the* WATER *of* PONDS *and* TUBS *in summer-time?*

A. Ponds and tubs are often left dry in summer-time, because their water is *evaporated by the air.*

Q. *How is this* EVAPORATION PRODUCED *and carried on?*

A. The heat of the air changes the *surface of the water into vapor*, which (blending with the air) *is soon wafted away;* and *similar evaporation* is repeatedly produced, till the pond or tub is left quite dry.

Q. *Why are the* WHEELS *of some machines kept* CONSTANTLY WET *with* WATER?

A. *To carry off* (by evaporation) *the heat* which arises from the *rapid motion* of the wheels.

Q. *Why is* MOULD HARDENED *by the* SUN?

A. Because the moisture of the mould is exhaled by *evaporation;* and, as the earthy particles are brought *closer* together, the mass becomes more solid.

Q. *Show the* WISDOM *of* GOD *in this arrangement.*

A. If the soil did not become *crusty* and *hard in dry weather*, the heat and drought would *penetrate the soil*, and kill both seeds and roots.

Q. *Why is* TEA *cooled* FASTER *in a* SAUCER *than in a cup?*

A. Because *evaporation is increased*

by *increasing the surface;* and, as tea in a saucer presents *a larger surface to the air*, its heat is more rapidly carried off by evaporation.

(The subject of "convection" will be treated of in a future chapter; it would scarcely be understood in this place. See p. 213.)

Q. *Why is not the* VAPOR *of the* SEA SALT?

A. Because the *salt* is always *left behind*, in the process of evaporation.

Q. *What is that* WHITE CRUST, *which appears (in hot weather) upon* CLOTHES *wetted by sea water?*

A. The *salt of the water*, left on the clothes by evaporation.

Q. *Why does this* WHITE CRUST *always* DISAPPEAR *in* WET *weather?*

A. Because the *moisture of the air dissolves the salt;* in consequence of which, it is no longer visible.

Q. *Why should* NOT *persons, who take violent exercise,* WEAR *very* THICK CLOTHING?

A. Because it prevents the perspiration from evaporating. When the heat of the body is increased by exercise, *perspiration reduces the heat* (by evaporation) *to a healthy standard;* as thick clothing *prevents* this evaporation, it is injurious to health.

COMMUNICATION OF HEAT.

CHAPTER XV.

1—CONDUCTION.

Q. *How is* HEAT COMMUNICATED *from one body to another?*

A. 1.—By Conduction. 2.—By Absorption. 3.—By Reflection. 4—By Radiation. And 5.—By Convection.

Q. *What is meant by* CONDUCTION *of heat?*

A. Heat communicated from one body to another by *actual contact.*

Q. *Why does a* PIECE *of* WOOD (*blazing at* ONE *end*) NOT *feel* HOT *at the* OTHER?

A. Because *wood is so bad a conductor*, that heat does not traverse freely through it; hence, though one end of a stick be blazing the other end may be quite cold.

Q. *Why do* SOME THINGS *feel* COLDER *than others?*

A. Principally because they are *better conductors;* and draw off heat from our body much faster.

Q. *What are the* BEST CONDUCTORS *of* HEAT?

A. *Dense, solid bodies*, such as metal and stone.

Q. *Which* METALS *are the most* RAPID CONDUCTORS *of* HEAT?

A. The *best* conductors of heat are 1. gold, 2. silver, 3. copper:

The *next* best are 4. plat'inum, 5. iron, 6. zinc, 7. tin. Lead is a very *inferior* conductor to any of the preceding metals.

Q. *What are the* WORST CONDUCTORS *of* HEAT?

A. All *light* and *porous bodies;* such as hair, fur, wool, charcoal, and so on.

Two of the *worst* conductors known are hare's fur and eider down;—the two next worst are beaver's fur and raw silk;—then wood and lamp-black;—then cotton and fine lint;—then charcoal, wood ashes, &c.

Q. *Why are* COOKING VESSELS *often furnished with* WOODEN HANDLES?

A. Because wood *is not a good conductor*, like metal; and, therefore, *wooden handles* prevent the heat of the vessel from rushing into our hands, to burn them.

Q. *Why is the* HANDLE *of a* METAL TEA-POT *made of* WOOD?

A. Because *wood is a bad conductor;* therefore, the heat of the boiling water is *not so quickly conveyed* to our hand by a wooden handle, as by one made of metal.

Q. *Why would a* METAL HANDLE BURN *the* HAND *of the tea-maker?*

A. Because metal is an *excellent conductor;* therefore, the heat of boiling water would *rush so quickly* into the *metal handle*, that it would burn our hand.

Q. *Prove that a* METAL HANDLE *would be* HOTTER *than a* WOODEN ONE.

A. If we *touch the metal collar* into which the wooden handle is fixed, we shall find that the wooden handle *feels cold*, but the metal collar *intensely hot.*

Q. *Why do persons use paper or* WOOLLEN KETTLE-HOLDERS?

A. Because paper and woollen are both very *bad conductors of heat;* in consequence of which, the heat of the kettle does not *readily pass through them* to the hand.

Q. *Does the heat of the boiling kettle* NEVER *get through the woollen or paper kettle-holder?*

A. Yes; but though the kettle-holder became as hot as the kettle itself, it would never *feel* so hot.

Q. *Why would not the kettle-holder* FEEL *so hot as the kettle, when both are of the same temperature?*

A. Because it is a very *bad* conductor, and *disposes of its heat too slowly* to be *perceptible;* but metal (being an *excellent* conductor) disposes of its heat *so quickly*, that the sudden influx is painful.

Q. *Why does* HOT METAL FEEL MORE *intensely* WARM *than* HOT WOOL?

A. Because metal gives out a much

greater quantity of heat in the *same space of time;* and the *influx* of heat is, consequently, *more perceptible.*

Q. *Why does* MONEY *in our pocket feel very* HOT *when we stand* BEFORE *a* FIRE?

A. Because metal is an *excellent* conductor, and becomes rapidly heated. For the same reason, it becomes *rapidly cold*, whenever it comes in contact with a body *colder than itself.*

Q. *Why does a* PUMP-HANDLE *feel intensely* COLD *in* WINTER?

A. Because it is an *excellent* conductor, and draws off the heat of our hand so rapidly, that the sudden loss produces a sensation of intense coldness.

Q. *Is the iron* HANDLE *of the pump really* COLDER *than the wooden* PUMP *itself?*

A. No; every inanimate substance (exposed to the same temperature) possesses in reality the *same degree of heat.*

Q. *Why does the* IRON HANDLE *seem so* MUCH COLDER *than the* WOODEN PUMP?

A. Merely because the *iron is a better conductor;* and, therefore, *draws off the heat* from our hand more rapidly than wood does.

Q. *Why does a* STONE *or marble* HEARTH *feel to the feet* COLDER *than a* CARPET *or hearth-rug?*

A. Because *stone* and *marble* are *good*

conductors; but *woollen carpets* and *hearth-rugs* are very *bad* conductors.

Q. *How does the* STONE HEARTH *make our* FEET COLD?

A. As soon as the hearth-stone has absorbed a portion of heat from our foot, it instantly disposes of it, and calls for a *fresh supply;* till the hearth-stone has become of the *same temperature as the foot placed upon it.*

Q. *Do not also the woollen* CARPET *and* HEARTH-RUG *conduct heat from the human body?*

A. Yes; but being very *bad* conductors, they convey the heat away *so slowly*, that the loss is scarcely perceptible.

Q. *Is the* COLD HEARTH-STONE *in reality of the* SAME TEMPERATURE *as the* WARM CARPET?

A. Yes; every thing in the room is really of *one temperature;* but some things *feel* colder than others, because they are *better conductors.*

Q. *How* LONG *will the hearth-stone feel cold to the feet resting on it?*

A. Till the *feet* and the *hearth-stone* are *both of the same temperature;* and then the sensation of cold in the hearth-stone will go off.

Q. *Why would not the* HEARTH-STONE *feel* COLD, *when it is of the* SAME *temperature as our* FEET?

A. Because the heat would no longer *rush out of our feet into the hearth-stone*, in order to produce equilibrium.

Q. *Why does the* HEARTH-STONE (*when the fire is lighted*) *feel* HOTTER *than the* HEARTH-RUG?

A. Because the hearth-stone is an *excellent conductor*, and parts with its heat *very readily*; but the woollen hearth-rug (being a *bad* conductor) parts with its heat very *reluctantly*.

Q. *Why does* PARTING *with* HEAT RAPIDLY *make the* HEARTH-STONE *feel* WARM?

A. Because the rapid influx of heat raises the temperature of our body *so suddenly*, that we cannot *help perceiving the increase*.

Q. *Why does the non-conducting power of the* HEARTH-RUG *prevent its feeling* SO HOT *as it really is?*

A. Because it parts with its heat *so slowly* and *gradually*, that we scarcely *perceive its transmission* into our feet.

Q. *When we plunge our* HANDS *into a basin of* WATER *why does it produce a sensation of* COLD?

A. Because water is a *better conductor* than air; and, as it draws off the heat from our hands *more rapidly*, it *feels colder*.

Q. *Why does the* CONDUCTING *power of water make it feel* COLDER *than* AIR?

A. Because it *abstracts heat from our*

hands so rapidly, that we *feel* its loss; but the air abstracts heat *so very slowly*, that its *gradual loss is hardly perceptible.*

Q. *Is water a* GOOD CONDUCTOR *of heat?*

A. No; *no* liquid is a *good* conductor of heat; but yet water is a *much better conductor* than *air*.

Q. *Why is* WATER *a* BETTER CONDUCTOR *of heat than* AIR?

A. Because *it is less subtile;* and the conducting power of any substance depends upon its *solidity*, or the *closeness of its particles*.

Q. *How do you know that* WATER *is* NOT *a* GOOD CONDUCTOR *of heat?*

A. Because it may be made to *boil at its surface*, without imparting sufficient heat to *melt ice a quarter of an inch below the surface.*

Q. *Why are* NOT LIQUIDS GOOD CONDUCTORS *of heat?*

A. Because the heat (which should be transmitted) *produces evaporation*, and *flies off in the vapor.*

Q. *Why does a* POKER (*resting on a fender*) *feel* COLDER *than the* HEARTH-RUG, *which is further off the fire?*

A. Because the poker is an *excellent conductor*, and draws heat from the hand much *more rapidly* than the woollen hearth-rug, which is a very *bad conductor:* though both, therefore, are *equally warm,* the *poker* seems to be the *colder.* (See also p. 173.)

Q. *Why are* HOT BRICKS (*wrapped in cloth*) *employed in cold weather to* KEEP *the* FEET WARM?

A. Because bricks are *bad conductors* of heat, and cloth or flannel *still worse:* in consequence of which, a hot brick (wrapped in flannel) will *retain its heat a very long time.*

Q. *Why is a* TIN PAN (*filled with* HOT WATER) *employed as a* FOOT-WARMER?

A. Because *polished tin* (being a bad radiator of heat) *keeps hot a very long time;* and warms the feet resting upon it.

Q. *What is meant by being a "bad* RADIATOR *of heat?"*

A. To radiate heat is to *throw off heat by rays,* as the sun; a polished tin pan does *not throw off the heat of boiling water* from its surface, but *keeps it in.*

Q. *Why are* TIN FOOT-WARMERS *covered with* FLANNEL?

A. 1st—That the *polish* of the tin may not be injured:

2dly—Because the flannel (being a *very bad conductor*) helps to keep the tin hot *longer:* and

3dly—Lest the conducting surface of the tin should *feel painfully hot.*

Q. *What disadvantage would it be, if the* POLISH *of the tin were injured?*

A. If the tin foot-warmer were to *lose its polish*, it would get cold in a *much shorter time.*

Q. *Why would the tin foot-warmer get* COLD SOONER, *if the* POLISH *were* INJURED?

A. Because *polished* tin throws off its heat *very slowly;* but dull, scratched, painted, or dirty tin, *throws off its heat very quickly.*

Q. *Why are* FURNACES *and stoves (where much* HEAT *is required) built of porous* BRICK?

A. Because bricks are bad conductors, and *prevent the escape of heat;* in consequence of which, they are employed where great heat is required.

Q. *Why are* FURNACE DOORS, *&c., frequently* COVERED *with a paste of* CLAY *and* SAND?

A. Because this paste is a *very bad conductor of heat;* and, therefore, prevents the *escape of heat from the furnace.*

Q. *If a stove be placed in the* MIDDLE *of a room should it be made of bricks or* IRON?

A. A stove in the *middle of a room* should be made of *iron;* because iron is an *excellent conductor*, and rapidly communicates heat to the air around.

Q. *Why does the Bible say, that God "giveth* SNOW *like* WOOL?"

A. Because *snow* (being a *very bad conductor of heat*) protects vegetables and seeds from the frost and cold.

Q. *How does the non-conducting power of* SNOW PROTECT VEGETABLES *from the* FROST *and cold?*

A. It prevents the *heat* of the earth from being *drawn off* by the cold air which rests upon it.

Q. *Why are* WOOLLENS *and* FURS *used for* CLOTHING *in* COLD *weather?*

A. Because they are *very bad conductors* of heat; and, therefore, *prevent the warmth of the body from being drawn off* by the cold air.

Q. *Do not woollens and furs actually* IMPART *heat to the body?*

A. No; they merely *prevent the heat of the body from escaping.*

Q. *Where would the heat* ESCAPE *to, if the body were* NOT *wrapped in wool or fur?*

A. The heat of the body would *fly off* into the air; for the cold air (coming in contact with our body) would *gradually draw away its heat,* till it was as cold as the air itself.

Q. *What then is the* PRINCIPAL USE *of* CLOTHING *in winter-time?*

A. 1st—To prevent the animal heat from escaping too freely; and

2dly—To protect the body from the *external air* (or wind), which would carry away its heat too rapidly.

Q. *Why are* BEASTS COVERED *with* FUR, HAIR *or* WOOL?

A. Because fur, hair and wool, are *very slow* conductors of heat; and (as dumb animals cannot be clad, like human beings) God has given them *a robe of hair* or wool, to *keep them warm.*

Q. *Why are* BIRDS *covered with* DOWN *or* FEATHERS?

A. Because down and feathers are *very bad* conductors of heat; and (as birds cannot be clad, like human beings) God has given them a *robe of feathers, to keep them warm.*

Q. *Why are* WOOL, FUR, HAIR, *and* FEATHERS, *such* SLOW CONDUCTORS *of heat?*

A. Because a *great quantity of air* lurks entangled between the fibres; and *air* is a *very bad* conductor of heat.

The warmest clothing is that which fits the body very *loosely* in every part except at the *extremities:* Because more hot air will be confined by a *loose* garment than by one which fits the body *tightly.*

Q. *If* AIR *be a* BAD CONDUCTOR *of heat, why should we not feel as warm* WITHOUT *clothing, as when we are wrapped in wool and fur?*

A. Because the air (which is cooler than our body) *is never at rest;* and every fresh particle of air *draws off a fresh portion of heat.*

Q. *How does the ceaseless* CHANGE *of air tend to* DECREASE *the* WARMTH *of a naked body?*

A. Thus:—the air (which cases the body) absorbs as much heat from it as it can, while it remains in contact; being then blown away, it makes room for a *fresh coat of air*, which absorbs *more* heat.

Q. *Does the* AIR *which encases a naked body become* (*by contact*) *as* WARM *as the* BODY *itself?*

A. It would do so, if it remained *motionless;* but, as it remains only a *very short time*, it absorbs as much heat as it can in the time, and passes on.

Q. *Why do we feel* COLDER *in* WINDY WEATHER *than in a* CALM *day?*

A. Because the particles of air *pass over us more rapidly;* and every *fresh* particle takes from us *some* portion of heat.

Q. *Show the wisdom of God in making the* AIR *a* BAD CONDUCTOR.

A. If air were a *good conductor* (like iron and stone) heat would be drawn *so rapidly from our body*, that we should be *chilled to death.* Similar evils would be felt also by *all* the animal and vegetable world.

Q. *Does not the bad conducting power of air*

enable persons to judge whether an EGG *be* NEW *or* STALE ?

A. Yes; touch the larger end of the shell with your tongue; if it *feels warm*, the *egg is stale;* if *not*, it is new-laid.

Q. *Why will the* SHELL *of a* STALE EGG *feel* WARM *to the tongue?*

A. Because the thick end of an egg contains *a small quantity of air* (between the shell and the white); when the egg is stale the white *shrinks*, and the confined *air* accordingly *expands*.

Q. *Why does the expansion of air (at the end of an egg) make it feel* WARM *to the tongue?*

A. Because air is a very bad conductor, and the more *air* an egg contains, the *less heat will be drawn from the tongue* when it touches the shell.

Q. *Why will a* NEW-LAID *egg feel* COLDER *to the tongue at the thick end than a stale one?*

A. Because it contains *more white* and *less air;* and as the *white* of an egg is a better conductor than *air*, the heat of the tongue will be drawn off *more rapidly*, and the egg feel *colder*.

Q. *Why does* FANNING *the face in summer make it* COOL ?

A. Because the fan *puts the air in motion*, and makes it pass more *rapidly over the face;* and (as the temperature of the *air is always lower* than that of the human *face*) each puff of air *carries off some portion of its heat.*

Q. *Does* FANNING *make the* AIR *itself* COOLER?

A. No; fanning makes the *air hotter and hotter.*

Q. *How does* FANNING *the face increase the* HEAT *of the air?*

A. By driving the air more rapidly over the human body, and causing it, consequently, to *absorb more heat.*

Q. *If fanning makes the* AIR HOTTER, *why can it make a* PERSON *feel* COOLER?

A. Because it takes the heat *out of the face,* and gives it to the *air.*

Q. *Why is* BROTH COOLED *by* BLOWING *it?*

A. Because the breath causes a rapid *change of air* to pass over the broth; and (as the air is colder than the broth) it continually *absorbs heat* from it, and makes it cooler and cooler.

Q. *Would not the air absorb heat from the broth just as well* WITHOUT BLOWING?

A. No; *air is a very bad conductor;* unless, therefore, *the change be rapid,* the air nearest the surface of the broth *would soon become as hot as the broth itself.*

Q. *Would not hot air* PART *with its heat instantly to the* CIRCUMJACENT *air?*

A. No; not instantly. Air is so bad

a conductor, that it parts with its heat *very slowly:* unless, therefore, the air be kept in *continual motion,* it would *cool the broth very slowly indeed.*

Q. *Why does* WIND *generally feel* COOL?

A. Because it drives the air more rapidly over our body; and this rapid *change* of air draws off a large quantity of heat.

Q. *Why does* AIR ABSORB *heat more* QUICKLY *by being set in* MOTION?

A. Because every fresh gust of air *absorbs a fresh portion of heat;* and the more rapid the *succession of gusts,* the greater will be the quantity of heat absorbed.

Q. *If the* AIR *were* HOTTER *than our body would the* WIND *feel* COOL?

A. No; the air would feel *insufferably hot,* if it were *hotter than our body.*

Q. *Why would the* AIR *feel* INTENSELY HOT, *if it were* WARMER *than our* BODY?

A. Because it would *add* to the heat of our body, instead of *diminishing* it.

Q. *Is the* AIR EVER *as* HOT *as the human* BODY?

A. Not in *this* country: in the hottest summer's day, the air is at least 10 or 12 degrees *cooler than the human body.*

Q. *Is the* EARTH *a good conductor of heat?*

A. No; the earth is a very *bad* conductor of heat.

Q. *Why is the* EARTH *a* BAD *conductor of heat?*

A. Because its particles are not *continuous:* and the power of *conducting* heat depends upon the *continuity of matter.*

Q. *Why is the earth* (BELOW *the* SURFACE) WARMER *in* WINTER *than the surface itself?*

A. Because the earth is a *bad* conductor of heat; and, therefore, (although the ground be frozen,) the frost never penetrates more than a *few inches below the surface.*

Q. *Why is the earth* (BELOW *the* SURFACE) COOLER *in* SUMMER *than the surface itself?*

A. Because the earth is a *bad* conductor of heat; and, therefore, (although the *surface be scorched* with the burning sun,) the intense heat cannot penetrate to the *roots* of the plants and trees.

Q. *Show the* WISDOM *of* GOD *in making the* EARTH *a* BAD CONDUCTOR?

A. If the *heat and cold could penetrate the earth* (as freely as the heat of a fire penetrates iron), the springs would be dried up in summer, and frozen in winter; and all vegetation would perish.

Q. *Why is* WATER *from a* SPRING *always* COOL *even in* SUMMER?

A. Because the earth is *so bad a conductor*, that the burning rays of the sun can penetrate only a few inches below the surface; in consequence of which, the *springs of water are not affected* by the heat of summer.

Q. *Why is it* COOL *under a* SHADY *tree in a hot summer's day?*

A. 1st—Because the overhanging foliage *screens off the rays of the sun:*

2dly—As the rays of the sun are warded off, *the air* (beneath the tree) is not heated by the *reflection of the earth:* and

3dly—The leaves of the trees, being *non-conductors*, allow no heat to penetrate them.

Q. *Why do the* LAPLANDERS *wear* SKINS *with the* FUR INWARDS?

A. Because the *dry skin* prevents the *wind* from penetrating to their body; and the *air* (between the hairs of the fur) soon becomes *heated by the body:* in consequence of which, the Laplander in his fur is clad in *a case of hot air*, impervious to the *cold* and *wind.*

Q. *Why does a* LINEN SHIRT *feel* COLDER *than a* COTTON ONE?

A. Because *linen* is a *much better*

conductor than cotton; and, therefore, (as soon as it touches the body) it draws away the heat *more rapidly*, and produces a greater sensation of cold.

Q. *Why is the* FACE COOLED *by wiping the temples with a fine* CAMBRIC HANDKERCHIEF?

A. Because the fine fibres of the cambric have a *strong capillary attraction for moisture*, and are *excellent conductors* of heat: in consequence of which, the moisture and heat are *abstracted from the face* by the cambric, and a sensation of coolness produced.

"Capillary attraction," i. e., *the attraction of a thread or hair.* The wick of a candle is wet with grease, because the melted tallow runs up the cotton from capillary attraction.

Q. *Why would not a* COTTON *handkerchief do as well?*

A. Because the coarse fibres of cotton have very little capillary attraction, and are *very bad conductors;* in consequence of which, the heat of the face would be *increased* (rather than *diminished*) by the use of a *cotton* handkerchief.

CHAPTER XVI.

2.—ABSORPTION OF HEAT.

Q. *What is the difference between* CONDUCTING *heat, and* ABSORBING *heat?*

A. To *conduct* heat is to *transmit it* from one body to another through a *conducting* medium. To *absorb* heat is to *suck it up*, as a sponge sucks up water.

Q. *Give me an example.*

A. *Black cloth absorbs*, but does not *conduct heat;* thus, if black cloth be laid in the sun, it will *absorb the rays* very rapidly; but if *one end* of the black cloth be made hot, it would not *conduct the* heat to the *other* end.

Q. *Are good* CONDUCTORS *of heat good* ABSORBERS *also?*

A. No; every *good conductor* of heat is a *bad absorber* of it; and *no good absorber* of heat can be a *good conductor* also.

Q. *Is* IRON *a good* ABSORBER *of heat?*

A. No; *iron* is a *good conductor*, but a very *bad absorber* of heat.

Q. *Why do the* FIRE-IRONS (*which lie upon a* FENDER) *remain* COLD, *although they are before a good fire?*

A. Because they are *bad absorbers* of

heat; in consequence of which, they remain *cold*, unless they come in *contact* with the stove or fire.

Q. *Why are the* FIRE-IRONS *intensely* HOT, *when they* REST AGAINST *the* STOVE *which contains a good fire?*

A. Because they are *excellent conductors of heat*, and draw it rapidly from the stove with which they are in contact.

Q. *Why does a* KETTLE *boil faster, when the bottom and back are* COVERED *with* SOOT?

A. Because the *black soot absorbs heat* very quickly from the fire, and the metal *conducts* it to the water.

Q. *Why will not a* NEW KETTLE *boil so fast as an* OLD *one?*

A. Because the *bottom* and *sides* of a new kettle are *clean* and *bright:* but in an *old* kettle they are *covered with soot.*

Q. *Why will a* KETTLE *be* SLOWER BOILING *if the* BOTTOM *and* BACK *are* CLEAN *and bright?*

A. Because *bright* metal does *not absorb heat*, but *reflects* it; and (as the heat is *thrown off* from the surface of *bright* metal by reflection) therefore, a new kettle takes a longer time to boil.

Reflects heat, i. e., throws it off.

Q. *Why do we wear* WHITE LINEN *and a* BLACK *outer* DRESS, *if we want to be warm?*

A. Because the *black outer dress*

quickly *absorbs heat* from the sun; and the *white linen* (being a *bad* absorbent) abstracts no heat from the warm body.

Q. *Why do persons* WEAR WHITE *dresses in* SUMMER *time?*

A. Because white *throws off the heat* of the sun by *reflection*, and is a very bad absorbent of heat; in consequence of which, white dresses never become *so hot from the scorching sun* as dark colors do.

Q. *Why do* NOT *persons* WEAR WHITE *dresses in* WINTER *time?*

A. Because *white will not absorb heat*, like black and other dark colors; and, therefore, *white dresses are not so warm as dark* ones.

Q. *What* COLORS *are* WARMEST *for dresses?*

A. For *outside* garments *black* is the *warmest*, and then such colors as approach nearest to black, (as dark blue and green.) *White is the coldest color* for external clothing.

Q. *Why are* DARK COLORS (*for external wear*) *so much* WARMER *than* LIGHT ONES?

A. Because *dark colors absorb heat* from the sun more abundantly than *light* ones.

Q. *How can you prove that* DARK *colors are* WARMER *than* LIGHT *ones?*

A. If a piece of *black* and a piece of *white* cloth were laid upon snow, in a few hours the *black cloth will have melted the snow beneath;* whereas, the *white* cloth will have produced little or *no effect upon it at all.*

N. B. The *darker* any color is, the *warmer* it is, because it is a better absorbent of heat. The order may be thus arranged:—1.—Black (warmest of all).—2. Violet.—3. Indigo.—4. Blue.—5. Green.—6. Red.—7. Yellow: and 8. White (coldest of all).

Q. *Why are* BLACK KID GLOVES *unpleasantly* HOT *for summer wear?*

A. 1st—Because *black absorbs the solar heat;* and

2dly—*Kid* will not allow the heat of our hand to *escape through the glove.*

Q. *Why are* LISLE THREAD GLOVES *agreeably* COOL *for summer wear?*

A. 1st—Because thread *absorbs perspiration:* and

2dly—It *conducts away the* heat of our hot hands.

Q. *Are Lisle thread gloves* ABSORBENTS *of heat?*

A. No; Lisle thread gloves are generally of a *grey or lilac color;* and, therefore, do *not absorb solar heat.*

Q. *Why is a* PLATE-WARMER *made of* UNPAINTED BRIGHT TIN?

A. Because bright tin *reflects the heat*

(which issues from the fire in rays) upon the meat; and, therefore, greatly assists the process of roasting.

Reflects the heat, i. e., throws it *back* upon the meat.

Q. *Why would not the tin* REFLECTOR *do as well, if it were* PAINTED?

A. Because it would then *absorb* heat, and *not reflect it at all.* A plate-warmer should never be *painted,* but should be kept *very clean, bright,* and *free from all scratches.*

Q. *Why should a* REFLECTOR *be kept so very* CLEAN *and free from all* SCRATCHES?

A. Because if a reflector were *spotted, dull, or scratched,* it would *absorb* heat, instead of *reflecting* it; and, consequently, would be of no use whatsoever as a *reflector.*

Q. *Why does* HOAR FROST *remain on* TOMB-STONES *long after it has melted from the* GRASS *and* GRAVEL-WALKS *of a church-yard?*

A. Because tomb-stones (being *white*) will *not absorb heat,* like the darker grass and gravel; in consequence of which, they remain too *cold* to thaw the frost congealed upon their surface.

Q. *If black absorbs heat, why have those who live in* HOT *climates* BLACK SKINS, *and not* WHITE *skins, which would not absorb heat at all?*

A. Because *black* will not *blister* from

the heat of the sun. Although, therefore, the black skin of the negro *absorbs heat* more plentifully than the *white skin of a European;* yet the *blackness* prevents the sun from *blistering* or *scorching it.*

Q. *How is it known that the* BLACK *color prevents the sun from either* BLISTERING *or* SCORCHING *the skin?*

A. If you put a *white glove* on *one hand*, and a *black glove* on the *other* (when the sun is burning hot), the hand with the *white* glove will be *scorched*, but *not the other.*

Q. WHICH *hand will* FEEL *the* HOTTER?

A. The hand with the *black glove* will *feel* the *hotter*, but will not be *scorched* by the sun; whereas, the hand with the *white* glove (though much *cooler*) will be *severely scorched.*

Q. *Why does the* BLACK *skin of a* NEGRO NEVER SCORCH *or* BLISTER *with the hot sun?*

A. Because the *black color absorbs* the heat—conveys it *below the surface* of the skin—and converts it to *sensible heat* and *perspiration.*

Q. *Why does the* WHITE EUROPEAN SKIN BLISTER *and* SCORCH *when exposed to the hot sun?*

A. Because *white will not absorb* heat; and, therefore, the hot sun *rests on the surface of the skin,* and *scorches* it.

Q. *Why has a* NEGRO BLACK EYES?

A. Because the black color defends them from the strong light of the tropical sun. If a negro's eyes were not black, the sun would *scorch them*, and every negro would be blind.

Q. *Why is* WATER (*in hot weather*) KEPT COOLER *in a* BRIGHT TIN POT *than in an* EARTHEN *one?*

A. Because bright metal will *not absorb* heat from the hot air, like an *earthen* vessel; in consequence of which, the water is kept *cooler.*

Boiling water is also kept *hot* in bright metal better than in earthen vessels. *See p.* 187.

CHAPTER XVII.

3.—Reflection of Heat.

Q. *What is meant by* REFLECTING HEAT?

A. To reflect heat is *to throw it back in rays* from the surface of the reflecting body towards the place whence it came.

Q. *What are the* BEST REFLECTORS *of heat?*

A. All *bright* surfaces and *light colors.*

Q. *Are* GOOD ABSORBERS *of heat* GOOD REFLECTORS *also?*

A. No; those things which *absorb* heat *best*, *reflect* heat *worst;* and those which *reflect* heat *worst*, *absorb* it *best.*

Q. *Why are those things which* ABSORB HEAT *unable to* REFLECT *it?*

A. Because if anything *sucks in heat* like a sponge, it cannot *throw it off* from its surface; and if anything *throws off heat* from its surface, it cannot *drink it in.*

Q. *Why are* REFLECTORS *always made of* LIGHT COLORED *and highly* POLISHED METAL?

A. Because *light* colored and *highly polished metal* makes the best of all reflectors.

Q. *Why do not* PLATE-WARMERS BLISTER *and scorch the* WOOD *behind?*

A. Because the bright tin front throws the heat of the fire *back again*, and will not allow it to penetrate to the wood behind.

Q. *If metal be such an excellent* CONDUCTOR *of heat, how can it* REFLECT *heat, or throw it off?*

A. Polished metal is a *conductor of heat*, only when that heat is communicated by *actual contact:* But whenever heat falls upon bright metal *in rays*, it is *reflected back again*, and the metal remains *cool.*

Q. *What is meant "by heat falling upon metal* IN RAYS," *and not "by contact?"*

A. If a piece of metal were thrust *into* a fire, it would be *in actual contact with the fire;* but if it were *held before a fire*, the heat of the fire would fall upon it *in rays*.

Q. *What is the use of the* TIN SCREEN *or* REFLECTOR *used in* ROASTING?

A. It *throws the heat of the fire back upon the meat;* and, therefore, both assists the *process of roasting*, and helps to *keep the kitchen cool.*

Q. *How does a tin* REFLECTOR *tend to keep the* KITCHEN COOL?

A. By *confining the heat* of the fire *to the hearth*, and preventing its dispersion throughout the kitchen.

Q. *Why are* SHOES HOTTER *for being* DUSTY?

A. Because dull, dusty shoes will *absorb heat* from the sun, earth, and air; but shoes brightly polished *throw off* the heat of the sun by reflection.

Q. *Why does it always* FREEZE *on the* TOP *of a* MOUNTAIN?

A. 1st—Because the air on a mountain is very *rarefied;* and rarefied air retains more heat in the *latent* form than *denser* air does: and

2dly—Air is heated by the *reflection of the earth*, and not by solar rays; therefore a mountain-top (which is *deprived* of this reflection) remains intensely cold.

CHAPTER XVIII.

4.—Radiation.

Q. *What is meant by* RADIATION?

A. Radiation means *the emission of rays:* thus the sun radiates both light and heat; that is, it emits *rays of light and heat* in all directions.

Q. WHEN *is heat* RADIATED *from one body to another?*

A. When the two bodies are *separated* by a *non-conducting medium:* thus the sun *radiates* heat towards the earth, because the *air* (which is a very bad conductor) *comes between.*

Q. *On* WHAT *does* RADIATION DEPEND?

A. On the *roughness* of the radiating surface: thus, if metal be *scratched*, its radiating power is increased; because the *heat has more points to escape from.*

Q. *Does a* FIRE RADIATE *heat?*

A. Yes; and because *burning fuel emits rays of heat*, therefore we *feel warm* when we stand before a fire.

Q. *Why does our* FACE FEEL *uncomfortably* HOT *when we approach a* FIRE?

A. Because the fire radiates heat upon the face; which (not being covered) feels the effect immediately.

Q. *Why does the fire catch the* FACE *more than it does the* REST *of the body ?*

A. Because the *rest* of the body is *covered* with clothing; which (being a *bad* conductor of heat) prevents the same sudden and rapid transmission of heat to the skin.

Q. *Do those substances which* RADIATE *heat* ABSORB *heat also ?*

A. Yes. Those substances which *radiate most*, also *absorb most heat;* and those which *radiate least*, also *absorb the least* heat.

Q. *Does anything* ELSE *radiate heat* BESIDES *the* SUN *and* FIRE ?

A. Yes: *all* things radiate heat in *some* measure, but *not equally well.*

Q. WHAT *things* RADIATE *heat the* NEXT BEST *to the sun and fire ?*

A. All *dull* and *dark* substances are *good radiators* of heat; but all *light* and *polished* substances are *bad radiators.*

Q. *Why should the* FLUES *(connected with stoves, &c.,) be always* BLACKENED *with* BLACK LEAD ?

A. In order that the heat of the flue may be more readily *diffused* throughout the room. Black lead radiates heat more freely than any other known substance.

In heating a room with *steam* it would be absurd to use *black pipes* for conveying the steam, because they would tend to *cool* the hot vapor.

Q. *Why does a* POLISHED METAL TEA POT *make* BETTER TEA *than a black earthen one?*

A. Because polished metal (being a very *bad radiator* of heat) *keeps the water hot much longer;* and the hotter the water is, the better it "draws" the tea.

Q. *Why will not a* DULL BLACK TEA-POT *make good tea?*

A. Because the heat of the water *flies off so quickly* through the dull black surface of the tea-pot, that the water is very *rapidly cooled,* and cannot "draw" the tea.

Q. *Do not pensioners and aged cottagers generally prefer the little* BLACK EARTHEN TEA-POT *to the bright* METAL *one?*

A. Yes; because they *set it on the hob "to draw;"* in which case, the little *black tea-pot* will make the *best* tea.

Q. *Why will a* BLACK TEA-POT *make better tea than a bright metal one, if it be set upon the* HOB *to* DRAW?

A. Because the black tea-pot will *absorb heat plentifully* from the fire, and keep the water *hot:* whereas, a bright *metal* tea-pot (set upon the hob) would *throw off* the heat by *reflection.*

Q. *Then sometimes a* BLACK EARTHEN *tea-pot is the best, and sometimes a bright metal one?*

A. Yes; when a tea-pot is *set on the*

hob "to draw," black *earth* is the *best,* because it *absorbs heat:* But, when a tea-pot is *not* set on the hob, bright *metal* is the *best;* because it *radiates heat very slowly,* and therefore *keeps the water hot.*

Q. *Why does a* SAUCEPAN *which has been* USED *boil in a shorter time than a* NEW ONE?

A. Because the bottom and back are *covered with soot;* and *black soot* rapidly *absorbs the heat* of the glowing coals.

Q. *Why should the* FRONT *and* LID *of a* SAUCE PAN *be clean and* BRIGHT?

A. Because they cannot *absorb heat,* as they do not come in contact with the fire; and (being bright) they will not suffer the heat to *escape* by radiation.

Q. *In what state should a* SAUCEPAN *be in order that it may* BOIL QUICKLY?

A. All those parts which *come in contact with the fire,* should be covered with *soot,* in order to absorb heat; but all the *rest* of the saucepan should be as *bright* as possible, to prevent the *escape* of heat by radiation.

Q. *Why should* NOT *the* BOTTOM *and* BACK *of a kettle be* CLEANED *and polished?*

A. Because, *they come in contact with the fire,* and (while they are covered with black soot) *absorb heat freely* from the burning coals.

Q *Why should the* FRONT *and* TOP *of a kettle be* CLEAN *and well polished?*

A. Because polished metal *will not radiate heat;* and, therefore, (while the front and top of the kettle are well polished) *the heat is kept in,* and not suffered to escape by radiation.

Q. *Why is the* BOTTOM *of a* KETTLE *nearly* COLD *when the* WATER *is* BOILING HOT?

A. Because black soot is a very *bad conductor of heat;* and, therefore, the heat of the boiling water is some time before it gets *through the soot* which adheres to the bottom of the kettle.

Q. *Why is the* LID *of a* KETTLE *intensely* HOT *when the water boils?*

A. Because the bright metal lid is an *admirable conductor;* and, therefore, *the heat from the boiling water pours into our hand* the moment we touch it.

Q. *Show the benefit of* SMOKE *in* COOKING?

A. The carbon of the fuel (which flies off in smoke) naturally *blackens* all culinary vessels set upon the fire to boil, and thus renders them fit for use.

"Culinary vessels" are vessels used in kitchens for cooking, as saucepans, boilers, kettles, &c., (from the Latin word "Culina," *a kitchen.*)

Q. *How does* SMOKE *make culinary vessels* FIT *for* USE?

A. By absorbing heat. If it were not for the *smoke* (which gathers round a kettle or saucepan) *heat would not be absorbed*, and the process of boiling would be greatly retarded.

Q. *Why is boiling water* KEPT HOT *in a* BRIGHT METAL *pot better than in an earthen vessel?*

A. Because bright metal (being a *bad radiator*) will not *throw off from its surface* the heat of the boiling water.

Q. *Would a metal pot serve to keep water hot if it were* DULL *and* DIRTY?

A. No. It is the bright *polish* of the metal which makes it a bad radiator: if it were *dull*, *scratched*, or *dirty*, the heat would *escape* very rapidly.

Water in hot weather is also kept *cooler* in bright metal than in *dull* or earthen vessels. *See p.* 179.

Q. *Why are* DINNER-COVERS *made of* BRIGHT TIN *or* SILVER?

A. Because light-colored and highly-polished metal is a *very bad radiator of heat;* and, therefore, bright tin or silver will not allow the heat of the cooked food to *escape through the cover by radiation.*

Q. *Why should a* MEAT-COVER *be very brightly* POLISHED?

A. To prevent the heat of the food

from escaping by *radiation*. If a meat-cover be *dull* or *scratched*, it will *absorb heat from the food beneath;* and (instead of keeping it *hot*) *make it cold.*

Q. *Why should a* SILVER MEAT-COVER *be* PLAIN *and not* CHASED?

A. Because a *chased* meat-cover would *absorb heat from the food;* and (instead of *keeping it hot*) *make it cold.*

Q. *What is* DEW?

A. Dew is the *vapor of the air condensed* by coming in contact with bodies *colder than itself.*

Q. *Why is the* GROUND *sometimes* COVERED *with* DEW?

A. Because the surface of the earth (at sun-set) is made so very *cold* by radiation, that the warm vapor of the air is *chilled* by contact, and condensed into dew.

Q. *Why is the* EARTH *made colder than the* AIR *after the sun has set?*

A. Because the *earth radiates* heat very freely, but the air does not; in consequence of which, the earth is often 5 or 10 degrees colder than the air (after sun-set); although it was much *warmer* than the air, during the whole day.

Q. *Why is the* EARTH WARMER *than the* AIR *during the day?*

A. Because the earth *absorbs* solar heat very freely, but the air does not; in consequence of which, it is often many degrees warmer than the air, during the day.

Q. *Why is the surface of the* GROUND COLDER *in a* FINE *clear* NIGHT *than in a* CLOUDY *one?*

A. Because, on a fine, clear star-light night, *heat radiates from the earth freely*, and is lost in open space: but on a *dull* night, the clouds *arrest the process of radiation.*

Q. *Why is* DEW *deposited only on a* FINE, *clear* NIGHT?

A. Because the *surface of the ground radiates heat most freely* on a fine night; and (being cooled down by this loss of heat) *chills the vapor of the air into dew.*

Q. *Why is there* NO DEW *on a dull,* CLOUDY NIGHT?

A. Because the clouds *arrest the radiation of heat from the earth;* and (as the heat cannot freely escape) the surface is not sufficiently cooled down *to chill the vapor of the air into dew.*

Q. *Why is a* CLOUDY NIGHT WARMER *than a* FINE *one?*

A. Because the clouds *prevent the radiation of heat from the earth;* in consequence of which, the surface of the earth remains *warmer.*

Q. *Why is* DEW *most* ABUNDANT *in situations most* EXPOSED ?

A. Because the radiation of heat *is not arrested* by houses, trees, hedges, or any other thing.

Q. *Why is there scarcely any* DEW *under a shady* TREE ?

A. 1st—Because the shady head of a tree *arrests the radiation of heat from the earth :* and

2dly—A leafy tree radiates some of its own heat *towards the earth ;* in consequence of which, the ground underneath a tree is not sufficiently cooled down to chill the vapor of the air into dew.

Q. *Why is there never much* DEW *at the foot of* WALLS *and* HEDGES ?

A. 1st—Because they act as screens, *to arrest the radiation of heat from the earth :* and

2dly—They themselves *radiate some portion of heat* towards the earth ; in consequence of which, the ground at the foot of walls and hedges is not sufficiently *cooled down,* to chill the vapor of the air into dew.

Q. *Why is there little or* NO DEW *beneath a* FLOWER-AWNING, *although that awning be open on all four sides ?*

A. 1st—Because the awning *arrests*

the radiation of heat from the *ground* beneath: and

2dly—It *radiates* some of its own heat *downwards;* in consequence of which, the ground beneath an awning is not sufficiently cooled down, to chill the vapor of air into dew.

Q. *How can a thin covering of* BASS *or even* MUSLIN *protect trees from* FROST?

A. Because *any covering* prevents the radiation of heat from the tree; and if trees are *not cooled down* by radiation the vapor of the air will *not be frozen*, as it comes in contact with them.

Bass *pronounce* bas—a kind of matting used by gardeners.

Q. *Why is the* BASS *or* CANVASS *itself (which covers the tree) always* DRENCHED *with* DEW?

A. Because it *radiates heat* both *upwards* and *downwards;* in consequence of which, it is *so cooled down* that it readily *chills the vapor* of the *air* into *dew.*

Q. *Why does* SNOW *(at the foot of a* HEDGE *or* WALL*) melt sooner than that in an open field?*

A. Because the hedge or wall *radiates heat into the snow beneath*, which melts it.

Q. *Why is there* NO DEW *after a* WINDY NIGHT?

A. 1st—Because the wind *evaporates*

the moisture, as fast as it is deposited. and

2dly—It *disturbs* the *radiation of heat;* and thus diminishes the deposition of dew.

Q. *Why are* VALLEYS *and* HOLLOWS *often thickly covered with* DEW, *although they are sheltered?*

A. Because the surrounding hills prevent the *repose* of air from being *disturbed;* but do not *overhang* and *screen* the valleys sufficiently to *arrest* their radiation.

Q. *Why does* DEW *fall more* ABUNDANTLY *on* SOME THINGS *than on* OTHERS?

A. Because some things radiate heat *more freely* than others; and, therefore, become *much cooler* in the night.

Q. *Why are things which* RADIATE HEAT MOST FREELY *always the most* THICKLY COVERED *with* DEW?

A. Because the vapor of the air is *chilled into dew*, the moment it comes in contact with them.

Q. WHAT *kind of things* RADIATE HEAT *most* FREELY?

A. Grass, wood, and the leaves of plants, radiate heat *very freely:* but polished metal, smooth stones, and woollen cloth, part with their heat *very tardily.*

Q. *Do the leaves of* ALL *plants radiate heat* EQUALLY WELL?

A. No. Rough, *woolly leaves* (like those of a holly-hock) radiate heat much *more freely* than the *hard, smooth, polished leaves* of a common laurel.

Q. *Show the* WISDOM *of* GOD *in making grass, the leaves of trees, and* ALL VEGETABLES, EXCELLENT RADIATORS *of heat?*

A. As vegetables *require much moisture*, and would often *perish* without a plentiful deposit of dew, God wisely made them to *radiate heat freely*, so as to *chill the vapor* (which touches them) *into dew.*

Q. *Will polished* METAL, *smooth* STONES, *and woollen* CLOTH, *readily collect* DEW?

A. No. While grass and the leaves of plants *are completely drenched with dew* a piece of *polished metal*, or of *woollen cloth* (lying on the same spot), will be *almost dry.*

Q. *Why would* POLISHED METAL *and* WOOLLEN CLOTH *be* DRY, *while grass and leaves are drenched with* DEW?

A. Because the polished metal and woollen cloth *part with their heat so slowly*, that the vapor of the air is *not chilled into dew* as it passes over them.

Q. *Why is a* GRAVEL WALK *almost* DRY, *when a grass plat is covered thick with* DEW?

A. Because *grass* is a *good radiator*

and throws off its heat very *freely;* but *gravel* is a *very bad radiator*, and parts with its heat very slowly.

Q. *Is that the reason why* GRASS *is* SATURATED *with* DEW, *and the* GRAVEL *is* NOT?

A. Yes. When the vapor of warm air comes in contact with the *cold grass*, it is instantly chilled into dew; but it is *not so freely condensed* as it passes over gravel, because gravel is not so *cold* as the grass.

Q. *Why does* DEW *rarely fall upon hard* ROCKS *and* BARREN *lands?*

A. Because rocks and barren lands are so *compact* and *hard*, that they can neither *absorb nor radiate much heat;* and (as their *temperature varies but very little*) very little *dew* distils upon them.

Q. *Why does* DEW *fall more abundantly on* CULTIVATED *soils than on* BARREN *lands?*

A. Because cultivated soils (being *loose and porous*) very freely *radiate* by night the heat which they absorbed by day; in consequence of which, they are *much cooled* down, and plentifully *condense* the vapor of the passing air *into dew.*

Q. *Show the* WISDOM *of* GOD *in this arrangement.*

A. Every plant and inch of land,

which *needs* the moisture of dew, is adapted to *collect* it; but *not a single drop* is *wasted* where its refreshing moisture is *not required.*

Q. *Show the advantage to us in having polished* METAL *and woollen* CLOTH BAD RADIATORS *of heat.*

A. If polished metal collected dew as easily as grass, it *could never be kept dry* and *free from rust.* Again, if woollen garments collected dew as readily as the leaves of trees, we should be *often soaking wet,* and subject to *constant colds.*

Q. *Show how this affords a beautiful illustration of* GIDEON'S MIRACLE, *recorded in the book of Judges,* VI. 37, 38.

A. The *fleece of wool* (which is a very *bad* radiator of heat) was soaking *wet* with dew, when the *grass* (which is a most *excellent* radiator) was *quite dry.*

Q. *Was not this* CONTRARY *to the laws of* NATURE?

A. Yes; and was, therefore, a plain *demonstration* of the *power of God,* who could thus change the very *nature of things* at his will.

Q. *Why do our* CLOTHES FEEL DAMP, *after walking in a fine evening in* SPRING *or* AUTUMN?

A. Because the vapor (condensed by the cold earth) lights upon them like dew.

Q. *Why are* WINDOWS *often covered with thick* MIST, *and the frames wet with standing* WATER ?

A. Because the temperature of the *external air* always *falls* at sunset, and *chills* the *window-glass* with which it comes in contact.

Q. *How does this account for the* MIST *and* WATER *on a* WINDOW ?

A. As the warm vapor of the room *touches* the *cold glass* it is *chilled* and *condensed* into *mist ;* and the mist (collecting into drops) *rolls down* the window-frame in little streams of water.

Q. *Does the* GLASS *of a window* COOL *down more* RAPIDLY *than the* AIR *of the room itself?*

A. Yes; because the air is *kept warm by fires*, and by the *animal heat* of the people in the room ; in consequence of which, the air of a room suffers *very little* diminution of heat from the setting of the sun.

Q. *Whence arises the* VAPOR *of a* ROOM ?

A. 1st—The very *air* of the room contains *vapor :*

2dly—The *breath* and *insensible perspiration* of the inmates *increase* this vapor : and

3dly—*Hot dinners*, the *steam of tea*, and so on, *increase it* still more.

Q. *What is meant by "the* INSENSIBLE PERSPIRATION?"

A. From every part of the human body, an *insensible* and *invisible perspiration issues* all night and day; not only in the hot weather of *summer*, but also in the coldest day of *winter.*

Q. *If the perspiration be both* INSENSIBLE *and* INVISIBLE, *how is it* KNOWN *that there* IS *any such perspiration?*

A. If you put your naked arm into a *clean, dry glass tube*, the *perspiration* will *condense* on the glass like mist.

Q. *Why are* CARRIAGE WINDOWS *very* SOON *covered with thick* MIST?

A. Because the warm vapor of the carriage is *condensed* by the *cold glass*, and covers it with a thick mist.

Q. WHY *is the glass window* COLD *enough to condense the vapor of the carriage?*

A. Because the *inside* of a carriage is much *warmer* than the *outside;* and the glass window is made cold by contact with the *external air.*

Q. WHERE *does the* WARM *vapor of the carriage come from?*

A. The warm *breath* and insensible *perspiration* of the persons riding, load the air of the carriage with warm vapor.

Q. *What is the cause of the pretty* FROST-WORK, *seen on bed-room* WINDOWS *in winter-time?*

A. The *breath* and insensible *perspiration* of the sleeper (coming in contact with the ice-cold window) are *frozen* by the cold glass, and form those beautiful appearances seen in our bed-rooms on a winter morning.

Q. *Why is the* GLASS *of a window colder than the* WALLS *of a room?*

A. Because glass is so *excellent a radiator*, that it parts with its heat more *rapidly* than the *walls* do.

Q. *Why is a* TUMBLER *of cold* WATER *made quite* DULL *with mist, when brought into a room* FULL *of* PEOPLE?

A. Because the *hot vapor* of the room is *condensed* upon the cold tumbler, with which it comes in contact; and changes its invisible and gaseous form into that of a *thick mist.*

Q. *Why is a* GLASS *made quite* DULL *by laying a* HOT HAND *upon it?*

A. Because the insensible *perspiration* of the hot hand is *condensed* upon the cold glass, and made perceptible.

Q. *Why are* WINE-GLASSES *made quite* DULL, *when they are brought into a room* FULL *of* COMPANY?

A. Because the *hot vapor* of the room (coming in contact with the cold wine-glasses) is condensed upon them, and covers them with vapor, like dew.

Q. *Why does this misty appearance* GO OFF, *after a little time?*

A. Because the glass becomes of the same *temperature* as the *air* of the room; and will no longer *chill* the *vapor* which touches it, and *condense* it into *mist.*

Q. *Why is a* WINE GLASS (*which has been brought out of a* CELLAR *into the* AIR) *covered with a thick* MIST *in summer-time?*

A. Because the vapor of the hot air is *condensed* into a thick mist, by contact with the cold glass.

Q. *Why does* BREATHING *on a* GLASS *make it quite* DULL?

A. Because the hot breath is *condensed* by the cold glass; and therefore covers it with a thick mist.

Q. *Why are the* WALLS *of a house covered with* WET *in a sudden* THAW?

A. Because the walls (being thick) cannot *change* their *temperature* so fast as the air; in consequence of which, they *retain* their *cold* after the thaw has set in.

Q. *How does* "RETAINING *their* COLD" *account for their being so* WET?

A. As the vapor of the warm air touches the *cold walls*, it is *chilled* and *condensed* into *water;* which either *sticks* to the walls or trickles down in little streams.

Q. *Why does a thick* WELL-BUILT HOUSE *contract more* DAMP *of this kind than an* ORDINARY *one?*

A. Because the walls are much thicker; and (if the frost has penetrated far into the *bricks*) they will be some time before they are reduced to the same *temperature* as the *air*.

Q. *Why are* BALUSTERS, *&c.,* DAMP *after a* THAW?

A. Because they are made of some very close-grained varnished wood, which cannot *change* its *temperature* so *fast* as the air.

Balusters—corruptly called banisters.

Q. *How does* THIS *account for the* BALUSTERS *being* DAMP?

A. The vapor of the warm air (coming in *contact* with the *cold balusters*) is *chilled* and condensed into *water* upon them.

Q. *Why is our* BREATH VISIBLE *in* WINTER, *and* NOT *in* SUMMER?

A. Because the intense cold condenses our breath into *visible vapor;* but in *summer* the air is *not cold enough* to do so.

Q. *Why are our* HAIR *and the* BRIM *of our* HAT *often covered with little drops of pearly* DEW *in winter-time?*

A. Because our breath is condensed

as soon as it comes in contact with our cold hair or hat, and hangs there in little dew-drops.

Q. *Why does the* STEAM *of a* RAILWAY BOILER *often pour down, like fine rain, when the steam is "let off?"*

A. Because in cold weather the steam from the chimney is *condensed* by the *chill air* and falls like fine rain.

Q. *Why is there* LESS DEW *when the* WIND *is* WESTERLY, *than when the wind is* EASTERLY?

A. Because *westerly* winds cross the *continent*, and, (as they pass over *land*) are dry and arid: But *easterly* winds cross the *Atlantic Ocean*, and (as they pass over *water*) are *moist* and *full of vapor*.

Q. *How does the* DRYNESS *of a westerly wind* PREVENT DEW-FALLS?

A. As westerly winds are very dry, they imbibe the moisture of the air; in consequence of which, there is *very little* left to be condensed into *dew*.

Q. *How does the* MOISTNESS *of an eastern wind* PROMOTE *dew-falls?*

A. As easterly winds are *saturated* with *vapor*, they require very little *reduction of heat* to cause a *copious deposition of dew*.

Q. *When is* DEW *most* COPIOUSLY *distilled?*

A. After a hot day in summer or autumn, especially if the *wind* be easterly.

Q. *Why is* DEW *distilled most* COPIOUSLY *after a* HOT *day?*

A. Because the surface of the hot earth *radiates* heat very freely at sunset, and (being made much *colder* than the *air*) *chills* the *passing vapor* and condenses it into dew.

Q. *Does not* AIR *radiate heat, as well as the* EARTH *and its various plants?*

A. No. The air never *radiates heat;* nor is the air made *hot* by the *rays* of the *sun.*

Q. *How is the* AIR *made* HOT *or* COLD?

A. By convection of *hot* or *cold* currents.

Q. *Explain this.*

A. The air which has been heated by the surface of the earth ascends, warming the air through which it passes. Other air (being warmed in a similar way) also *ascends,* carrying *heat;* and this is repeated, till all the air is made hot.

Q. *How is the* AIR *made* COLD?

A. The air resting on the earth is made *cold* by *contact:* this cold air makes the *air above* it *cold;* and cold currents (or winds) *shake* the *whole together,* till all becomes of one temperature.

Q. *Why is* MEAT *very subject to* TAINT *on a* MOONLIGHT *night?*

A. Because it *radiates heat very* freely in a bright moonlight night; in consequence of which, it is soon covered with *dew*, which produces rapid *decomposition*.

Q. *How do* MOONLIGHT *nights conduce to the rapid* GROWTH *of* PLANTS?

A. Radiation is carried on very rapidly on bright moonlight nights; in consequence of which, *dew* is very plentifully *deposited* on young plants, which conduces much to their growth and vigor.

Q. *Why is evening* DEW INJURIOUS *to* HEALTH?

A. Because it is always laden with *noxious exhalations* from the *earth*; especially in *marshy* countries.

Q. *Is* HONEY-DEW *a similar thing to* DEW?

A. No. Honey-dew is a sweet liquid shed by a very small *insect* (called the a'phis) and deposited in autumn on the under surface of favorite leaves.

Frequently also on Lime Trees, in the Spring.

Q. *Does* HONEY-DEW INJURE *leaves, or do them good?*

A. It injures them very much, by filling the *pores* with a thick, clammy liquid; in consequence of which, the leaf can neither *transpire* nor *absorb* its needful food.

Q. *What* EFFECT *has honey-dew upon the* APPEARANCE *of a leaf?*

A. After a little time, the leaf (being *smothered* and *starved*) begins to turn a *dingy yellow.*

Q. *Are not* ANTS *very* FOND *of* HONEY-DEW?

A. Yes; and crawl up the loftiest trees in order to obtain it.

Q. *What is the cause of* MIST (*or earth-fog*)?

A. If the *night* has been very *calm*, the radiation of heat from the earth has been very abundant; in consequence of which, the *air* (resting on the earth) has been *chilled*, and its vapor condensed into a thick mist.

Q. *Why does not the* MIST *become* DEW?

A. Because the chill of the air is so *rapid*, that vapor is condensed *faster* than it can be *deposited;* and (covering the earth in a mist) prevents any further *radiation of heat* from the earth.

Q. *When the earth can no longer* RADIATE *heat upwards, does it continue to* CONDENSE *the vapor of the air?*

A. No; the air (in contact with the earth) becomes about equal in *temperature* with the surface of the earth itself for which reason, the mist is not *con-*

densed into *dew*, but remains *floating* above the *earth* as a thick cloud.

Q. *This* MIST *seems to* RISE HIGHER *and* HIGHER, *and yet remains quite as dense below as at first. Explain the cause of this.*

A. The air resting on the *earth* is first chilled, and *chills* the air resting on *it;* the air which touches this *new layer* of mist being *also* condensed, layer is added to layer: And thus the mist seems to be *rising*, when (in fact) it is only *deepening*.

Q. *Why do* MIST *and* DEW VANISH, *as the* SUN *rises?*

A. Because the air becomes *warmer* at sun-rise, and *absorbs* the vapor.

Q. *Why is a* DEW-DROP ROUND?

A. Because every part of it is *equally balanced;* and, therefore, there is no cause why *one part* of the drop should be further from the centre than *another*.

Q. *Why is the* DEW-DROP (*on a broad leaf*) *sometimes* FLATTENED?

A. Because two or more drops of dew *roll together*, and make one large *spheroid* (or flattened drop).

Q. *Why will* DEW-DROPS ROLL ABOUT CABBAGE-PLANTS, POPPIES, *&c., without wetting the surface?*

A. Because the leaves of cabbages

and poppies are covered with a very *fine waxen powder*, over which the dew-drop rolls without wetting the surface, as a drop of rain would over dust.

Q. *Why does not a drop of* RAIN WET *the* DUST *over which it rolls?*

A. Because dust has no *affinity* for water, and, therefore, repels it.

Q. *Why does not the* DEW-DROP WET *the* POWDER *of the* CABBAGE-PLANT?

A. Because the fine powder which covers the cabbage-leaves has no *affinity* for water, and, therefore, repels it.

Q. *Why will* DEW-DROPS ROLL *over a* ROSE, *&c., without wetting the petals?*

A. Because the leaves of a rose contain an *essential oil*, which has no *affinity* for water, and, therefore, repels it.

Q. *Why can* SWANS *and* DUCKS *dive under water* WITHOUT *being* WETTED?

A. Because their feathers are covered with an *oily secretion*, which has no *affinity* for water, and, therefore, repels it.

Q. *What is the cause of* MIST?

A. Currents of air from the water coming in contact with *colder land* currents.

Q. *Why are the currents of air from the* LAND COLDER *than those blowing over* WATER?

A. Because the earth radiates heat after sun-set more freely than water; consequently the *air* which comes in contact with the land is more cold than that which comes in contact with water.

For other questions respecting land and sea breezes see Chapter XXIV.

Q. *Why is not the* AIR *which passes over* WATER *so* COOL *as that which passes over* LAND?

A. Because *water* does not cool down at *sun-set* so fast as *land* does; and, therefore, the air in contact with it *remains warmer*.

Q. *Why does not* WATER *cool down so fast as* LAND?

A. 1st—Because the *surface* of water is perpetually *changing;* and, as fast as one surface is made cold, *another* is presented: and

2dly—The moment water is made cold *it sinks*, and *warmer* portions of water *rise* to occupy its place: therefore, before the *surface of water is cooled*, the *whole volume* must be made cold: which is not the case with land.

Q. *What is the cause of a "pea-soup"* LONDON FOG?

A. These fogs (which occur generally in the winter time) are occasioned thus:—Some current of air (being suddenly cooled) *descends* into the *warm streets*, forcing back the smoke in a *mass* towards the earth.

Q. *Why are there not* FOGS EVERY *night?*

A. Because the air will always hold in solution a certain quantity of vapor, (which varies according to its temperature:) and, when the air is not *saturated*, it may be cooled without parting with its vapor.

Q. *When do* FOGS *occur at night?*

A. When the air is saturated with *vapor* during the day. When this is the case, it deposits some of its superabundant moisture in the form of dew or fog as soon as its capacity for holding vapor is lessened by the *cold night.*

Q. *Why is there very* OFTEN *a fog over* MARSHES *and* RIVERS, *at night-time?*

A. Because the air of marshes is almost always near *saturation;* and, therefore, the least depression of *temperature* will compel it to relinquish some of its moisture in the form of dew or fog.

Q. *What is the* DIFFERENCE *between* DEW *ana* RAIN?

A. In *dew*, the condensation is made near the *earth's surface.*

In *rain*, the drops fall from a considerable height.

Q. *What is the* CAUSE *of both dew and rain?*

A. Cold *condensing* the vapor of the *air* when near the point of *saturation.*

Q. *Why do* MIST *and* FOG VANISH *at sun-rise?*

A. Because the condensed particles are again *changed* into *invisible* vapor by the heat of the sun.

Q. *What is the difference between a* MIST *and a* FOG?

A. MIST is generally applied to *vapors* condensed on *marshes*, *rivers*, and *lakes*.

FOG is generally applied to *vapors* condensed on *land;* especially if those vapors are laden with smoke.

Q. *What is the reason why condensed vapor sometimes forms into* CLOUDS, *and sometimes into* FOG?

A. If the surface of the EARTH is hotter than the *air*, the vapor of the earth is *chilled* by the *cold air*, and becomes FOG: But if the AIR is hotter than the *earth*, the vapor *rises through the air*, and becomes CLOUD.

Q. *If cold air produces* FOG, *why is it not foggy on a* FROSTY MORNING?

A. 1st—Because *less vapor* is formed on a *frosty day:* and

2dly—The vapor is *frozen* upon the *ground*, before it can rise from the earth, and becomes HOAR-FROST.

Q. *Why are* FOGS *more general in* AUTUMN *than in spring?*

A. 1st—Because the air in spring is generally much *drier* than it is in autumn; in consequence of which, it is not so near the point of *saturation:* and

2dly—The *earth* in spring is not so *hot* as it is in autumn; in consequence of which, its vapor is not chilled into fog as it issues into the air.

Q. *Why are* FOGS *more common in* VALLEYS *than on* HILLS?

A. 1st—Because valleys contain more *moisture* than *hills:* and

2dly—They are *not exposed* to sufficient *wind* to dissipate the vapor.

Q. *How does* WIND *dissipate* FOGS?

A. Either by *blowing* them away; or else by *dissolving* them into *vapor* again.

Q. *What is* HOAR-FROST?

A. There are two sorts o' hoar-frost; 1.—FROZEN DEW: and 2.—F OZEN FOG.

Q. *What is the cause of the* GROUND HOAR-FROST, *or frozen* DEW?

A. Very *rapid radiation* of heat from the earth; in consequence of which, the *surface* is so *cooled down* that it *freezes the dew* condensed upon it.

Q. *Why is* HOAR-FROST *seen only after a very* CLEAR NIGHT?

A. Because the earth will not have thrown off heat enough by radiation to *freeze* the vapor condensed upon its surface, unless the night has been very clear indeed.

Q. *Why does* HOAR-FROST *very often* COVER *the* GROUND *and* TREES, *when the water of rivers is not frozen?*

A. Because it is not the effect of cold in the *air*, but cold on the surface of the *earth* (produced by excessive radiation), which *freezes the dew* condensed upon it.

Q. *Why is the* HOAR-FROST *upon* GRASS *and* VEGETABLES *much thicker than that upon lofty* TREES?

A. Because the air (resting on the *surface* of the ground) is much colder after sun-set than the *air higher up;* in consequence of which, more *vapor* is *condensed* and *frozen* there.

Q. *Why is the* AIR *(resting on the surface of the* EARTH) *colder than that in the* HIGHER *regions?*

A. Because the *earth* radiates more heat than the *leaves* of lofty trees; and, therefore, more *rapidly condenses* and *freezes* the vapor of the air.

Q. *Why are* EVERGREENS *often* FROST-BITTEN *when lofty trees are* NOT?

A. Because they do not rise far above the surface of the earth; and (as the air *contiguous* to the earth is made *colder* by radiation than that in the *higher* regions), therefore, the *low evergreen* is often *frost-bitten*, when the lofty tree is uninjured.

Q. *Why is there little or* NO HOAR-FROST *under* SHRUBS *and shady* TREES?

A. 1st—Because the leafy top *arrests* the process of radiation from the earth:

2dly—Shrubs and trees radiate *heat* towards the earth: and, therefore, the *ground beneath* is never *cold enough* to *congeal* the little dew which rests upon it.

Q. *What is the cause of that* HOAR-FROST *which arises from* FROZEN FOG?

A. The thick fog which invested the earth during the night (being condensed by the *cold frost* of early morning), is *congealed* upon *every object* with which it comes in contact.

CHAPTER XIX.

5.—CONVECTION.

Q. *What is meant by the* CONVECTION *of* HEAT?

A. Heat communicated by being *carried* to another thing or place; as the hot water resting on the *bottom* of a kettle carries heat to the water through which it ascends. (*See p.* 226.)

Q. *Are* LIQUIDS *good* CONDUCTORS *of heat?*

A. No; liquids are bad *conductors;* and are, therefore, made hot by *convection.*

Q. *Why are* LIQUIDS BAD CONDUCTORS *of heat?*

A. Because heat *converts a liquid* into *steam;* and flies off with the vapor instead of being *conducted through* the liquid.

Q. *Explain how* WATER *is made* HOT.

A. The water *nearest the fire* is *first* heated, and (being heated) *rises* to the *top;* while its place is supplied by *colder* portions, which are heated in turn, till *all* the water is boiling hot.

Q. *Why is* WATER *in such continual* FERMENT, *when it is* BOILING?

A. This commotion is mainly produced by the *ascending* and *descending currents* of hot and cold water.

The escape of *steam* from the water contributes also to increase this agitation.

Q. *How do these two currents* PASS *each other?*

A. The *hot ascending current* rises up through the *centre* of the mass of water; while the *cold descending currents* pass down by the metal *sides of the kettle.*

For other questions on the subject of boiling water, see from page 109 to 115.

Q. *Why is* HEAT *applied to the* BOTTOM, *and not to the top of a* KETTLE?

A. Because the heated water always *ascends* to the *surface*, heating the water through which it passes; if, therefore, heat were applied to the *top* of a vessel, the water *below the surface* would never be *heated.*

Q. *As the lower part of a* GRATE *is made* RED-HOT *by the fire* ABOVE, *why would not the* WATER *boil, if fire were applied to the* TOP *of a kettle?*

A. The *iron* of a grate is an excellent *conductor;* if, therefore, *one* part be heated, the heat is conducted to *every* other part: But *water* is a very *bad conductor*, and will not diffuse heat in a similar way.

Q. *Prove that* WATER *is a* BAD CONDUCTOR *of heat.*

A. When a blacksmith immerses his red-hot iron in a tank of water, the water which surrounds the iron is made *boiling hot*, while that *below the surface* remains quite cold.

Q. *If you wish to* COOL LIQUIDS, *where should the cold be applied?*

A. To the *top* of the *liquid;* because the *cold* portions will always *descend*, and allow the warmer parts to come in contact with the cooling substance.

Q. *Does* BOILING *water get hotter by being* KEPT *on the* FIRE?

A. No:—not if the steam be suffered to escape.

Q. WHY *does not boiling water get* HOTTER, *if the steam be suffered to* ESCAPE?

A. Because the *water* is converted into *steam* as fast as it boils; and the steam *carries away* the additional heat.

Q. *Why does* SOUP *keep* HOT *longer than boiling water?*

A. Because the grease and various ingredients floating in the soup, oppose the ascending motion of the hot particles, and prevent their rising so freely to the surface.

Q. *If you wanted to keep* WATER HOT *for a long time, how could it be done?*

A. By adding a little *starch* or flour to the water.

Q. *Why would a little* STARCH, *added to boiling water, serve to keep it* HOT?

A. Because it would oppose the ascending motion of the hot particles of water, and prevent their rising so freely to the surface.

Q. *Why do* THICK MILK, RICE MILK, *&c., remain* HOT *longer than water?*

A. Because the ascending motion of the hot particles is opposed by the flour or rice, and cannot so quickly reach the surface.

Q. *Is* STEAM *visible or* INVISIBLE?

A. Steam is *invisible;* but when it comes in contact with the air (being *condensed* into small drops) it instantly becomes visible.

Q. *How do you know that* STEAM *is* INVISIBLE?

A. If you look at the spout of a boiling kettle, you will find that the steam (which issues from the spout) is always invisible for about *half an inch;* after which *it becomes visible.*

Q. WHY *is the steam* INVISIBLE *for* HALF AN INCH?

A. Because the air is not able to condense it, as it first issues from the spout; but when it *spreads* and comes in contact with a larger volume of air, the *invisible steam* is readily condensed into *visible drops.*

Q. WHY *do* STEAM-ENGINES *sometimes* BURST?

A. Because steam is very *elastic*, and this elasticity increases in a greater proportion than the that which produces it; unless, therefore, some *vent* be freely allowed, steam will burst the vessel which confines it.

Q. *Is* AIR *a good* CONDUCTOR?

A. No; *air* is a very *bad conductor;* and is heated (like water) by *convection.*

Q. *How is a* ROOM WARMED *by a* STOVE?

A. The air *nearest* the fire is made hot *first* and rises; *cold air* then *descends,* is heated, and *ascends* in like manner; and this interchange goes on till *all* the air of the room is *warmed.* (*See p.* 56.)

Q. *Why are* FIRES *placed on the* FLOOR *of a room, and not towards the* CEILING?

A. Because heated air always *ascends.* If, therefore, the fire were not *near the floor*, the air of the *lower* part of the room would never be heated by the fire at all.

Q. *If you take a* POKER *out of the fire, and hold the* HOT END DOWNWARDS, *why is the* HANDLE *intensely* HOT?

A. Because the hot end of the poker *heats the air* around it; and this hot air (in its ascent) *scorches* the *poker* and the *hand* which holds it.

Q. *How should a* RED-HOT POKER *be carried, o as not to* BURN *our fingers?*

A. With the hot end *upwards;* for then the air (heated by the poker) would not pass over our hand and scorch it.

PART II.

AIR.

CHAPTER XX.

THE ATMOSPHERE.

Q. *Of what is atmospheric* AIR *composed?*

A. Principally of two gases, *oxygen* and *nitrogen*, mixed together in the following proportion: viz., 1 gallon of oxygen to 4 of nitrogen.

It must not be forgotten that the air contains small quantities of other gaseous substances also, as *vapor of water*, *carbonic acid*, and *ammonia*.

Q. *What do you mean by a* GAS?

A. A *permanent elastic* fluid resembling air.

N. B. MOST GASES ARE INVISIBLE OR COLORLESS, LIKE AIR.

"PERMANENT,"—In this respect gas differs from *vapor*, which is *not* permanent; for vapor may be easily condensed by cold into a *liquid*, but gas never changes its gaseous form.

"ELASTIC,"—In this respect gas differs from a *liquid*, which is almost inelastic; whereas gas is exceedingly elastic.

"RESEMBLING AIR," or aeriform.—The word "Gas" means *air*, but air is a compound of two gases. Some few gases are visible, as CHLORINE, which is a greenish yellow.

Q. *What is the difference between a* GAS *and a* LIQUID ?

A. Gases are *elastic*, but liquids *not.*

Q. *Illustrate what is meant by "the* ELASTICITY *of* GAS."

A. If from a vessel full of gas *half* were taken out—the *other* half would immediately spread itself out, and fill the same space as was occupied by the *whole.*

Q. *Prove that a* LIQUID *is* NOT ELASTIC.

A. If from a gallon of water you take *half*, the remaining 4 pints will take up only *half* the room that the whole gallon previously did: a *liquid*, therefore, is not elastic like *gas.*

Strictly speaking, a liquid is *slightly* elastic; inasmuch as it may be *compressed* and will afterwards recover its former dimensions.

Q. *What are the uses of the* OXYGEN *of the air* ?

A. To *support* combustion and *sustain* life.

Q. *What is meant, when it is said, that the* OXYGEN *of the air* "SUPPORTS COMBUSTION ?"

A. It means this: It is the *oxygen* of the air which makes *fuel burn.*

Q. *How does the* OXYGEN *of the air make* FUEL BURN ?

A. The fuel is decomposed (by heat) into *hydrogen* and *carbon;* and these elements combining with the *oxygen* of the air produce combustion.

Q. *What* GAS *is produced by the combination of carbon and oxygen?*

A. CARBONIC ACID GAS. (*See p.* 43.)

Q. *What becomes of the* HYDROGEN *of the* FUEL?

A. The *hydrogen* of the fuel combines with the *oxygen* of the air, and forms WATERY VAPOR; but the combination is attended by the production of *flame*, owing to the very inflammable nature of hydrogen gas.

Q. *What becomes of the* NITROGEN *of the air, amidst all these changes and combinations?*

A. The nitrogen escapes *unchanged*, to be again mixed with *oxygen*, and converted into common AIR.

Q. *What is meant, when it is said, that* OXYGEN "SUSTAINS LIFE?"

A. It means this: If a person *could not inhale oxygen*, he would *die*.

Q. *What* GOOD *does this inspiration of* OXYGEN *do?*

A. 1st—It gives *vitality* to the *blood*: and

2dly—It is the *cause* of *animal heat*.

Q. *How is* FOOD *converted into* BLOOD?

A. After it is swallowed, it is dissolved in the stomach into a *grey pulp*, called CHYME; it then passes into the intestines, and is converted by the "bile" into a *milky substance*, called CHYLE.

Chyme—*pronounce* kyme—chyle *pronounce* kyle—*each as one syllable.*

Q. *What* BECOMES *of the milky substance called* CHYLE ?

A. It is absorbed by the vessels called "*lacteals*," and poured into the veins on the *left side of the neck.*

Lac'teals—*pronounce* Lac`-te-als.

Q. *What becomes of the chyle,* AFTER *it is* POURED *into the* VEINS ?

A. It *mingles* with the *blood,* and is itself *converted* into blood also.

Q. *How does the* OXYGEN *we inhale* MINGLE *with the* BLOOD ?

A. The oxygen of the air mingles with the blood *in the lungs,* and converts it into a *bright red color.*

Q. *What color is the blood* BEFORE *it is oxidized in the lungs ?*

A. *A dark purple.* The oxygen turns it to a *bright red.*

Oxidized, i. e., impregnated with oxygen.

Q. *Why are* PERSONS *so* PALE, *who live in* CLOSE ROOMS *and* CITIES ?

A. Because the blood derives its redness from the *oxygen* of the air inhaled; but, as the air in close rooms and cities is not *fresh,* it is *deficient in oxygen,* and cannot turn the blood to a beautiful bright red.

Q. *Why are* PERSONS, *who live in the* OPEN AIR *and in the country, of a* RUDDY *complexion ?*

A. Because they inhale fresh air which has its full proportion of oxygen: and the blood derives its bright red color from the *oxygen* of the air inhaled.

Q. *Why is not the air in* CITIES *so* FRESH *as that in the* COUNTRY?

A. Because it is impregnated with the *breath* of its numerous *inhabitants*, the *odor* of its *sewers*, the *smoke* of its *fires*, and many other impurities.

Q. *How does* OXYGEN *convert the color of blood into a bright* RED?

A. The *coloring* matter of the blood is formed by very minute *globules* floating in it; the oxygen (uniting with the *coats of these globules*) makes them *milky*—and the dark coloring matter of the blood (seen through this *milky coat*) appears of a *bright red*.

Exp.:—If you put some dark *venous* blood into a *milky* glass, and hold it up towards the light, it will appear of a *bright florid* color like *arterial* blood.

Q. *How does the* COMBINATION *of* OXYGEN *with the* BLOOD *produce animal* HEAT?

A. The principal element of the blood is *carbon;* and this carbon (combining with the oxygen of the air inhaled) produces *carbonic acid gas*, in the same way as burning fuel. (*See p.* 43.)

Q. *What becomes of the* NITROGEN *of the air, after the oxygen enters the blood?*

A. It is thrown out from the lungs unchanged, by the act of breathing; to be again mixed with *oxygen* and converted into common AIR.

Q. *Why does the vitiated air (after the oxygen has been absorbed)* COME OUT *of the* MOUTH, *and not sink into the stomach?*

A. Because a mechanical provision is made in the upper part of the wind-pipe and gullet for this purpose.

N. B. The lungs are a *hollow, spongy mass*, capable of confining air and of being *dilated* by it. They are so situated in the thorax (or chest), that the air *must* enter into them, whenever the cavities of the thorax are enlarged. The process of breathing is performed thus: When we INHALE, the thorax (or chest) is expanded; in consequence of which, a *vacuum is formed round the lungs*, and heavy external air instantly enters (through the mouth and throat) *to supply* this vacuum.

When we EXHALE, the thorax *contracts* again; in consequence of which, it can no longer contain the *same quantity* of air as it did before; and some of it is necessarily *expelled*. When this expulsion of air takes place, the lungs and *muscular fibres* of the wind-pipe and gullet *contract* in order to assist the process.

Q. *If (both in combustion and respiration) the* OXYGEN *of the air is* CONSUMED, *and the* NITROGEN REJECTED—*Why are not the* PROPORTIONS *of the* AIR DESTROYED?

A. Because the *under surface of vegetable leaves* (during the day) gives out *oxygen;* and thus restores to the air the very element of which it has been deprived.

Q. *Whence do leaves* OBTAIN *the oxygen which they exhale?*

A. From the *carbonic acid* absorbed by the *roots* from the soil, and carried to the leaves by the rising *sap*.

N. B. Carbonic acid (it must be remembered) is a compound of carbon and oxygen.

Q. *How do plants contrive to absorb carbonic acid from the soil?*

A. It rises (by capillary attraction) through the small fibrous roots, after it has been dissolved in the soil by water.

Q. *Whence does the* SOIL *obtain carbonic acid?*

A. 1st—From the air; from which it is driven by falling showers:

2dly—From the decomposition of vegetable and animal matters, which always produces this gas in abundance: and

3dly—All lime-stone, chalk, and calcareous stones, contain vast quantities of carbonic acid in a *solid* state.

Calcareous, i. e., of a limy nature.

Q. *If leaves throw off the* OXYGEN *of the carbonic acid, what becomes of the carbon?*

A. It is retained to give *firmness* and *solidity* to the plant itself.

Q. *Show how God has made* ANIMAL *life dependent on that of* VEGETABLES.

A. *Animals* require *oxygen* to keep them alive, and *draw it from the air* by inspiration: The under surface of *leaves gives out oxygen;* and thus supplies the air with the *very gas* required for the use of animals.

Q. *Show how God has made* VEGETABLE *life dependent on that of animal.*

A. Plants require *carbonic acid,* which is their *principal food;* and all animals exhale the same gas from their lungs. Thus *plants* supply animals with *oxygen,* and *animals* supply plants with *carbonic acid.*

Q. *How is* AIR HEATED?

A. By "convective currents."

Q. *Explain what is meant by* "CONVECTIVE CURRENTS."

A. When a portion of air is heated, it *rises upwards in a current,* carrying the heat with it; other *colder air succeeds,* and (being *heated* in a similar way) *ascends also:* These are called "convective currents."

("Convective currents;" so called from the Latin words, cum-vectus (*carried with*); because the *heat* is "carried with" the current.)

Q. *Is* AIR HEATED *by the* RAYS *of the* SUN?

A. No; air is *not heated* (in any sensible degree) *by the action of the sun's rays* passing through it.

Q. *Why then is the* AIR HOTTER *on a* SUNNY DAY, *than on a* CLOUDY *one?*

A. Because the sun *heats the surface* of the *earth*, and the air (resting on the earth) is *heated by contact:* as soon as it is heated *it ascends;* while its place is supplied by *colder* portions which are heated in turn also.

Q. *If* AIR *be a* BAD CONDUCTOR, *why does hot* IRON *become* COLD *by* EXPOSURE *to the* AIR?

A. Because it is made cold—1st—By "convection;" and 2dly—By "radiation."

Q. *How is hot iron made cold by* CONVECTION?

A. The air resting on the hot iron (being intensely heated), rapidly ascends with the heat it has absorbed; *colder* air succeeding *absorbs more heat* and ascends also; and this process is repeated till the hot iron *is cooled completely down.*

Q. *How is hot iron cooled by* RADIATION?

A. While its heat is being carried off by "convection," the hot iron *throws off heat* (on all sides) *by radiation* also.

Q. *What is meant by* RADIATION?

A. Heat emitted (in all directions) from any surface by *rays.*

Q. *How is* BROTH COOLED *by being left exposed to the* AIR?

A. It throws off *some* heat by *radiation;* but it is *mainly* cooled down by *convection.*

Q. *How is hot* BROTH *cooled down by* CONVECTION?

A. The air *resting* on the *hot broth* (being heated) *ascends; colder* air succeeding *absorbs more heat*, and *ascends also;* and this process is repeated till the broth is *made cool.*

The particles on the surface of the broth *sink* as they are cooled down, and *warmer* particles rise to the surface; which gradually assists the cooling process.

Q. *Why is hot* TEA *and* BROTH COOLED *faster by being* STIRRED *about?*

A. 1st—Because the agitation assists in bringing its *hottest particles* to the *surface.*

2dly—The action of stirring *agitates the air*, and brings it more *quickly* to the broth or tea: and

3dly—As the hotter particles are more rapidly brought into contact with the air, therefore, *convection is more rapid.*

Blowing tea or broth cools it also. (*See p.* 168.)

Q. *If a shutter be closed in the day-time, the stream of light (piercing through the crevice) seems in* CONSTANT AGITATION. WHY *is this?*

A. Because little *motes* and *particles of dust* (thrown into agitation by the violence of the *convective currents*) are made *visible* by the strong beam of light thrown into the room through the crevice of the shutter.

Q. *Why is the* GALLERY *of a* CHURCH *or theatre* HOTTER *than the* AISLE *or pit?*

A. Because the hot air ascends from the *bottom* to the *top of the building;* while cold air flows to the *bottom* from the doors and windows.

Q. *Why do persons who ascend in balloons feel intense pain in their eyes and ears?*

A. Because the air of the upper regions is *more rarefied* than that on the earth; and the air inside their bodies (seeking to become of the same rarity) *bursts through their eyes and ears,* producing intense pain.

Q. *Why is it often* PAINFUL *and difficult to* BREATHE, *on a* MOUNTAIN-TOP?

A. Because the pressure of air on the mountain-top is *not so great as it is on the plain;* and the air inside our bodies (seeking to become of the same rarity) *bursts through the pores of the body* and produces great pain.

Q. *Why do we feel* OPPRESSED *just* PREVIOUS *to a storm?*

A. Because the air is greatly *rarefied by heat and vapor;* and the air inside us (seeking to become of the same rarity) produces an oppressive and suffocating feeling.

Q. *Why do* DIVERS, *when they are under water, suffer great pain in their eyes and ears?*

A. Because the air at the bottom of the sea *is more dense* than the air on the *surface;* and (till the air inside the diver's body is settled into the same density) he feels oppressed with pain, especially in the ears.

Q. *Why is this* PAIN *felt especially about the* EARS *of a* DIVER?

A. Because the ear is fitted with a small membrane called *the drum* (or tym'-panum), through which the dense air bursts: The rupture of this membrane very often *produces incurable deafness.*

When the diver is not in a *bell* the dense *water* bursts into his ears and ruptures the tympanum.

Q. *Why do our* CORNS *ache just previous to* RAIN?

A. Because *our feet swell* from the sudden depression in the density of air; and the hard corn (*not being elastic*) is painfully stretched and pressed.

Some of this pain is due to electricity.

Q. *How do you know that the density of the air is lowered, previous to a storm?*

A. Because the *mercury* of a barometer rapidly *falls.*

Q. *Why do* CELLARS *feel* WARM *in* WINTER?

A. Because the external air has not

free access into them; in consequence of which, they remain almost at an *even temperature*—which (in winter time) is about 10 degrees *warmer* than the external air.

Q. *Why do* CELLARS *feel* COLD *in* SUMMER?

A. Because the external air has not free access into them; in consequence of which, they remain almost at an *even temperature*—which (in summer time) is about 10 degrees *colder* than the external air.

Q. *Why does* AIR *rust* IRON?

A. Because the *oxygen of the air* combines with the *surface* of the metal, and produces *oxide of iron;* which is generally called "rust."

An oxide of iron, copper, &c., is oxygen in *combination* with iron, copper, &c.

Q. *Why does hot iron* SCALE *and* PEEL *off, when struck with a* HAMMER?

A. Because the *oxygen of the air* very readily unites with the surface of the *hot iron*, and forms a metallic oxide (or rust), which scales off when struck with a hammer.

Q. *Does iron* RUST *in* DRY *air?*

A. No; iron undergoes no change in dry air.

Q. *Why do* STOVES *and* FIRE-IRONS *become* RUSTY *in rooms, which are not* OCCUPIED?

A. Because the air is damp; and moist air *oxidizes* iron and steel.

Oxidizes, i. e., rusts.

Q. *In what part of the year is it most difficult to keep* STOVES *and* FIRE-IRONS BRIGHT?

A. In *autumn* and *winter*.

Q. *Why is it more difficult to keep* STOVES *and* FIRE-IRONS *bright in* AUTUMN *and* WINTER *than in spring and summer?*

A. Because the capacity of the air for holding water is constantly on the *decrease*, after the summer is over; in consequence of which, vapor is deposited on everything with which the air comes in contact.

Q. *Why does* GREASING *iron prevent its be coming* RUSTY?

A. Because *grease* prevents the humidity of air from coming in contact with the *surface* of the *iron*.

Q. *Why do not* STOVES *rust so frequently as* POKERS *and* TONGS?

A. Because stoves are generally *covered with plumbago*, or black lead.

Q. *What is plumbago, or black lead?*

A. A mixture of charcoal and iron.

Plumbago (strictly speaking) is a chemical union of *carbon* and *iron*, in the following proportions:—91 parts carbon and 9 iron. But the BLACK LEAD sold in shops is a mixture of charcoal and iron filings.

N. B. A most excellent varnish to prevent rust is made of 1 pint of fat oil varnish, mixed with 5 pints of highly rectified spirits of turpentine, rubbed on the iron or steel with a piece of sponge. This varnish may be applied to bright stoves, and even mathematical instruments, without injuring their delicate polish.

Q. *Why does ornamental* STEEL *(of a purple or* LILAC *color) rust more readily than polished* WHITE *steel?*

A. Because the lilac tinge is produced by *partial oxidation;* and the process which forms rusts has, therefore, already commenced.

Q. *How can lilac* STEEL *be kept* FREE *from* RUST?

A. By keeping it in a very *dry place.*

Q. *If* DRY AIR *contains* OXYGEN, *why does it* NOT RUST IRON, *as well as* MOIST *air?*

A. Because moisture is always needed, in order to bring into action the affinity of oxygen for steel.

Q. *Do any* OTHER *metals (besides iron) combine rapidly with oxygen?*

A. Yes; copper, lead, mercury, and even silver to some extent.

Q. *Why does* COPPER TARNISH?

A. The tarnish of copper is caused by its *oxidation:* that is, the oxygen of the air combines with the surface of the copper, and (instead of *rusting* it) covers it with a *dark tarnish.*

Q. *Why does* LEAD *become of a* DARKER *hue by being exposed to the air?*

A. Because the vapor of the air combines with the lead, and *oxidizes its surface*; but instead of becoming *rusty*, the surface assumes a *darker hue.*

Q. *Why does* LEAD *lose its* BRIGHTNESS, *and become* DULL, *by being exposed to the air?*

A. The *dullness* of the lead is caused by the presence of a *carbonate* of the oxide. When the oxide is formed, it attracts *carbonic acid* from the air, and (combining with it) produces a *carbonate*, which gives the *dull* tint to old lead.

Q. *Why is it difficult to keep* SILVER BRIGHT?

A. Because the vapor of the air oxidizes its surface, and *tarnishes* it.

Q. *Why do silver* TEA-POTS *and* SPOONS *tarnish more quickly than silver ore or bullion?*

A. Because alloy of some *baser* metal is used, to make them more *hard and lasting*; and this *alloy* oxidizes more quickly than silver itself.

Q. *Why does* GERMAN *silver turn a dingy yellow in a few hours?*

A. Because German silver has a great affinity for oxygen; and shows its oxidation by a *sickly yellow tarnish*, instead of rust.

Q. *If quicksilver (or mercury) will tarnish lik copper and lead—why does it preserve its* BRILLIANCY *in* BAROMETERS *and* THERMOMETERS?

A. Because the *air* is excluded; and no moisture can come in contact with it, to *oxidize* (or *tarnish*) it.

Q. *Is* GOLD *affected by the atmosphere?*

A. Not readily; gold will never combine with oxygen of itself, (i. e., without aid.)

Q. WHICH *of the* METALS *is capable of resisting oxidation altogether?*

A. Plat'inum; in consequence of which, the graduated arcs of delicate "instruments-for-observation" are made of plat'inum instead of any *other* metal.

Q. *Why is* PLAT'INUM *used for the graduated arcs of delicate mathematical instruments, instead of any other metal?*

A. Because it will never oxidize; but retains its *bright surface* in all weathers, free from both *rust* and *tarnish.*

Q. *Before plat'inum was discovered, which of the metals was employed for the same purpose?*

A. Gold.

Plat'inum (a white metal), so called from "plata," the Spanish word for *silver.* It was introduced from South America into England by Mr. Wood, (A. D. 1749.)

Q. *For what other* SCIENTIFIC *purpose is* PLAT'INUM *now used?*

A. For crucibles in which *acids* are employed: and for galvanic batteries.

Q. *Why are* CRUCIBLES (*in which acids are employed*) *made of* PLAT'INUM?

A. Because the acid would act upon *other metals*, or upon *glass;* and prevent the experimenter's success.

Q. *Which of the* METALS *have the* GREATEST *affinity for* OXYGEN?

A. Those called *potas'sium* and *so'dium.*

Potas'sium and so'dium derive their names from potash and soda. Potas'sa is the oxide of potas'sium; and soda is the oxide of so'dium.

Q. *How is the affinity of potas'sium and so'dium for oxygen shown?*

A. They *decompose water* immediately they are brought into contact with it.

Q. *What* EFFECT *has* POTAS'SIUM *on* WATER?

A. It catches *fire* the moment it is thrown into water, and burns with a vivid flame—which is still further increased by the combustion of *hydrogen*, separated from the water.

N. B. Water is composed of oxygen and hydrogen; and potas'sium *separates* the two gases.

Q. *What effect has* SO'DIUM *on* WATER?

A. It does not take *fire*, as potassium does; but undergoes very rapid *oxidation.*

Q. *Is the* FURR *of* KETTLES *an oxide?*

A. No; the furr (or deposit of boiling water) is a precipitate of *lime and mineral salt*, separated from the water by the process of boiling.

Q. *Is not this* FURR *of boiling water often* DANGEROUS?

A. Yes; especially in *tubular boilers,* such as those employed in railways.

Q. *Why is this* FURR *especially* TROUBLESOME *in* RAILWAY *engines?*

A. Because it is a *bad conductor of heat;* in consequence of which, it hinders the *evaporating effect* of the fire, and prevents the economy of fuel.

Q. *Why is this* FURR *especially* DANGEROUS *in* RAILWAY *engines?*

A. Because, when it is deposited in the boilers, they are likely to become *over-heated;* and then *explosion* will take place, from the sudden generation of highly elastic steam.

Q. *Why cannot* RAILWAY *engines be fed with* BRACKISH WATER?

A. Because *brackish* water contains *mineral salt;* which makes a much larger deposit of furr than water which contains *only vegetable matters.*

CARBONIC ACID GAS.

CHAPTER XXI.

Q. *What is* CARBONIC ACID GAS?

A. A gas formed by the union of *carbon* and *oxygen*: It used to be called "FIXED AIR."

3 lbs. of carbon and 8 lbs. of oxygen will form 11 lbs. of carbonic acid.

Q. *Under what circumstances does* CARBON *most readily* UNITE *with* OXYGEN?

A. 1st—When its *temperature* is *raised:* Thus if carbon be *red-hot*, oxygen will most readily unite with it: and

2dly—When it forms part of the fluid *blood.*

Q. *Why do oxygen and carbon so readily unite in the* BLOOD?

A. Because the atoms of carbon are so *loosely attracted* by the *other* materials of the blood, that they unite very readily with the oxygen of the air inhaled.

Q. *Is carbonic acid* WHOLESOME?

A. No; it is *fatal to animal life;* and (whenever it is inhaled) acts like a narcotic poison—producing drowsiness, which sometimes ends in death.

Q. *How can any one* KNOW, *if a place be infested with* CARBONIC ACID GAS?

A. If a pit or well contain carbonic acid, *a candle* (let down into it) will be *instantly extinguished.* The rule, therefore, is this—Where a *candle will burn, a man can live;* but *what will extinguish a candle,* will also *destroy life.*

Q. *Why does a* MINER *lower a* CANDLE *into a mine, before he descends?*

A. Because the *candle will be extinguished,* if the mine contains carbonic acid gas: but if the candle is *not extinguished,* the mine is *safe,* and the man may fearlessly descend.

Q. *Why does a* CROWDED ROOM *produce* HEAD-ACHE?

A. Because we breathe air *vitiated* by the crowd.

Q. *Why is the* AIR *of a room* VITIATED *by a* CROWD?

A. Because it is deprived of its due proportion of *oxygen,* and laden with *carbonic acid.*

Q. How *is the air of a room affected thus by a crowd?*

A. The *elements* of the air inhaled are *separated* in the *lungs:*—the *oxygen* is converted in the blood into *carbonic acid;* and the carbonic acid (together with the nitrogen) is thrown back again by the breath into the room.

Q. *Is* ALL *the* NITROGEN REJECTED *by the lungs?*

A. Yes; *all* the nitrogen of the air is always *expired.*

Q. *Why is a* CROWDED ROOM UNWHOLESOME?

A. Because the oxygen of the air is *absorbed* by the *lungs;* and carbonic acid gas (which is a noxious poison) is substituted for it.

Q. *Mention the historical circumstances, so well known in connexion with the* "BLACK HOLE *of* CALCUTTA."

A. In the reign of George II., the Raja (or Prince) of Bengal* marched suddenly to Calcutta, to drive the English from the country; as the attack was unexpected, the English were obliged to submit, and 146 persons were taken prisoners.

Q. *What became of these prisoners?*

A. They were driven into a place about 18 feet square, and 15 or 16 feet in height, with only two small grated windows. 123 of the prisoners died in one night; and (of the 23 who survived) the larger portion died of putrid fevers, after they were liberated.

Q. *Why were so many persons* SUFFOCATED *in*

* The Sur Raja, at Dowlat; a young man of violent passions, who had but just succeeded to the throne. A. D. 1756.

a few hours, from confinement in this close, hot PRISON-HOLE?

A. Because the *oxygen* of the air was soon *consumed* by so many lungs, and its place supplied by *carbonic acid*, exhaled by the hot breath.

Q. *Why did the captives in the* BLACK HOLE *die* SLEEPING?

A. 1st—Because the *absence of oxygen* quickly affects the vital functions, depresses the nervous energies, and produces a lassitude which ends in death: and

2dly — *Carbonic acid gas* (being a narcotic poison) produces *drowsiness* and *death*, in those who inhale it.

Q. *Why are the* JUNGLES *of Java and Hindostan so* FATAL *to life?*

A. Because vast quantities of *carbonic acid* are thrown off by decaying *vegetables* in these jungles; and (as the wind cannot penetrate the thick brushwood to blow the pernicious gas away) it *settles* there, and destroys animal life.

Q. *Why do persons in a crowded* CHURCH *feel* DROWSY?

A. 1st—Because the crowded congregation *inhale a large portion* of the *oxygen* of the air, which alone can sustain vitality and healthy action: and

2dly—The air of the church is impregnated with carbonic acid gas, which (being a strong narcotic) produces drowsiness in those who inhale it.

Q. *Why do* PERSONS *who are much in the* OPEN AIR *enjoy the best* HEALTH ?

A. Because the air they inhale is *much more pure.*

Q. *Why is* COUNTRY AIR *more* PURE *than the air in* CITIES ?

A. 1st—Because there are fewer inhabitants to vitiate the air :

2dly—There are more trees to restore the equilibrium of the vitiated air : and

3dly—The free circulation of air keeps it pure and wholesome ; (In the same way as running streams are pure and wholesome, while stagnant waters are the contrary.)

Q. *Why does the* SCANTINESS *of a country* POPULATION *render the* COUNTRY AIR *more* PURE ?

A. Because the fewer the inhabitants, the *less carbonic acid* will be *exhaled ;* and thus country people inhale *pure oxygen,* instead of air impregnated with the narcotic poison, called carbonic acid gas.

Q. *Why do* TREES *and* FLOWERS *help to make country* AIR WHOLESOME ?

A. 1st—Because trees and flowers

absorb the carbonic acid, generated by the lungs of animals, putrid substances, and other obnoxious exhalations: and

2dly—Trees and flowers restore to the air the *oxygen*, which has been inhaled by man and other animals.

Q. *Why is the* AIR *of* CITIES LESS *wholesome, than* COUNTRY *air?*

A. 1st—Because there are more *inhabitants* to vitiate the air:

2dly—The *sewers*, *drains*, *bins*, and *filth* of a *city*, very greatly vitiate the air:

3dly—The streets and alleys prevent a free circulation: and

4thly—There are fewer trees to absorb the excess of carbonic acid gas, and restore the *equilibrium*.

Q. *Why are* PERSONS, *who live in* CLOSE ROOMS *and crowded* CITIES, *generally* SICKLY?

A. Because the air they breathe is not pure, but is (in the 1st place) *defective in oxygen*; and (in the 2d) is impregnated with *carbonic acid gas*.

Q. *Where does the* CARBONIC ACID *of close* ROOMS *and* CITIES COME *from?*

A. From the lungs of the inhabitants, the sewers, drains, and other like places, in which organic substances are undergoing *decomposition*.

Q. *What* BECOMES *of the* CARBONIC ACID *of crowded cities?*

A. Some of it is *absorbed by vegetables;* and the rest is *blown away* by the *wind*, and diffused through the whole volume of the air.

Q. *Does not this constant diffusion of carbonic acid affect the* PURITY *of the* WHOLE AIR?

A. No; because it is wafted by the wind from place to place, and *absorbed* in its passage by the *vegetable world.*

Q. *What is* CHOKE DAMP?

A. *Carbonic acid gas* accumulated at the bottom of wells and pits, which renders them noxious, and often fatal to life.

Q. *Why is not this carbonic acid* TAKEN UP *by the* AIR *and* DIFFUSED, *as it is in cities?*

A. Because (being *heavier than common air*) it cannot *rise from the well or pit:* and no wind can get to it, to blow it away.

Q. *Why are* PERSONS *sometimes* KILLED *by leaning over* BEER VATS?

A. Because vats (where beer has been made) contain a large quantity of *carbonic acid gas*, produced by the "vinous fermentation" of the beer; and when a man incautiously *leans over a beer vat*, and inhales the carbonic acid, he is immediately *killed* thereby.

Q. *Why are* PERSONS *often* KILLED, *who enter* BEER VATS *to clean them?*

A. Because carbonic acid (being heavier than *atmospheric air*) often rests upon the *bottom of a vat:* when, therefore, a person enters the vat, and *stoops to clean the bottom*, he inhales the pernicious gas, which *kills* him.

Q. *Why are* PERSONS *sometimes* KILLED, *by having a* CHARCOAL FIRE *in their bedrooms?*

A. Because the *carbon of the burning charcoal* unites with the *oxygen of the air*, and forms *carbonic acid gas*, which is a narcotic poison.

Q. *If carbonic acid settles at the* BOTTOM *of a room, how can it injure a person* LYING *upon a* BED, *raised considerably above the floor?*

A. Because all gases *diffuse* themselves *through each other*, as a drop of *ink* would diffuse itself through a cup of water. If, therefore, a person slept for 6 or 8 hours in a room containing carbonic acid, quite enough of the gas will be diffused throughout the room to produce death.

The *heat* of the fire assists the process of diffusion.

Q. *What are the chief* SOURCES *of* CARBONIC ACID?

A. 1st—The breath of animals.

2dly—The decomposition of vegetable and animal matter.

3dly—Lime-stone, chalk, and all calcareous stones,—in which it exists in a *solid* form.

Q. *From which of these sources is* CARBONIC ACID *most likely to* ACCUMULATE *to a noxious extent?*

A. From the fermentation and putrefaction of decaying vegetable and animal matters.

Q. *How can this* ACCUMULATION *of* CARBONIC ACID *be* PREVENTED?

A. By throwing *quick-lime* into places, where such fermentation and putrefaction are going on.

Q. *How will* QUICK-LIME PREVENT *the accumulation of* CARBONIC ACID?

A. Quick-lime will *absorb* the carbonic acid; and produce a combination called "carbonate of lime."

Q. *Does not heavy* RAIN *prevent the* ACCUMULATION *of* CARBONIC ACID, *as well as quick-lime?*

A. Yes; an abundant supply of *water* will prevent the accumulation of carbonic acid, by *dissolving* it.

N. B. Red heat (as a pan of red-hot coals, or a piece of red-hot iron) will soon absorb the carbonic acid gas, accumulated in a pit or well.

Q. *What effect has* CARBONIC ACID *on the* WATER *in which it is dissolved?*

A. It renders it slightly *acid* to the taste.

Q. *Can the* CAPACITY *of water for dissolving carbonic acid be increased?*

A. Yes. Carbonic acid may be *forced* into water by *pressure* to a considerable extent.

Q. *To what practical* USES *has this capacity of water (for dissolving carbonic acid) been applied?*

A. *Effervescing draughts* are made upon this principle.

Q. *Explain the cause of* EFFERVESCENCE *in these beverages?*

A. The carbonic acid of the beverage (being prevented by the cork from *escaping*) is *forced* into the liquor by pressure, and *absorbed* by it: but when the cork (or pressure) is removed, some of the carbonic acid flies off in *bubbles* or *effervescence.*

Q. *Why does* AERATED WATER *effervesce when the* CORK *is removed?*

A. While the bottle remains *corked*, carbonic acid is *forced* into the water by pressure, and absorbed by it: but, when the cork (*or pressure*) is *removed*, some of the carbonic acid flies off in *effervescence.*

Q. *Why does* SODA WATER *effervesce?*

A. In soda water there is forced 8

times its own bulk of carbonic acid gas, which makes its escape in *effervescence*, as soon as the *cork is removed.*

Q. *Why does* GINGER POP *fly about in froth, when the string of the cork is cut?*

A. Because it contains carbonic acid gas. While the *cork is fast*, the carbonic acid is *forced into* the liquor; but when the *pressure is removed* the gas is given off in *effervescence.*

N. B. All vinous fermentation produces carbonic acid.

Q. *Why does* BOTTLED ALE *froth more than* DRAUGHT *ale?*

A. Because the *pressure* is greater in a *bottle* than in a tub which is continually tapped; and effervescence is always increased by *pressure.*

Q. *What produces the* FROTH *of* BOTTLED PORTER?

A. *Carbonic acid* generated by the *vinous fermentation* of the *porter*: This gas is *absorbed* by the *liquor*, so long as the bottle is well *corked;* but is given off in froth, when the pressure of the cork is removed.

Q. *What gives the pleasant* ACID *taste to soda water, ginger beer, champagne, and cider?*

A. The presence of *carbonic acid*, generated by fermentation; and liberated by effervescence, when the pressure of the cork is removed.

Q. *Why does fresh* SPRING WATER SPARKLE, *when poured from one vessel to another?*

A. Because fresh spring and pump water contain carbonic acid; and it is the presence of this gas which makes the water *sparkle.*

Much of the froth and bubbling of ale, beer, WATER, &c., when they are "poured high," is due to simple *mechanical* action.

Q. *What is the* FERMENTATION *of* BEER *and* WINE?

A. The escape of carbonic acid, produced by the change of *sugar* into *al'cohol.*

Q. *What is* AL'COHOL?

A. The *spirit* of beer and wine, obtained by fermentation.

Q. *Of what* ELEMENTS *is* AL'COHOL *composed?*

A. Of carbon, oxygen, and hydrogen.

Of AL'COHOL, 4 parts are carbon, 2 oxygen, and 6 hydrogen.

Q. *What are the* ELEMENTS *of grape* SUGAR?

A. Carbon, oxygen, and hydrogen, all in equal proportions.

Q. *What* CHANGES *does* SUGAR *undergo by* FERMENTATION?

A. It is first decomposed, and then its elements re-unite in different proportions, producing *al'cohol, carbonic acid,* and *water.*

Of SUGAR, one portion is alcohol; and another carbonic acid; as may be seen by the following table.

	Carb.	Oxy.	Hyd.
Every atom of anhydrous sugar contains	12	12	12
Two atoms of alcohol contain	8	4	12
Four atoms of carbonic acid contain	4	8	0
	12	12	12

N. B. "Anhydrous sugar" is sugar *dried* at 300°

Q. *How does* SUGAR *form* AL'COHOL *by fermentation?*

A. *Two-thirds* of its carbon and *one-third* of its oxygen re-unite with the hydrogen, and generate *al'cohol.*

Q. *How does* SUGAR *form* CARBONIC ACID *by fermentation?*

A. The remaining *one-third* of its carbon and *two-thirds* of its oxygen re unite, and generate *carbonic acid.*

Q. *What* BECOMES *of the* AL'COHOL *which is thus generated by fermentation?*

A. It mixes with the *water*, and forms the *intoxicating* part of beer and wine.

Q. *What becomes of the* CARBONIC ACID, *which is generated by fermentation?*

A. It makes its *escape into the air.*

Q. *Why is* BARLEY MALTED?

A. Because *germination* is produced by the artificial heat; and in germination, the *starch* of the *grain* is converted into *sugar.*

Q. How *is barley malted?*

A. It is *moistened with water*, and *heaped up;* by which means, great heat is produced, which makes the *barley sprout.*

(See "spontaneous combustion.")

Q. *Why is not the* BARLEY *suffered to* GROW *as well as* SPROUT ?

A. Because plants in the *germ* contain more sugar than in any *other* state: as soon as the germ *puts forth shoots*, the *sugar* of the plant is *consumed*, to support the shoot.

Q. *How is* BARLEY PREVENTED *from* SHOOTING *in the process of* MALTING?

A. It is put into a *kiln*, as soon as it sprouts; and the heat of the kiln checks or destroys the young shoot.

Q. *What is* YEAST?

A. The foam of beer (or of some similar liquor) produced by *fermentation.*

Q. *Why is* YEAST *used in* BREWING?

A. Because it consists of a substance called glu'ten, undergoing putrefaction; in which state it possesses the peculiar property of exciting *fermentation.*

If the gluten were not in a putrefying state, it could not produce fermentation.

Q. *What is glu'ten?*

A. A tough, elastic substance, composed of carbon, oxygen, hydrogen, and nitrogen.

Q. *Does* MALT *contain glu'ten?*

A. Yes. The infusion of malt, called "sweet-wort" contains an *abundance* of glu'ten; and the yeast (which converts its *sugar* into *al'cohol*) converts this *glu'ten* into *yeast.*

Q. *Why is* YEAST *needful in order to make malt into* BEER?

A. Because the presence of a putrefying body containing nitrogen is essential, in order to convert sugar into al'cohol.

Q. *What* EFFECT *has yeast upon the* SWEET-WORT?

A. It causes the SUGAR to be converted into *al'cohol* and *carbonic acid;* and its GLUTEN into yeast.

Q. *What change is produced in gluten by* PUTREFACTION?

A. Its elements are loosened from their former *conditions of combination*, and re-arranged (with the addition of oxygen from the air) into a *new series.*

Q. *What is the* DIFFERENCE *between* FERMENTATION *and* PUTREFACTION?

A. FERMENTATION is a change effected in the elements of a body composed of carbon, oxygen, and hydrogen, *without nitrogen.* PUTREFACTION is a change effected in the elements of a body composed of carbon, oxygen, hydrogen, and *nitrogen.*

Q. *What* NEW COMPOUNDS *are produced by the change called* FERMENTATION?

A. *Al'cohol* and *carbonic acid.*—The alcohol is still further changed (unless the process be checked) into *ace'tic* acid or *vinegar.*

Q. *What new compounds are produced by the change called* PUTREFACTION?

A. The carbon, oxygen, hydrogen, and nitrogen, of the original substance (being separated by decomposition) reunite in the following manner. 1. Carbon and oxygen unite to form *carbonic acid.* 2. Oxygen and hydrogen unite to form *water.* 3. Hydrogen and nitrogen unite to form *ammonia.*

Hartshorn is a solution of ammonia in water.

N. B. When bodies containing sulphur and phosphorus putrefy, the *sulphur* and *phosphorus* unite with *hydrogen,* and form *sulphuretted* and *phosphuretted hydrogen* gases.

Q. *What* BECOMES *of these several products of putrefaction?*

A. They are all elastic bodies, and *escape into the air.*

N. B. *Water* is elastic and gaseous when in the condition of *vapor.*

Q. *What is the cause of the* OFFENSIVE SMELL *which issues from putrefying bodies?*

A. The evolution of *ammonia*, or of *sulphuretted* and *phosphuretted hydrogen* gases; all of which have pungent and offensive odors.

Q. *Why do boiled* EGGS DISCOLOR *a* SILVER SPOON?

A. Because they contain a small portion of *sulphur*, which *unites with the silver* (for which it has a great *affinity*) and *tarnishes it.*

Both the white and yolk contain sulphur—the latter more abundantly.

Q. *What causes the offensive smell of* STALE *hard boiled* EGGS?

A. The *hydrogen* of the egg combining with the *sulphur* and phosphorus, form *sulphuretted* and *phosphuretted hydrogen;* both of which gases have an offensive odor.

Of an egg 55 parts are carbon, 16 nitrogen, 7 hydrogen, and the remaining 22 are oxygen, phosphorus, and sulphur.

Q. *Why is it* NOT *needful to put* YEAST *into* GRAPE *juice, in order to produce fermentation?*

A. Because grape juice contains a sufficient quantity of a nitrogenized substance (like *yeast*) to produce fermentation.

Nitrogenized, i. e., containing nitrogen.

Q. *Why do* NOT GRAPES *ferment, while they hang on the* VINE?

A. Because the *water of the juice* evaporates through the skin, and allows the grapes to shrivel and dry up, after they are ripe.

Fermentation cannot occur unless the sugar be dissolved in a sufficient quantity of *water.*

Q. *What is the* FROTH *or* SCUM *of fermented* LIQUORS?

A. Putrefying glutinous substances (of a nature similar to yeast), which rise to the surface from their *lightness.*

Q. *Why is* BEER FLAT *if the cask be left open too long?*

A. Because too much of the *carbonic acid gas* (produced by fermentation) is suffered to escape.

Q. *Why are* BEER *and* PORTER *made* STALE *by being exposed to the* AIR?

A. Because too much of the *carbonic acid gas* (produced by fermentation) is suffered to escape.

Q. *Why does* BEER *turn* FLAT *if the* VENT PEG *be left out of the tub?*

A. Because the *carbonic acid gas escapes* through the vent hole.

Q. *Why will* NOT *beer* RUN OUT *of the tub till the* VENT PEG *is taken out?*

A. Because the upward pressure of the external air (admitted through the *tap*) holds the liquor back—not being counterbalanced by any pressure of air on the *surface* of the liquid.

The *upward* pressure of air is illustrated by the following simple experiment:—Fill a wine glass with water; cover the top of the glass with a piece of writing paper turn the glass upside down, and the water will not run out. The paper is used merely to give the air a medium sufficiently dense to act against.

Q. *Why does the* BEER RUN FREELY, *immediately the* VENT PEG *is taken out?*

A. Because air rushes immediately *through the vent hole* at the *top of the tub*, to counterbalance the air admitted by the tap; in consequence of which the liquid escapes by its own downward pressure.

Q. *Why does liquor flow reluctantly out of a* BOTTLE *held upside down?*

A. Because the *upward pressure of the air* prevents the liquor from flowing out.

Q. *Why should a bottle be held* OBLIQUELY *in order to be emptied of its liquor?*

A. Because *air* will then *flow into the bottle*, and help the liquor out, by *counterbalancing the upward pressure.*

Q. *Why does wine* (*poured from a bottle* QUICKLY) SPIRT *about, without going into the decanter?*

A. Because it fills the *top of the decanter* (like a *cork*), and leaves *no room* for the air inside *to escape ;* the decanter, therefore, (being *full of air*) refuses to admit the *wine.*

Q. *Why does the* EFFERVESCENCE *of soda water and ginger beer so soon go off?*

A. Because the *carbonic acid,* (which produced the effervescence) very rapidly *escapes* into the air.

Q. *Why is* BOILED WATER FLAT *and insipid?*

A. Because the whole of the *carbonic acid* is expelled by boiling, and escapes *into the air.*

Q. *Why does* YEAST *make* BREAD LIGHT?

A. Because it produces a species of fermentation on the starch and glu'ten of flour, as it does in the sugar of malt.

Q. *How does* FERMENTATION *make the* DOUGH RISE?

A. During fermentation, *carbonic acid gas is evolved;* but the sticky texture of the dough will not allow it to *escape;* so it *forces up little bladders* all over the dough.

Q. *Why is* DOUGH *placed* BEFORE *the* FIRE?

A. 1st—Because the heat of the fire *increases the fermentation ;* and

2dly—It *expands the gas,* confined in the little bladders; in consequence of which, the bladders are *enlarged,* and the dough becomes lighter and more porous.

Q. *Why is* BREAD HEAVY, *if the dough be removed from the fire?*

A. Because the dough *gets cold*, and then the air in the bladders *condenses*—the paste falls—and the bread becomes close and heavy.

Q. *What causes the* HEAT *of* FIRE?

A. The *carbon of fuel* (when heated) *combines* with the *oxygen* of the *air*, and produces *carbonic acid gas:* Again, the *hydrogen* of the *fuel* combining with *other portions* of oxygen, condenses *into water;* by which chemical actions *heat is evolved.*

Q. *What causes the* HEAT *of our own* BODY?

A. The *carbon* of our *blood* combines with the *oxygen* of the *air inhaled*, and produces *carbonic acid gas;* which evolves heat in a way similar to burning fuel.

Q. *Whence does the* HEAT *of a* DUNGHILL *arise?*

A. As the *straw*, &c., of the *dunghill* decays, it undergoes *fermentation*, which produces *carbonic acid gas;* and heat is evolved by a species of combustion, (as in the two former cases.)

Q. *How does the formation of* CARBONIC ACID *(in all these cases) produce* HEAT?

A. *Carbonic acid* has less power of holding *latent heat* than *carbon* and *oxygen* have: When, therefore, these elements are changed into carbonic acid, latent heat is given off, and made *sensible.*

Q. *Why do persons throw* LIME *into* BINS *and* SEWERS, *to* PREVENT *their offensive* SMELL, *in summer time?*

A. Because they contain large quantities of *carbonic acid gas,* which readily *combines with lime;* and producing "*carbonate of lime,*" neutralizes the offensive gases.

Q. *Why should* WATER *(used for washing) be exposed to the air?*

A. Because it is made more *soft* by exposure to the air.

Most spring water holds lime in solution as a *bicarbonate,* in consequence of the presence of abundant carbonic acid. Carbonic acid escapes by exposure to air—and the lime is, consequently, deposited as a carbonate.

Q. *Why is hard* WATER *made more* SOFT *by exposure to air?*

A. 1st—Because the *mineral salts* (which cause its hardness) *subside:* and

2dly—Because the carbonic acid of the water makes its escape into the air.

Q. *How is the carbonic acid of water produced?*

A. From the presence of *lime*, which is frequently held in solution by hard water: When the carbonic acid *escapes* by exposure to the air, the *lime* is deposited as a *carbonate.*

Q. *Why is* HARD WATER *more agreeable to* DRINK *than soft water?*

A. Chiefly because it contains carbonic acid.

Q. *Why is water* FRESH *from the pump more* SPARKLING, *than after it has been drawn some time?*

A. Because water fresh from the pump contains carbonic acid, which soon escapes into the air, and leaves the water flat and stale.

Q. *Why is* QUICK-LIME *formed by burning chalk and marl in a* KILN?

A. Because the *carbonic acid* (which rendered it *mild*) is driven off by the heat of the kiln: and the lime becomes *quick* or *caustic.*

Q. *What is* MORTAR?

A. Quick-lime mixed with sand and water.

Q. *Wherein does* LIME-STONE *differ in appearance from quick-lime?*

A. LIME-STONE is a hard, *rocky* substance; but QUICK-LIME a loose *powder.*

Q. *Why does* MORTAR *become* HARD *after a few days?*

A. Because the lime *re-imbibes* from the air the carbonic acid which had been *expelled by fire;* and the loose *powder* again becomes as hard as the original *lime-stone.*

Q. *Explain in what way* MORTAR *is adhesive.*

A. When the carbonic acid is expelled, the hard lime-stone is *converted into a loose powder*, which (being mixed with sand and water) becomes a *soft and sticky plaster;* but as soon as it is placed between bricks, it *imbibes carbonic acid again*, and hardens into *lime-stone.*

CARBURETTED HYDROGEN GAS.

CHAPTER XXII.

Q. *What is* CHOKE-DAMP?

A. *Carbonic acid gas* accumulated at the bottom of wells and pits. It is called CHOKE damp, because it *chokes* (or suffocates) *every animal* that attempts to *inhale it.* (*See p.* 238.)

It suffocates without getting into the *lungs*, by closing the outer orifice *spasmodically.*

Q. *What is marsh-gas or* FIRE-DAMP?

A. *Carburetted hydrogen gas* accumulated on marshes, in stagnant waters, and coal-pits; it is frequently called "inflammable air."

Q. *What is* CARBURETTED HYDROGEN GAS?

A. *Carbon* combined with *hydrogen.*

Q. *How may* CARBURETTED HYDROGEN GAS *be* PROCURED *on marshes?*

A. By *stirring the mud* at the bottom of any stagnant pool, and collecting the gas (as it escapes upwards) in an inverted glass vessel.

Q. *What is* COAL GAS?

A. *Carburetted hydrogen* extracted from coals by the heat of *fire.*

Q. *Why is carburetted hydrogen gas called* FIRE-DAMP *or inflammable air?*

A. Because it very readily *catches fire and explodes,* when a light is introduced to it.

Provided atmospheric air be present.

Q. *Why is carburetted hydrogen gas frequently called* MARSH-GAS?

A. Because it is generated in *meadows and marshes* from putrefying vegetable substances.

See ignis fatuus, p. 266.

Q. *What gas is evolved by the* WICK *of a burning* CANDLE?

A. *Carburetted hydrogen gas:* The *carbon* and *hydrogen* of the tallow *com-*

bine into a gas from the heat of the flame; and this gas is called *carburetted hydrogen* or inflammable air.

Q. *Why do* COAL-MINES *so frequently* EXPLODE?

A. Because the *carburetted hydrogen gas* (which is generated in these mines by the coals) explodes, when a light is incautiously introduced.

Q. *How can miners* SEE *in the coal-pits if they may never introduce a* LIGHT?

A. Sir Humphrey Davy invented a lantern for the use of miners, called "the Safety Lamp," which may be used without danger.

Q. *Who was* SIR HUMPHREY DAVY?

A. A very clever chemist, born in Cornwall, 1778, and died in 1829.

Q. *What kind of thing is the* SAFETY-LAMP?

A. A kind of lantern, *covered with a fine gauze wire*, instead of glass or horn.

Q. *How does this fine* GAUZE WIRE *prevent an* EXPLOSION *in the coal-mine?*

A. By preventing the flame of the lamp from communicating with the inflammable gas of the mine.

N. B. The interstices of the gauze wire must not exceed the 7th of an inch in diameter.

Q. *Why will not* FLAME PASS THROUGH *very fine wire* GAUZE?

A. Because the metal wire is a very *rapid conductor of heat;* and when the flame (of gas burning in the lamp) reaches the wire gauze, so much heat is *conducted away by the wire*, that the flame is *extinguished.*

Q. *Does the gas of the* COAL-PIT *get* THROUGH *the wire gauze* INTO *the* LANTERN?

A. Yes; and the inflammable gas ignites, and burns *inside the lamp:* As soon as this is the case, *the miner is in danger*, and should withdraw.

Q. *Why is the miner in* DANGER *if the gas ignites and burns in the* INSIDE *of the safety lamp?*

A. Because the heat of the burning gas will soon *destroy the wire gauze;* and then the flame (being free) will set fire to the mine.

N. B. When the carburetted hydrogen gas takes fire from the miner's candle, the miner sometimes perishes in the *blast of the flame*, and sometimes suffers *suffocation* from the carbonic acid which is thus produced.

PHOSPHURETTED HYDROGEN GAS.

CHAPTER XXIII.

Q. *From what do the very* OFFENSIVE EFFLUVIA *of* CHURCH-YARDS *arise?*

A. From a gas called PHOSPHURETTED HYDROGEN; which is *phosphorus* combined with *hydrogen gas.*

Q. *What is* PHOSPHORUS?

A. A pale amber-colored substance, resembling wax in appearance. The word is derived from two Greek words, which mean "to *produce or carry light.*" (φως-φέρειν).

Q. *How is* PHOSPHORUS OBTAINED?

A. By heating bones to a white heat; by which means, the animal matter and charcoal are *consumed*, and a substance called "*phosphate of lime*" is left behind.

Q. *What is the* PHOSPHATE OF LIME?

A. Phosphorus united to oxygen and lime; when *sulphuric acid* is added, and the mixture heated, the lime is attracted to the acid, and pure *phosphorus* remains.

If powdered charcoal be added, phosphorus may be procured by distillation.

Q. *Of what is the ignitible part of* LUCIFER MATCHES *made?*

A. Of phosphorus: and above 250 thousand lbs. are used every year in London alone, merely for the manufacture of lucifer matches.

Q. *Why does a* PUTREFYING *dead* BODY SMELL *so offensively?*

A. Because *phosphuretted hydrogen gas* always rises from putrefying animal substances.

The escape of *ammonia* and *sulphuretted* hydrogen contributes also to this offensive effluvia.

Q. *What is the cause of the* IGNIS FATUUS, *Jack o'Lantern, or Will o'the Wisp?*

A. This luminous appearance (which haunts meadows, bogs, and marshes) arises from the *gas of putrefying animal and vegetable substances;* especially from decaying fish.

Q. *What gases arise from these* PUTREFYING *substances?*

A. *Phosphuretted hydrogen* from putrefying *animal* substances: and

Carburetted hydrogen, from decaying *vegetable* matters. (*See p.* 262.)

Q. *How is the gas of the ignis fatuus* IGNITED *on bogs and meadows?*

A. Impure phosphuretted hydrogen bursts *spontaneously* into flame, whenever it mixes with *air* or *pure oxygen* gas.

Pure phosphuretted hydrogen will *not* ignite spontaneously—this spontaneous ignition is due to the presence of a small quantity of the vapor of an exceedingly volatile liquid-compound of phosphorus with hydrogen, which is occasionally produced with the gas itself.

If phosphorus be boiled with milk of lime, and the beak of the retort be placed under water, bubbles of phosphuretted hydrogen will rise successively through the water, and (on reaching the surface) burst into flame.

Q. *Why does an ignis fatuus or Will o'the Wisp* FLY *from us when we* RUN *to* MEET *it?*

A. Because we produce a current of air in front of ourselves, (when we run *towards* the ignis fatuus) which drives the light gas *forwards.*

Q. *Why does an ignis fatuus run* AFTER *us when we* FLEE *from it in a fright?*

A. Because we produce a current of air in the way we run, which *attracts* the light gas in the *same course;* drawing it *after* us as we run away *from* it.

Q. *Is not a kind of Jack o'Lantern sometimes produced by an* INSECT?

A. Yes; swarms of luminous insects sometimes pass over a meadow, and produce an appearance similar to the ignis fatuus.

Q. *May not many* GHOST *stories have arisen from some ignis fatuus lurking about church-yards?*

A. Perhaps all the ghost stories (which deserve any credit at all) have arisen from the ignited gas of church-yards, lurking about the tombs; to which *fear* has added its own creations.

WIND.

CHAPTER XXIV.

Q. *What is* WIND?

A. Wind is *air in motion.*

Q. *What* PUTS *the air in motion, so as to produce* WIND?

A. The principal causes are the *variations of heat and cold,* produced by the succession of *day and night,* and of the *four seasons.*

Q. *What effect has* HEAT *upon the air?*

A. Heat *rarefies* the air and causes it to expand.

Q. *How do you* KNOW *that heat causes the air to* EXPAND?

A. Thus, if a bladder *half full of air* (tied tight round the neck) be laid before a *fire,* the air will expand by the heat, and *fill* the bladder.

Q. *What* EFFECT *is produced upon air by* RAREFACTION?

A. It is made *lighter* and *ascends through colder strata;* as a cork (put at the bottom of a basin of water) rises to the surface.

Q. *Prove that rarefied air* ASCENDS.

A. When a boy sets fire to the cotton or sponge of his balloon, the flame *heats the air;* which becomes *so light,* that it ascends, and *carries the balloon with it.*

Q. *What effect is produced upon* AIR *by* COLD?

A. It is *condensed,* or squeezed into a smaller compass: in consequence of which, *it becomes heavier,* and descends towards the ground.

Q. *Prove that air is condensed by* COLD.

A. Lay a bladder half full of air before a fire, till it has become fully *inflated;* if it be now removed *from* the fire, the bladder will *collapse* again, because the air condenses into its former bulk.

Q. *What is meant by the bladder* "COLLAPSING?"

A. The skin becoming *wrinkled, shrivelled, and flabby;* because there is not sufficient air inside to *fill* it.

Q. *How do you* KNOW *that* CONDENSED *air will* DESCEND?

A. Because a fire balloon *falls* to the earth, so soon as the spirit in the cotton is *burnt out,* and the air of the balloon has become *cold again.*

Q. *Does the* SUN HEAT *the* AIR *as it does the* EARTH?

A. No; the air is *not heated* by the *rays of the sun;* because air (like water) is a very *bad conductor.*

Q. *How is the* AIR HEATED?

A. By *convection*, thus:—The *sun* heats the *earth*, and the *earth* heats the *air resting upon it;* the air thus heated *rises*, and is succeeded by *other air*, which is heated in a similar way; till the whole volume is *warmed* by "convective currents."

Q. *What is meant by* "CONVECTIVE CURRENTS" *of hot air?*

A. Streams of air heated by the earth, which *rise upwards*, and *carry heat with them.* (*See p.* 226.)

Q. *Is the air in a* ROOM *in perpetual motion as the air* ABROAD *is?*

A. Yes; there are always *two currents of air* in the room we occupy; one of *hot* air flowing *out* of the room, and another of *cold* air flowing *into* the room.

Q. *How do you* KNOW *that there are these* TWO *currents of air in every occupied* ROOM?

A. If I hold a lighted candle near the crevice at the *top of the door*, the flame will be blown *outward* (towards the *hall*); but if I hold the candle at the *bottom of the door*, the flame will be blown *inwards* (into the *room*).

N. B. This is not the case if a *fire* be in the room. When a fire is lighted, an inward current is drawn through *all* the crevices.

Q. *Why would the flame be blown* OUTWARDS

(towards the HALL), *if a candle be held at the* TOP *of the door?*

A. Because the air of the room being heated, &c., *ascends;* and (floating about the upper part of the room) some of it escapes *through the crevice* at the *top of the door*, producing a current of air *outwards* (into the *hall*).

Q. *Why would the flame be blown* INWARDS *(into the* ROOM), *if the candle be held at the* BOTTOM *of the door?*

A. Because a partial *vacuum* is made at the *bottom of the room*, as soon as the warm air of the room has ascended to the ceiling, or made its escape from the room: and cold air from the hall *rushes under the door*, to supply the void.

Q. *What is meant by a "partial* VACUUM *being made at the* BOTTOM *of the* ROOM?"

A. A vacuum means a place *from which the air has been taken:* and a "partial vacuum" means a place from which a *part* of the air has been taken away. Thus, when the air on the floor *ascends* to the ceiling, a partial vacuum is made on the *floor*.

Q. *And how is the* VACUUM *filled* UP *again?*

A. It is filled up by *colder* air, which rushes (under the *door*, and through the *window* crevices) into the room.

Q. *Give me an* ILLUSTRATION.

A. If I dip a pail into a pond and fill it with water, a hole (or vacuum) is made in the pond as *big as the pail;* but the moment I *draw the pail out*, the hole is *filled up* by the water around.

Q. *Show how this illustration* APPLIES.

A. The heated air, which ascends from the bottom of a room, is as much taken away as the water in the pail; and (as the void was instantly supplied by *other water in the pond*) so the *void of air is supplied* by the air around.

Q. *What is the* CAUSE *of* WIND?

A. The *sun* heats the *earth*, and the *earth* heats the *air* resting upon it; as the warm air ascends, the void is filled up by a *rush of cold air* to the place; and this *rush of air* we call WIND.

Q. *Does the* WIND ALWAYS *blow?*

A. Yes; there is always *some* motion in the air; but the *violence* of the motion is perpetually varying.

Q. *Does the rotation of the earth upon its axis affect the motion of the air?*

A. Yes, in two ways. 1st—As the earth moves round its axis, the thin moveable air is left somewhat *behind*; and, therefore, seems (to a stationary object) to be blowing in the *opposite* direction to the earth's motion: and

2dly—As the earth revolves, different portions of its surface are continually passing under the vertical rays of the sun.

Q. *When are the rays of the sun called* "VERTICAL RAYS?"

A. When the sun is in a *direct line* above any place, his rays are said to be "vertical" to that place.

Q. *Illustrate the manner in which the earth's surface passes under the vertical sun.*

A. Suppose the brass meridian of a globe to represent the vertical rays of the sun; as you turn the globe round, *different parts* of it will pass under the brass rim, in constant *succession.*

Q. *Why is it* NOON-DAY *to the place over which the* SUN *is* VERTICAL?

A. Because the sun is *half-way* between rising and setting to that place.

Q. *Show how this* ROTATION *of the earth affects the* AIR.

A. If we suppose the brass meridian to be the vertical sun, the whole column of air *beneath* will be heated by the *noon-day rays;* that part which the sun has *left,* will become gradually *colder and colder;* and that part to which the sun is *approaching*, will grow constantly *warmer and warmer*.

Q. *Then there are* THREE *qualities of air about this spot?*

A. Yes; the air over the place, which has *passed* the meridian, is *cooling;* the air under the *vertical sun* is the *hottest;* and the air, which is over the place *about to pass* under the meridian, is *increasing in heat*.

See fig. on next page. The column A (which the sun has passed) is cooling—B is under the vertical sun; and C is *increasing in heat*.

Q. *How does this* VARIETY *in the* HEAT *of* AIR *produce* WIND?

A. The air always seeks to *preserve an equilibrium;* so *cold air* rushes into the *void* made by the *upward current of the warm air*.

Q. *Why does not the wind* ALWAYS BLOW ONE *way, following the direction of the* SUN?

A. Because the direction of the wind is subject to perpetual interruptions from *hills*, and *valleys*, *deserts*, *seas*, &c.

Q. *How can* HILLS *and* MOUNTAINS ALTER *the course of the* WIND?

A. Suppose a wind (blowing from the north) comes to a mountain; as it cannot pass *through it*, it must either rush *back again*, or *fly off at one side*, (as a *marble*, when it strikes against a *wall*.)

Q. *Do* MOUNTAINS *affect the wind in any* OTHER *way?*

A. Yes; many mountains are *capped with snow*, and the *warm air* is *condensed*, when it comes in contact with them; but so soon as the *temperature of the wind* is changed, its *direction* may be changed also. (See *Fig.*)

THE SUN.

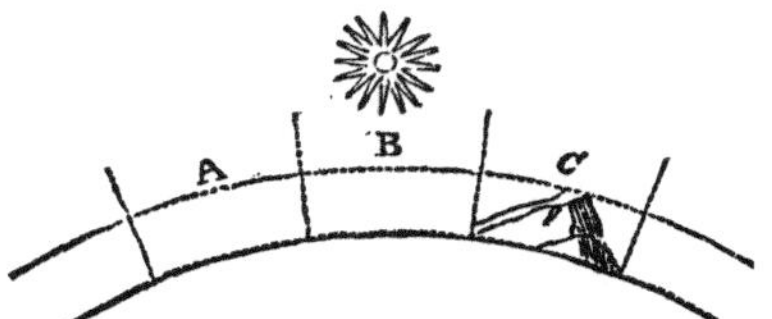

Suppose A B C to be *three columns of air.* A, the column of air which is *cooling down*; B, the column to which the *sun is vertical;* and C the column which *is to be heated next.* In this case the *cold* air of A will rush towards B C; because the air of B and C is *hotter* than A. But suppose now C to be a *snow-capped mountain:* As the hot air of B reaches C, it is *chilled;* and (being now *colder* than the air *behind*) it rushes *back again* towards A, instead of following the sun.

Q. *How can the* OCEAN *affect the direction of the* WIND?

A. When the ocean rolls beneath the *vertical sun*, the water is *not made so hot* as the *land;* in consequence of which, the general direction of the wind is directed from tracts of *ocean* towards tracts of *land*.

Q. *Why is not the* WATER *of the sea made so*

HOT, *by the vertical sun, as the surface of the* LAND?

A. 1st—Because the *evaporation* of the sea is greater than that of the land:

2dly—The constant *motion* of the water prevents the increase of temperature at the surface: and

3dly—The rays of the sun strike *into* the water; in consequence of which the immediate *surface* is much less affected.

Q. *Why does the* EVAPORATION *of the sea prevent its surface from being* HEATED *by the vertical sun?*

A. Because its heat is *absorbed* in the generation of *vapor* and carried off into the air.

Q. *Why does the* MOTION *of the sea prevent its surface from being* HEATED *by the vertical sun?*

A. Because each portion *rolls away*, as soon as it becomes heated, and is succeeded by *another;* and this constant motion prevents the *surface* of the sea from being *more* heated than the water *below* the surface.

Q. *Do* CLOUDS *affect the* WIND?

A. Yes. As passing clouds screen the direct heat of the sun from the earth, they diminish the *rarefaction of the air also;* and this is *another* cause why neither the strength nor direction of the wind is *uniform:*

Q. *Would the wind blow regularly from east to west, if these* OBSTRUCTIONS *were* REMOVED ?

A. Without doubt. If the whole earth were covered with *water* the winds would always *follow the sun*, and blow uniformly in one direction.

Q. *Do winds* EVER *blow* REGULARLY ?

A. Yes: in those parts of the world, which present a large surface of water, as in the Atlantic and Pacific Oceans.

Q. *What are the winds, which blow over the* ATLANTIC *and* PACIFIC *Oceans, called?*

A. They are called "Trade Winds."

Q. *Why are they called* "TRADE WINDS."

A. Because they are very convenient to merchants, who have to cross the ocean, inasmuch as they always blow in one direction.

Q. *In what* DIRECTION *do the* TRADE WINDS *blow?*

A. That in the *northern* hemisphere blows from the *north-east;* that in the *southern* hemisphere from the *south-east.*

Q. *Why do they not blow from the* FULL NORTH *and* SOUTH ?

A. Because currents of air *flowing from the poles*, give them an *easterly* direction.

This effect is due in some measure to the rotation of the earth on its axis.

Q. *What is the cause of these currents of air from the* POLES *to the* EQUATOR ?

A. The air about the equator constantly ascends, in consequence of being rarefied by the heat of the sun : as the hot equatorial air ascends, cold air from the north and south flows towards the equator, to restore the equilibrium.

Q. *Is there an* UPPER *as well as a* LOWER CURRENT *in the atmosphere?*

A. Yes ; the *upper* current of rarefied air is *from the equator to the poles ;* where it is condensed—and then returns again to the *equator*, forming the *lower* current.

Q. *These* LOWER CURRENTS (*from the poles to the equator*) *have an* EASTERLY *tendency. Explain the cause of this.*

A. All the atmosphere revolves *with the earth ;* but when a current of air from the *poles* flows towards the *equator*, it comes to a part of the earth's surface which is moving *faster than itself;* in consequence of which it is *left behind*, and thus produces the effect of a current moving in the opposite direction.

Thus, to a person in a carriage, the hedges and trees seem to be running in an opposite direction.

As the circumference of the earth at the equator is

much larger than the circumference of the earth at the poles, therefore every spot of the earth's *equatorial* surface must move *much faster* than the corresponding one at the poles.

N. B. As the earth revolves on its axis from west to east, therefore the air which is carried with it will seem to blow *from the west:* As, however, the current of air from the poles seems to blow in the *opposite* direction, it will seem to blow from the *east* (or to be an *easterly* wind).

Q. *By what means are the north-east and south-east* TRADE WINDS *produced?*

A. By a combination of the two motions of the *polar currents:* which produces the intermediate directions of the *north-east* and *south-east.*

Q. *Are* BOTH *these motions of the polar currents* REAL?

A. No. The motion from the east to west is only *apparent.* As the earth revolves from *west* to *east,* the air carried with it will be a *west* wind; but the polar currents seem to blow in the *opposite direction,* merely because they have not *acquired the same velocity.*

Q. *Do trade winds blow from the north-east and south-east* ALL *the* YEAR ROUND?

A. Yes, *in the open sea;* that is, in the Atlantic and Pacific Oceans, for about 30° each side of the equator.

Q. *What do the north-easterly and south-easterly trade winds produce when they meet near the equator?*

A. A region of *calms,* in which thick

foggy air prevails, with sudden showers and thunder-storms.

Q. *Is this region of calms* FIXED *in its position?*

A. No; it shifts its place according to the sun's distance, and position in regard to the *equator:* being sometimes entirely to the *north* of the equator, and occasionally reaching as far as 2° *south* of it.

Q. *Do the* TRADE WINDS *blow uniformly from north-east and south-east in the* INDIAN OCEAN?

A. No; nor yet in those parts of the *Atlantic* and ***Pacific*** which *verge on the continents.*

Q. *How do the* TRADE WINDS *in the* INDIAN OCEAN *blow?*

A. From April to October a *south-west* wind prevails; but from October to April, a *north-east.*

Q. *What are these periodical currents of air (which affect the neighborhood of the Arabian, Indian, and Chinese Seas) called?*

A. They are called MONSOONS.

Q. *How far do the limits of the* MONSOONS *extend?*

A. They extend from the African shore to the longitude of New Guinea; and are felt *northward* as far as the parallel of latitude, which crosses the Loochoo Isles.

The Loochoo Isles are about 24° north latitude, and 130° east longitude.

Q. *Why do not the trade winds in the* INDIAN OCEAN *blow south-west from April to October?*

A. Because the air of Arabia, Persia, India, and China, *is so rarefied* by the enormous heat of their summer sun, that the cold air from the south rushes *towards these nations*, across the *equator*, (during these *six months*,) and produces a SOUTH-WEST wind.

Q. *To what distance does this* SOUTH-WEST *wind prevail?*

A. From 3° south of the equator, to the shores of the Arabian, Indian, and Chinese Seas.

Q. *Why do the trade winds (in the* INDIAN OCEAN) *blow north-east from October to April?*

A. Because the *southern part of the torrid zone* is most heated, when the sun has left the *northern* side of the equator for the *southern:* and the cold air from the north (rushing towards the southern tropic) is diverted into the direction of NORTH-EAST, where it continues for the *other* six months of the year.

Q. *Are the monsoons as* POWERFUL *as the trade winds?*

A. They are far *more* so, and very often amount to violent gales.

Q. *Why are the* MONSOONS *more* USEFUL *to the mariner than the fixed* TRADE WINDS?

A. Because the mariner is able to avail himself of these periodic changes, to go in *one* direction during *one* half of the year, and to *return* in the *opposite* direction during the *other* half.

Q. *How is the change of the monsoons marked?*

A. By an interval of alternating calms and storms.

Q. *When are the* WINDS *at the* NORTH *generally the* HIGHEST?

A. The winds in December and January are generally the highest. Those in February and November the next; and those in August and September are the *least* boisterous.

Q. *Why are the winds at the North generally* HIGHEST *in* DECEMBER *and* JANUARY?

A. Because the sun is *furthest south* in those months; and (as the heat in these northern regions rapidly *decreases*) the contrast between our temperature and that of the *torrid zone* is greater in December and January, than in any other two months throughout the year.

Q. *Why does this* CONTRAST *of heat increase the* VIOLENCE *of the* WIND?

A. Because the air always seeks to *preserve an equilibrium;* therefore the greater the contrast, the more violent will be the rush of air to *equalize* the two volumes.

Q. *Why are the winds at the North generally most* PLACID *during the months of* SEPTEMBER *and* AUGUST ?

A. Because August and September are the *warmest months*, when we approach nearest to the heat of the torrid zone; therefore the air (to and from the equator) *moves with less velocity* in our northern hemisphere in those two months than in any other.

Q. *Show the* GOODNESS *and* WISDOM *of* GOD *in this constant tendency of air to equilibrium.*

A. If the torrid zone were not tempered by cold air from the polar regions, *it would become so hot*, that no human being could endure it. If (on the other hand) the polar regions were never warmed by hot air from the torrid zone, they would soon become *insufferably cold*.

Q. *In what* OTHER *way does the mingling of the polar and equatorial atmosphere act* BENEFICIALLY?

A. In the *equatorial* regions, the great abundance of *vegetable* life is productive of a very large amount of *oxygen:* In the *colder* regions, artificial *fires* and dense masses of *animal life*, produce large quantities of *carbonic acid:* The mingling of the polar and equatorial atmosphere assists in supplying each of these regions with the very gas in which it would be otherwise defective.

Q. *How does the mingling of the* POLAR *and* EQUATORIAL *atmosphere serve to supply each region with the* GAS *it most requires?*

A. The *plants* of the EQUATORIAL regions require *carbonic acid;*—The *animals* of the COLDER regions require oxygen:—The currents of air from the *Poles* carry *carbonic acid* to the equatorial *plants;* and the currents of air from the *Equator* carry *oxygen* to the *animals* which abound nearer the *poles*.

Q. *Why are* EAST WINDS *in Europe, and* WEST WINDS *in the United States, generally* DRY?

A. Because they come over *vast continents*, and therefore absorb *very little water;* and being thirsty, they readily imbibe moisture from the air and clouds, and therefore *bring dry weather.*

Q. *Why is the* NORTH WIND *generally* COLD?

A. Because it comes from the *polar regions*, over mountains of snow and seas of ice.

Q. *Why are* NORTH WINDS *generally* DRY *and biting?*

A. Because they come from *colder* regions, and being *warmed* by the heat of our climate, *absorb moisture* from every thing they touch; in consequence of which, they are both *dry and parching.*

Q. *Why are* SOUTH WINDS *generally* WARM?

A. Because they come from the torrid zone, where they are much heated.

Q. *Why do* SOUTH WINDS *often bring* RAIN?

A. Because, coming from the torrid zone, they are much *heated*, and *imbibe water very plentifully*, as they pass over the Ocean.

Q. *How does this account for the* RAINY *character of* SOUTH *winds?*

A. As soon as they reach a cold climate they are *condensed*, and can no longer hold all their vapor in suspension; in consequence of which, some of it is deposited as rain.

Q. *Why are* WEST WINDS *in Europe, and* EAST WINDS *in the United States, generally* RAINY?

A. Because they come over the *Atlantic Ocean*, and are laden with *vapor;* if, therefore, they meet with the least *chill*, some of the vapor is deposited as rain.

Q. *Why is a fine* CLEAR DAY *sometimes* OVERCAST *in a few minutes?*

A. Because some *sudden change of temperature* has condensed the vapor of the air *into clouds.*

Q. *Why are* CLOUDS *sometimes* DISSIPATED *very suddenly?*

A. Because some *dry wind* (blowing over the clouds) *imbibes their moisture*, and carries it off in invisible vapor.

Q. *Why do* SOUTH-EAST *winds bring us* RAIN?

A. Because they come from the *torrid zone*, and get *laden with vapor* in their transit across the *ocean.* But when they reach our colder climate, (being condensed by the chill) some of the vapor is precipitated in rain.

Q. *Why do* NORTH-WEST *winds* RARELY *bring* RAIN?

A. Because they come from a climate *colder than our own*, and their capacity for imbibing vapor is *increased*, when they reach a warmer climate; in consequence of which, north-west winds *dry the air*, dispel the clouds, and promote evaporation.

Q. *Why does* WIND *sometimes bring* RAIN *and sometimes* FINE *weather?*

A. If the wind be *colder than the clouds*, it will condense their vapor into *rain:* But if the wind *is warmer than the clouds*, it will *dissolve* them, and cause them to disappear.

Q. *What is the* USE *of dry* MARCH *winds?*

A. They *dry the soil*, which is saturated with the floods of February, *break up the heavy clods*, and fit the land for the *seed* committed to it.

Q. *Why is it said, that* "MARCH COMES IN *like a* LION?"

A. Because it comes in with *blustering winds*, so essential to dry the soil, lest it *rot the seeds* committed to it.

Q. *Why does* "MARCH GO OUT *like a* LAMB?"

A. Because the water (evaporated by the high winds) falls again in *showers*, to fertilize the earth; and these constant showers *break the violence* of the *winds*.

Q. *Why is it said, that* "*A bushel of* MARCH DUST *is worth a king's ransom?*"

A. Because it indicates that there has been a continuance of *dry weather*; and unless *March be dry*, the seed will rot in the wet soil.

Q. *Why is it said,* "*A* DRY, *cold* MARCH *never* BEGS BREAD?"

A. Because the *dry, cold winds* of March prepare the soil for *seeds*; which germinate and produce fruit in the autumn.

Q. *It is said, that "A* WET MARCH *makes a* SAD *autumn." Explain the reason of this.*

A. If *March* is *wet*, so much seed *rots* in the ground, that the autumn crops are spoiled.

Q. *It is said, that* "MARCH FLOWERS *make* NO *summer* BOWERS." *Explain the reason of this.*

A. If the *spring be very mild*, vegetation gets too forward, and is *pinched* by the *nightly frosts*, so as to produce neither fruits nor flowers.

Q. *It is said, " A* LATE SPRING *makes a* FRUITFUL YEAR." *Explain the reason of this.*

A. If the vegetation of spring be *backward*, the frosty nights will *do no harm;* for the fruits and flowers will not put forth their tender shoots, till the nights become *too warm to injure them.*

Q. *Why is it said, that* " APRIL SHOWERS *bring* MAY FLOWERS?"

A. Because April showers supply the principal nourishment, on which seeds depend for their development.

Before seeds can germinate, *three* things are essential:—Darkness, Heat, and Moisture.

Q. *Does* RAIN-WATER *possess any fertilizing properties,* BESIDES *that of mere* MOISTURE ?

A. Yes ; rain-water contains an abundance of *carbonic acid*, and a small quantity of *ammo'nia;* to which much of its fertilizing power may be attributed.

Ammonia is a compound of nitrogen and hydrogen. Common hartshorn is only ammonia and water.

Q. *Why is there* MORE *rain* FROM SEPTEMBER *to* MARCH, *than from March to September?*

A. Because the temperature of the air is *constantly decreasing;* on which account, its *capacity for holding vapor* is on the *decrease*, and the vapor is precipitated as rain.

Q. *What good purpose is effected under* PROVIDENCE *by this increase of rain in* AUTUMN *and* WINTER?

A. Because rain hastens the *putrefaction* of the *fallen leaves;* and this makes the earth fertile.

Q. *Why is there* LESS *rain* FROM MARCH *to* SEPTEMBER, *than from September to March?*

A. Because the temperature of the air is *constantly increasing;* on which account its *capacity for holding vapor* is on the *increase*, and very little is precipitated as rain.

Q. *Why is the* RISING SUN *in summer accompanied with a* BREEZE?

A. Because the heat of the rising sun *stops the radiation of heat* from the earth, and *warms its surface.*

Q. *How does this* WARMTH *produce a* BREEZE?

A. The air (resting on the earth's surface) being *warmed by contact* ascends, and *colder air rushing in* to fill up the void, produces the *morning* breeze.

Q. *Why is there often an* EVENING BREEZE *during the summer months?*

A. Because the earth *radiates heat at sun-set* and the air is rapidly cooled down by contact: this condensation causes a *motion in the air*, called the evening breeze.

Q. *Why are* TROPICAL ISLANDS *subject to a* SEA BREEZE *every* MORNING: (*i. e., a breeze blowing from the sea to the land*)?

A. Because solar rays are unable to heat the surface of the *sea*, as they do the *earth;* therefore, the *air resting* on the *sea* is less *heated* than the *air resting* on the *earth;* and the colder sea air blows *inland* to restore the equilibrium.

Q. *Why is a* LAND BREEZE UNHEALTHY?

A. Because it is frequently laden with exhalations from *putrefying animal* and *vegetable* substances.

Q. *Why is a* SEA BREEZE *fresh and* HEALTHY?

A. Because it passes over the fresh sea, and is *not* laden with noxious exhalations.

It is particularly *healthy*, therefore, to walk on the sea-beach before ten o'clock in the morning; *but unhealthy after sun-set.*

Q. *Why is there generally a fresh breeze from the* SEA *during the summer and autumn* MORNINGS?

A. Because *land* is *more heated by the sun* than the *sea* is; and the *land* air becomes hotter than that over the *sea;* in consequence of which, the cooler sea air glides *inland* to restore the equilibrium.

Q. *Why does a* SEA BREEZE *feel* COOL?

A. Because the sun cannot make the surface of the *sea* so hot as the *land;* therefore, the air which blows from the sea is *cooler than the air of the land.*

Q. *Why are* TROPICAL ISLANDS *subject to a* LAND BREEZE *every* EVENING (*i. e., a breeze blowing from the land towards the sea*)?

A. Because the *surface of the land* cools down *faster* (after sun-set) than the surface of the *sea:* in consequence of which, the air of the cold land *is condensed—sinks down*—and spreads itself into the warmer *sea air*—causing the LAND BREEZE.

Q. *Why is the* LAND BREEZE COOL?

A. Because the surface of the land is cooled at sun-set *quicker than the surface of the sea;* therefore, seamen feel the air from the land to be chill.

Q. *Why is the* TEMPERATURE *of* ISLANDS *more* EQUABLE *than that of* CONTINENTS?

A. Because the *water* around the island *absorbs* the extreme heat of summer; and *gives out* heat to mitigate the extreme cold of winter.

Q. ISLANDS *are* WARMER *in winter than continents. Explain the reason of this.*

A. Unless the *sea be frozen* (which is rarely the case) it is warmer than the frozen land: and the warmth of the sea air helps to mitigate the intense cold of the land air.

Q. *Explain the cause of sea* WAVES?

A. The wind (acting on the surface of the sea) *piles up ridges of water*, leaving behind an *indentation:* as the water on all sides rushes to *fill up this indentation*, the disturbance spreads on all sides, and billow rolls after billow.

Q. *Why does* WIND *generally feel* COLD?

A. Because a *constantly changing surface* comes in contact with our body, to draw off its heat.

Q. *Why is a* ROOM *(even without a fire) generally* WARMER *than the* OPEN AIR?

A. Because the air in a room is *not subject to much change*, and soon becomes of the same temperature as our skin, when it no longer feels cold.

Q. *Why do we generally feel* COLDER *out-of-doors than in-doors?*

A. Because the air (which surrounds us) is *always changing;* and as fast as *one* portion of air has become warmer by contact with our body, *another colder portion* surrounds us, to absorb more heat.

Q. *How does* BLOWING HOT FOOD *make it* COOL?

A. It causes the air (which has been heated by the food) to *change more rapidly*, and give place to fresh *cold air*.

Q. *Why do ladies* FAN THEMSELVES *in hot weather?*

A. That *fresh particles of air* may be brought in contact with their faces by the action of the fan; and as every fresh particle of air *absorbs some heat* from the skin, this constant *change* makes them cool.

Q. *Does a fan* COOL *the* AIR?

A. No; it makes the air *hotter* by imparting to it the heat *out of our face;* but it cools our *face* by transferring its heat to the *air*.

Q. *How fast does wind travel?*

A. A gentle breeze goes at about the rate of 5 miles an hour. A high wind from 20 to 60. A hurricane from 80 to 100 miles an hour.

Q. *How is the* VELOCITY *of* WINDS *ascertained?*

A. By observing the velocity of the

clouds; and by an instrument for the purpose, called an Anemometer.

Pronounce An-e-mom′-e-ter. From two Greek words ανεμος (wind) and μετρον (a measure). This term is applied more frequently to an instrument which measures the *force* of wind.

Q. *How is the* VELOCITY *of the* CLOUDS *ascertained?*

A. By observing the speed of their shadow along the ground; which is found (in a high wind) to vary from 20 to 60 miles an hour.

Q. *Why is there a strong* DRAUGHT *through the* KEYHOLE *of a door?*

A. Because the air in the room we occupy is *warmer* than the air in the hall; therefore, the air from the hall *rushes through the keyhole* in the room, and causes a draught.

Q. *Why is there a strong* DRAUGHT UNDER *the* DOOR, *and through the crevice on each side?*

A. Because cold air *rushes from the hall*, to supply the *void* in the room, caused by the escape of warm air up the chimney, &c.

Q. *Why is there always a* DRAUGHT *through the* WINDOW *crevices?*

A. Because the external air (being colder than the air of the room we occupy) rushes through the window crevices *to supply the deficiency*, caused by the escape of warm air up the chimney, &c.

Q. *If you open the* LOWER SASH *of a window, there is more* DRAUGHT *than if you open the* UPPER *sash. Explain the reason of this.*

A. If the *lower* sash be open, *cold external air* will rush freely *into the room* and cause a great draught *inwards;* But if the *upper* sash be open, the *heated air of the room* will *rush out,* and (of course) there will be less draught inwards.

Q. *By which means is a* ROOM *better* VENTILATED—*By opening the upper or the lower sash?*

A. A room is better *ventilated* by opening the *upper sash;* because the hot vitiated air (which always ascends towards the ceiling) *can escape more easily.*

Q. *By which means is a* HOT ROOM *more quickly* COOLED—*By opening the upper or the lower sash?*

A. A hot room is *cooled more quickly* by opening the *lower sash;* because the cold air can enter more freely at the *lower* part of the room, than at the *upper.*

Q. *Why does* WIND DRY *damp* LINEN?

A. Because dry wind (like a dry sponge) imbibes the particles of vapor from the surface of the linen, as fast as they are formed.

Q. *Which is the* HOTTEST PLACE *in a church, chapel, or theatre?*

A. The gallery.

Q. *Why is the* GALLERY *of all public places* HOTTER *than the* LOWER *parts of the building?*

A. Because the heated air of the building *ascends;* and all the *cold air* (which can enter through the doors and windows) *keeps to the floor*, till it has become heated.

Q. *Why do* PLANTS *often grow out of* WALLS *and* TOWERS?

A. Because the *seed* has been blown there with the dust, by the *wind*, or dropped by some *bird* flying over.

BAROMETER.

CHAPTER XXV.

Q. *What is a* BAROMETER?

A. A weather-glass, or instrument to measure the variations in the *weight* of the *air;* by means of which *variations*, we may judge what weather may be expected.

BAROMETER is a compound of two Greek words, βαρος (weight) and μετρον (a measure).

Q. *What is a* THERMOMETER?

A. An instrument to show how *hot or cold* anything is.

THERMOMETER is a compound of two Greek words θερμος (heat) and μετρον (measure).

Q. *What is the* DIFFERENCE *between a* THERMOMETER *and a* BAROMETER?

A. In a THERMOMETER the mercury is *sealed up from the air;* and rises or falls, as the varying *temperature* of the air expands or contracts it: but

In a BAROMETER the mercury is left *exposed* (or open) *to the air;** and rises or falls, as the varying *weight* of the air presses upon the open column.

Q. *If the mercury of the thermometer be* SEALED UP *from the air, how can the air* AFFECT *it?*

A. The heat of the air passes *through the glass tube* into the mercury which causes the metal to expand and rise in the tube.

Q. *Why is the* TUBE *of a barometer left* OPEN?

A. That the air may *press upon it* freely; and, as this pressure varies, the mercury *rises or falls* in the tube.

The top of the tube must be a "*vacuum;*" otherwise the pressure of the external air upon the lower part of the column cannot affect the mercury.

Q. *How can a barometer, which measures the* WEIGHT *of air, be of service as a* WEATHER *glass?*

---

* At its lower extremity.

A. When air is *moist*, or filled with vapor, it is *lighter* than usual; and the column of mercury stands *low:*

When air is *dry* and free from vapor, it is *heavier* than usual; and the mercury stands *high:* Thus the barometer (by showing the variations in the *weight of the air*) indicates the changes of the *weather also.*

Q. *Why can you tell (by looking at a* BAROMETER) *what* KIND *of* WEATHER *it will be?*

A. Because the mercury in the tube *rises and falls*, as the air becomes heavier or lighter: and we can generally tell by the *weight* of the air, what kind of weather to expect.

Q. *Does the* WEIGHT *of the air* VARY MUCH?

A. Yes; the atmosphere varies as much as *one-tenth part* more or less.

Q. *What* USE *is a* BAROMETER *to sailors?*

A. It warns them to *regulate their ships*, before squalls come on.

Q. *How can a* BAROMETER *warn* SAILORS *to regulate their* SHIPS?

A. As it indicates when *wind*, *rain*, and *storm* are at hand, the sailor can make his ship trim before they overtake him.

Q. *Are there any* RULES *which can be depended on?*

A. Yes; there are *ten special rules* to direct us how to know the changes of weather, by marking the mercury of a barometer.

Q. *Mention the* 1ST SPECIAL RULE *with regard to the barometer?*

A. The barometer is *highest of all* during a *long frost;* and it generally rises with a *north-west wind.*

Q. *Why is the barometer* HIGHEST *of all during a long* FROST?

A. Because a long frost *condenses the air very greatly;* and the more *condensed* air is, the greater is its *pressure* on the mercury of a barometer.

Q. *Why does the barometer generally* RISE *with* NORTH-WEST *winds?*

A. Because NORTH-WEST winds make the air both *cold and dry:* and being both *condensed,* and *without vapor,* it is much heavier.

Q. *Mention the* 2D SPECIAL RULE *with regard to the barometer?*

A. The barometer is *lowest of all* during a *thaw, which follows a long frost:* and it generally falls with SOUTH or EAST wind.

Q. *Why does the barometer fall* LOWEST *of all at the* BREAKING UP *of a long* FROST?

A. 1st—Because the air (which had

been much *dried* by the frost) *absorbs the moisture* of the fresh warm current of wind from the south or south-west: and

2dly—The air (which had been much *condensed* by the frost) is suddenly *expanded* by the warm wind, which is introduced.

Q. *Why does the barometer fall very low with* SOUTH *and* EAST *winds?*

A. Because SOUTH and EAST winds come heavily *laden with vapor;* and *vaporized* air is lighter than *dry* air.

Q. *What effect has* WIND *on the mercury?*

A. The barometer is *high*, when the wind blows between the WEST and the NORTH; but it is *low*, when the wind blows between the SOUTH and the EAST.

Q. WHY *do these winds affect the mercury of a barometer?*

A. Because the pressure of the air is *increased* by *cold winds*, and diminished by *warm* ones.

Q. *Why is the pressure of air* INCREASED *with cold winds from the* NORTH?

A. Because the air *contracts*, when it is *cooled* by winds from the north and east, and *warmer* air flows in from all sides to fill up the vacuum; in consequence of which, its volume is increased, and the barometer *rises*.

Q. *Why is the* PRESSURE *of air* DIMINISHED *by warm winds from the* SOUTH?

A. Because the air *ascends* when it is *heated* by south winds, and flows away in all directions; in consequence of which, its volume is *diminished*, and the mercury *falls*.

Q. *What is the* 3D SPECIAL RULE *with regard to the barometer?*

A. While the barometer stands above 30, the air must be very *dry*, or very *cold*, or perhaps *both*—and *no rain* may be expected.

Q. *Why will there be* NO RAIN *if the* AIR *be very* DRY?

A. Because *dry* air will *absorb moisture*, and not part with it in *rain*.

Q. *Why will there be* NO RAIN *if the* AIR *be very* COLD?

A. Because it is *so much condensed*, that it has already parted with as much moisture as it can spare.

Q. *What is the* 4TH SPECIAL RULE *with regard to the barometer?*

A. When the barometer stands *very low* indeed, there will never be *much* rain; although a *fine day* will seldom occur at such times.

Q. *What kind of* WEATHER *is there likely to be, when the barometer is* UNUSUALLY LOW?

A. *Short heavy showers*, with sudden *squalls of wind* from the *west.*

Q. *Why will there be* VERY LITTLE RAIN, *if the barometer is* UNUSUALLY LOW?

A. Because the air must be very *warm*, or very *moist*, or perhaps *both.*

Q. *Why will there be little or no rain, if the* AIR *be very* WARM?

A. Because *warm* air has a tendency to imbibe *more* moisture and not to part with what it has.

Q. *Why will there be little or no rain, if the air be* MOIST *and the barometer very* LOW?

A. Because rain will never fall (even though the air be saturated), till *cold air* has been introduced to *condense the vapor:* And, as soon as *cold* air has been introduced, the barometer will *rise* instantly.

Q. *Name the* 5TH SPECIAL RULE *with regard to the barometer?*

A. In summer-time (after a long continuance of fair weather) the barometer will *fall gradually* for 2 or 3 days before *rain* comes: But if the fall of the mercury is very *sudden*, a *thunder-storm* may be expected.

Q. *What is the* 6TH SPECIAL RULE *with regard to the barometer?*

A. When the sky is cloudless, and seems to promise fair weather—if the barometer is *low*, the face of the sky will soon be suddenly *overcast.*

Q. *What is the* 7TH SPECIAL RULE *with regard to the barometer?*

A. Dark dense clouds will pass over *without rain*, when the barometer is *high;* but if the barometer be *low*, it will often rain *without* any appearance of clouds.

Q. *What is the* 8TH SPECIAL RULE *with regard to the barometer?*

A. The *higher* the barometer, the greater the probability of *fair weather.*

Q. *Why is the barometer* HIGH *in* FINE *weather?*

A. Because the air in fine weather contains *very little vapor.* The *drier* the air, the *higher* does the mercury of the barometer rise.

Q. *What is the* 9TH SPECIAL RULE *with regard to the barometer?*

A. When the mercury is in a *rising* state, *fine* weather is at hand; but, when the mercury is in a *sinking* state, *foul* weather is near.

Q. *Why does the mercury* RISE *at the approach of* FINE *weather?*

A. Because the air is becoming more

dry; and, therefore, its *pressure is increased.*

Q. *Why does the mercury* SINK *at the approach of* FOUL *weather?*

A. Because the air is *laden with vapor* or *disturbed by wind.*

Q. *Why does* VAPOR *in the air make the mercury* SINK?

A. Because vaporized air is *lighter than dry air;* and its *pressure* on the barometer *less.*

Q. *What is the* 10TH SPECIAL RULE *with regard to the barometer?*

A. If (in frosty weather) it *begins to snow,* the barometer generally rises to 30; where it remains, so long as the snow continues to fall: If, after this, the weather *clears up,* you may expect *very severe cold.*

Q. *How can you know if the* MERCURY *of the barometer is* RISING?

A. When the top of the column is *convex* (i. e., higher in the *middle* than at the *sides*), the mercury is in a *rising state.*

Q. *How can you tell if the* MERCURY *of the barometer is* FALLING?

A. When the top of the column is *concave* (i. e., *hollow* in the middle), the mercury is in a *falling state.*

Q. *Why is the mercury* CONVEX *when it is* RISING?

A. Because the parts of the mercury in contact with *the tube* are delayed by the glass; in consequence of which, the *middle* part *rises faster* than the *sides;* and the surface is CONVEX.

Q. *Why is the mercury* CONCAVE *when it is* FALLING?

A. Because the parts of the mercury in contact with *the tube* are delayed by *capillary attraction;* in consequence of which, the *middle* part *sinks faster* than the *sides:* and the surface is CONCAVE.

Q. *What effect does a* THUNDER-STORM *produce on the weather?*

A. It is generally *preceded by hot* weather, and *followed by cold* and showery weather.

Q. *What effect does a* SUDDEN CHANGE *of temperature produce on the weather?*

A. A great and sudden change (either from hot to cold, or from cold to hot) is generally followed by *rain within 24 hours.*

Q. *Why is a sudden* CHANGE *from* HOT *to* COLD *followed by* RAIN?

A. Because cold *condenses the air;* and some of its vapor is given off *in rain.*

Q. *Why is a sudden* CHANGE *from* COLD *to* HOT *followed by* RAIN?

A. Because the air is quickly *saturated* with *moisture*: but when *night* comes on, and *chills* the temperature, some of the abundant moisture is given off in rain.

Q. *Why is the air quickly* SATURATED *with* MOISTURE, *when* HEAT *rapidly succeeds to* COLD?

A. Because the evaporation (which was checked by the cold) is *carried on very rapidly*, in consequence of the *diminished* pressure of the air.

N. B. The *less the pressure* of the air, the more *rapid the evaporation* of moisture will be.

Q. *When does the barometer* VARY MOST?

A. In winter-time.

Q. *Why does the barometer vary* MORE *in* WINTER, *than in* SUMMER-*time?*

A. Because the *difference* of temperature between the torrid and temperate zones is much *greater* in winter than in summer: and produces a greater disturbance in the state of the air.

Q. *When does the barometer* VARY LEAST?

A. In summer-time.

Q. *Why does the barometer vary* LESS *in* SUMMER *than in* WINTER-*time?*

A. Because the temperature of the torrid and temperate zones in summer is *so nearly equal*, that its state is *not much* disturbed by interchange of currents.

Q. *Have* HEAT *and* COLD *any effect on the barometer?*

A. No, not of themselves; but because *cold* weather is generally either *dry*, or *rough* with north-west winds, therefore the mercury *rises* in cold weather: And because warm weather is often *moist*, or *fanned* by south-east winds, therefore the mercury *sinks* in warm weather.

Q. *Why is the mercury of a barometer* LOWER *in the* TORRID *than in the* FRIGID *zone?*

A. Because the warm air of the torrid zone contains much more *vapor* than the condensed air of the frigid zone; and the *moister* the air, the *less* is its pressure.

Q. *In what* MONTHS *is the barometer* HIGHEST?

A. In May and August; then in June, March, September, and April.

Q. *In what* MONTHS *is the barometer* LOWEST?

A. In November and February; then in October, July, December, and January.

Q. *Why is there* LESS *wet from* MARCH *to* AUGUST *than there is from August to March?*

A. Because the heat is *constantly increasing;* and the capacity of air to absorb and retain moisture increases likewise.

Q. *Why is there* MORE *wet from* AUGUST *to* MARCH *than from March to August?*

A. Because the heat is *constantly decreasing;* and the capacity of air to retain moisture decreases also; so that although it often rains, yet the air is always on the point of saturation.

Q. *Why does the mercury of a barometer* RISE *in a* FROST?

A. Because frost *condenses the air;* and condensed air is heavier than rarefied air.

Q. *Why does the mercury of a barometer* FALL *in a* THAW?

A. Because the air is filled with *vapor.*

Q. *What does a* SUDDEN *rise or fall of the barometer indicate?*

A. If the *rise* be sudden, fine weather will not continue long:

If the *fall* be sudden, foul weather will not continue long.

Q. *What sort of weather may we expect, if the barometer is very* FLUCTUATING?

A. If the mercury fluctuates much, the weather will be very *changeable* and *unsettled.*

THE FALL OF THE BAROMETER.

In very *hot* weather, the fall of the mercury denotes *thunder.* Otherwise, the sudden falling of the barometer denotes high wind.

In *frosty* weather, the fall of the barometer denotes *thaw.*

If *wet* weather happens soon after the fall of the barometer, expect but *little* of it.

In *wet* weather, if the barometer falls, expect much wet.

In *fair* weather, if the barometer falls and *remains* low, expect much wet in a few days, and probably *wind.*

N. B. The barometer sinks lowest of all for wind and rain together; next to that for wind, (except it be an east or north-east wind.)

THE RISE OF THE BAROMETER.

In *winter*, the rise of the barometer presages *frost.*

In *frosty* weather, the rise of the barometer presage *snow.*

If *fair* weather happens *soon* after the rise of the barometer, expect but little of it.

In *wet* weather, if the mercury rises high and *remains* so, expect continued *fine weather* in a day or two.

In wet weather, if the mercury rises suddenly very high, fine weather will not last long.

N. B. The barometer rises highest of all for north and west winds; for all *other* winds it sinks.

THE BAROMETER UNSETTLED.

If the motion of the mercury be *unsettled*, expect unsettled weather.

If it stand at "MUCH RAIN" and rise to "CHANGEABLE," expect *fair weather of short continuance.*

If it stand at "FAIR" and fall to "CHANGEABLE," expect *foul* weather.

N. B. Its motion *upwards* indicates the approach of fine weather; its motion *downwards* indicates the approach of foul weather.

SNOW. HAIL. RAIN.

CHAPTER XXVI.

Q. *What is* SNOW?

A. The condensed vapor of the air *frozen*, and precipitated to the earth.

Q. *What is the* CAUSE *of* SNOW?

A. When the air is nearly saturated with vapor, and condensed by a current of air *below freezing point*, some of the vapor is condensed, and frozen into snow.

A few years ago, some fishermen (who wintered at Nova Zembla) after they had been shut up in a hut for several days, *opened the window*, and the cold external air rushing in, instantly condensed the air of the hut, and its vapor fell on the floor *in a shower of snow.*

Q. *Why does* SNOW *fall in* WINTER *time?*

A. Because the sun's rays are too *oblique* to heat the surface of the earth; and (as the earth has no heat to radiate into the air) the air is very cold.

Q. *What is the cause of* SLEET?

A. When flakes of snow (in their descent) pass through a bed of air *above freezing point*, they partially melt; and fall to the earth as half-melted snow, or sleet.

Q. *What is the* USE *of* SNOW?

A. To keep the earth *warm*, and to *nourish* it.

Q. *Does snow keep the* EARTH WARM?

A. Yes, because it is a very *bad conductor;* in consequence of which, when the earth is covered with snow, its temperature very rarely descends *below freezing point*, even when the air is 15 or 20 degrees colder.

Q. WHY *is* SNOW *a* BAD CONDUCTOR *of heat and cold?*

A. Because *air* is confined and entangled among the crystals; and *air* is a very *bad* conductor: When, therefore, the earth is covered with snow, it cannot throw off its heat by radiation.

Q. *Tell me the words of the* PSALMIST (cxlvii. 16) *respecting snow; and explain what he means?*

A. The Psalmist says—"The Lord giveth snow like wool;" and he means, not only that snow is as *white as wool*, but that it is also as *warm as wool.*

Q. *Why is* WOOL WARM?

A. Because *air* is entangled among the fibres of the wool; and air is a very *bad conductor.*

Q. *Why is* SNOW WARM?

A. Because *air* is entangled among the crystals of the snow; and air is a very *bad conductor.*

Q. *Why does* SNOW NOURISH *the earth?*

A. Because it supplies *moisture* containing carbonic acid; which penetrates slowly into the soil, and insinuates itself through every clod, ridge, and furrow.

Q. *Why is there* NO SNOW *in* SUMMER *time?*

A. Because the *heat of the earth* melts it in its descent, and prevents it from reaching the surface of the earth.

Q. *Why are some* MOUNTAINS ALWAYS COVERED *with* SNOW?

A. 1st—Because the *air* on a high mountain is more *rarefied;* and rarefied air retains much heat in a latent state: and

2dly—Mountain-tops are not *surrounded by earth*, to radiate heat into the air; and, therefore, the snow is *not melted* in its descent, but falls on the mountain, and lies there.

Q. *Why is* SNOW WHITE?

A. Because it is formed of an infinite number of very minute crystals and prisms, which reflect all the colors of the rays of light from different points; and these colors, *uniting* before they meet the eye, cause snow to appear white.

The same answer applies to salt, loaf-sugar, &c. (*See p.* 372.)

Q. *What is* HAIL?

A. Rain, which has passed in its descent *through some cold bed of air*, and has been frozen into drops of ice.

Q. *What makes* ONE *bed of air* COLDER *than another?*

A. It is frequently caused by *electricity unequally distributed* in the air.

Q. *Why is* HAIL *frequently accompanied with* THUNDER *and* LIGHTNING?

A. 1st—Because the *congelation of water into hail* disturbs the electricity of the air: and

2dly—The *friction* (produced by the fall of hail) excites it still more.

Q. *Why does* HAIL *fall generally in* SUMMER *and* AUTUMN?

A. 1st—Because the air is *more highly electrified* in summer and autumn than in winter and spring: and

2dly—The vapors in summer and autumn (being rarefied) ascend to more elevated regions, which are *colder* than those nearer the earth.

Q. *What* TWO *things are essential to cause* HAIL?

A. Two *strata of clouds* having *opposite electricities*, and *two currents of wind.* The *lower cloud* (being negative) is the one *precipitated* in hail.

Q. *What is* RAIN?

A The vapor of the clouds or air *condensed*, and precipitated to the earth.

Q. *When is the vapor of the air or clouds* PRECIPITATED *in hail, rain, or snow?*

A. When the air is *saturated with vapor*, and a cold current *condenses* it; it is then no longer able to hold all its vapor in solution, and some of it falls as rain.

Q. *Why does* RAIN *fall in* DROPS?

A. Because the vapory particles in their descent *attract each other;* and those which are sufficiently near *unite*, and form into drops.

Q. *Why does not the* COLD *of* NIGHT ALWAYS *cause rain?*

A. Because the air is not always near saturation; and unless this be the case, it will be able to hold its vapor in solution, even after it is condensed by the chilly night.

Q. *Why does a* PASSING CLOUD *often drop* RAIN?

A. Because the cloud (travelling about on the wind) comes into contact with *something that chills it;* and its vapor being condensed, *falls to the earth* as *rain.*

Q. *Why are* RAIN-DROPS *sometimes much* LARGER *than at* OTHER *times?*

A. Because the rain-cloud is floating *near the earth;* when this is the case, the drops are large, because such a cloud is much more *dense* than one more elevated.

The size of the rain-drop is also increased, according to the *rapidity* with which the vapors are condensed.

Q. *Does not* WIND *sometimes* INCREASE *the* SIZE *of rain-drops?*

A. Yes; by blowing two or more drops into one.

Q. *Why do* CLOUDS FALL *in* RAINY *weather?*

A. 1st—Because they are *heavy* with abundant vapor: and

2dly—The density of the air being *diminished*, is less able to buoy the clouds up.

Q. *How do you* KNOW *that the* DENSITY *of the air is* DIMINISHED *in* RAINY *weather?*

A. Because the mercury of a barometer *falls*.

Q. *Why is* RAIN-WATER *more* FERTILIZING *than* PUMP-WATER?

A. 1st—Because it contains more carbonic acid: and

2dly—It contains also a small quantity of *ammonia*, with which it supplies the young plants.

It is probable that the ammonia of rain-water is merely that which escapes from putrefying animal matters, beaten back by the force of the shower.

Q. *Why does* RAIN PURIFY *the* AIR?

A. 1st—Because it *beats down* the

noxious exhalations collected in the air, and *dissolves* them:

2dly—It mixes the air of the *upper* regions with that of the *lower regions:* and

3dly—It *washes the earth*, and sets in motion the stagnant contents of sewers and ditches.

Q. *Why are* MOUNTAINOUS *countries more* RAINY *than flat ones?*

A. Because the air (striking against the sides of the mountains) is *carried up the inclined plane*, and brought in contact with the *cold air* of the higher regions: in consequence of which, its vapor is *condensed*, and deposited in rain.

Q. *Why does a* SPONGE SWELL *when it is* WETTED?

A. Because the water *penetrates the pores* of the sponge by capillary attraction, and drives the particles *further from each other;* in consequence of which, the *bulk* of the sponge is greatly *increased.*

Q. *Why do* FIDDLE-STRINGS SNAP *in* WET *weather?*

A. Because the moisture of the air (penetrating the string) causes it to *swell;* and (as the cord *thickens*) its *tension is increased*, and the string snaps.

Q. *Why does* PAPER PUCKER *when it is* WETTED?

A. Because the moisture (penetrating the paper) *drives its particles further apart;* and (as the moisture is absorbed *unequally* by the paper) some parts are more enlarged than others; in consequence of which, the paper *blisters* or *puckers.*

Q. *Why do the weather-toys (called* CAPUCHINS) *lift the cowl over the figures in wet weather, and remove it in dry?*

A. Because the cowl of the cap'uchin is attached to a *piece of cat-gut* in such a manner, that when the cat-gut is *shortened by moisture,* it pulls the cowl up; but in *dry* weather the string *is loosened,* and the cowl falls down by its own weight.

Q. *In another weather-toy the* MAN *comes out in* WET *weather, and the* LADY *in* FINE:—*Why is this?*

A. Because the two figures are attached to a piece of *cat-gut* in such a manner, that when the cat-gut is *shortened by moisture,* it pulls the *man out;* but when it is *loose,* the *woman falls out* by her own weight.

Q. *Why are* WET STOCKINGS DIFFICULT *to* PULL ON?

A. Because the moisture penetrates the threads of the stockings, and causes them to *shrink in size.*

Q. *In which* PART *of the* DAY *does the* MOST RAIN *fall?*

A. More rain falls by *night* than by day; because the cold night *condenses the air*, and diminishes its capacity for holding vapor in solution.

Q. *Does more rain fall in* SUMMER *or in* WINTER?

A. There are *more rainy days* from September to March; but *heavier* rains between March and September.

Q. *Why are there* MORE RAINY DAYS *from September to March than from March to September?*

A. Because the temperature of the air is *constantly decreasing*, and its capacity for holding vapor decreases also; in consequence of which, it is frequently obliged to part with some of its vapor in rain.

Q. *In what* PART *of the* WORLD *does* RAIN *fall* MOST ABUNDANTLY?

A. Near the *equator;* and the quantity of rain *decreases*, as we approach the *poles.*

Be it remembered that there are fewer rainy *days*, although more *rain* actually falls during the wet season of the equator, than falls in 12 months at any other part of the globe.

WATER.

CHAPTER XXVII.

Q. *Of what is* WATER *composed?*

A. Of *two gases*, oxygen and hydrogen.

In 9lbs. of water—8 are oxygen, and 1 is hydrogen.

Q. *Why is* WATER FLUID?

A. Because its particles are kept separate by *latent heat:* When a certain quantity of this latent heat is driven out, *water becomes solid*, and is called ice.

By increasing its *latent heat*, the particles of water are again subdivided into *invisible steam.*

Q. *Why is* PUMP-WATER *called* "HARD *water?*"

A. Because it is laden with foreign matters, and will not readily *dissolve substances* immersed in it.

Q. *What makes* PUMP-WATER HARD?

A. When it filters through the earth, it becomes impregnated with *sulphate of lime*, and many other impurities from the *earths and minerals* with which it comes in contact.

Q. *What is the cause of* MINERAL SPRINGS?

A. When water trickles through the ground, it dissolves some of the substances with which it comes in contact; if these substances are metallic, the water will partake of their mineral character.

Some water is imbued with *lime*; some with *salt*, &c., &c.

Q. *Why is it difficult to* WASH *our* HANDS *clean with* HARD *water?*

A. Because the *soda of the soap* combines with the *sulphuric acid* of the hard water—and the *oil of the soap* with the *lime*—and floats in flakes on the top of the water.

N. B. Sulphate of lime consists of sulphuric acid and lime.

Q. *Why is it difficult to wash in* SALT WATER?

A. Because it contains *muriatic acid*; and the *soda of soap* combines with the *muriatic acid of the salt water*, and produces a cloudiness.

Q. *What is the cause of* PETRIFACTIONS?

A. While water rolls underground, its impurities are held in solution by the presence of carbonic acid: but when the stream reaches the open air, its carbonic acid escapes, and these impurities are precipitated on various substances lying in the course of the stream.

These impurities are especially carbonate of lime and iron.

Q. *Why does a* BLACK HAT *turn* RED *at the* SEA-SIDE?

A. Because the *muriatic acid* of the

sea water disturbs the *gallic acid* of the black dye, and turns it red.

Q. *Of what is* SOAP *made?*

A. Of kelp (or the ashes of sea-weed dried and burnt in a pit) mixed with oil or fat.

YELLOW SOAP is made of whale oil, soda, and resin. SOFT SOAP is made of oil and potash. HARD SOAP, of oil and soda.

Q. *Why does* WATER CLEAN *dirty* LINEN?

A. Because it *dissolves* the stains, as it would dissolve salt.

Q. *Why does* SOAP *greatly* INCREASE *the cleansing power of water?*

A. Because many stains are of a *greasy nature;* and soap has the power of *uniting with greasy* matters, and rendering them soluble in water.

Q. *Why is* RAIN-WATER SOFT?

A. Because it is not impregnated with *earths and minerals.*

Q. *Why is it* MORE EASY *to* WASH *with* SOFT *water, than with* HARD?

A. Because soft water unites freely with soap, and *dissolves* it; instead of decomposing it, as hard water does.

Q. *Why do* WOOD ASHES *make* HARD *water* SOFT?

A. 1st—Because the *carbonic acid* of *wood ashes* combines with the *sulphate of lime* in the hard water, and converts it into *chalk:* and

2dly—Wood ashes convert some of the soluble salts of water into insoluble, and throw them down as a sediment; in consequence of which, the water remains more pure.

Q. *Why has* RAIN-WATER *such an* UNPLEASANT SMELL, *when it is collected in a rain-water tub or tank?*

A. Because it is impregnated with *decomposed* organic matters, washed from roofs, trees, or the casks in which it is collected.

Q. *Why does* WATER MELT SUGAR?

A. Because very minute particles of water insinuate themselves into the *pores* of the sugar, by capillary attraction; and force the crystals apart from each other.

Q. *Why does* WATER MELT SALT?

A. Because very minute particles of water insinuate themselves into the *pores* of the salt, by capillary attraction; and force the crystals apart from each other.

Q. *Why does melted* SUGAR *or* SALT *give a* FLAVOR *to water?*

A. Because the sugar or salt (being disunited into very minute pieces) *floats* about the water, and mixes with every part.

Q. *Why does* HOT *water melt sugar and salt* QUICKER *than* COLD *water?*

A. Because the *heat* (entering the pores of the sugar or salt) opens a passage for the water.

Q. *Why is* SEA-WATER *brackish?*

A. 1st—Because the sea contains *mines of salt* at the bottom of its bed:

2dly—It is impregnated with *bituminous matter*, which is brackish: and

3dly—It contains many *putrid substances* of a brackish nature.

Q. *Why is* NOT RAIN-WATER SALT, *although most of it is evaporated from the* SEA?

A. Because *salt* will not *evaporate;* and therefore when sea-water is turned into vapor, its *salt* is left behind.

Q. *Why does* STAGNANT *water* PUTREFY?

A. Because leaves, plants, insects, &c., are decomposed in it.

Q. *Why is* STAGNANT *water full of* WORMS, EELS, *&c.?*

A. Because numberless insects *lay their eggs* in the leaves and plants floating on the surface; these eggs are soon hatched, and produce swarms of worms, eels, and insects.

Q. *Why is* FLOWING *water* FREE *from these* IMPURITIES?

A. 1st—Because the motion of running water prevents *fermentation:*

2dly—It dissolves the *putrid substances* which happen to fall into it: and

3dly—It casts on the *bank* (by its current) such substances as it cannot dissolve.

Q. *Why does* RUNNING *water* OSCILLATE *and* WHIRL *in its current?*

A. 1st—Because it *impinges* against its *banks,* and is perpetually diverted from its forward motion: and

2dly—Because the *centre* of a river flows faster than its sides.

Q. *Why do the* SIDES *of a river flow more* TARDILY *than its* CENTRE?

A. Because they *rub* against the *banks,* and are delayed in their current by this friction.

Q. *Why does* SOAPY *water* BUBBLE?

A. Because soap makes the *water tenacious;* and prevents the bubbles from *bursting* as soon as they are formed.

Q. *Why will not water bubble* WITHOUT SOAP?

A. Because it is not tenacious enough to hold together the *bubbles* that are formed.

Q. *When* SOAP-BUBBLES *are blown from a pipe why do they* ASCEND?

A. Because they are *filled with warm breath*, which is lighter than air.

ICE.

CHAPTER XXVIII.

Q. *What is* ICE?

A. FROZEN WATER. When the air is reduced to 32 degrees of heat, water will no longer remain in a *fluid* state.

Q. *Why is* SOLID ICE LIGHTER *than* WATER?

A. Because water *expands* by freezing; and as the *bulk* is *increased*, the *gravity* must be *less*.

Nine cubic inches of water become *ten* when frozen.

Q. *Why do* EWERS BREAK *in a* FROSTY NIGHT?

A. Because the water in them *freezes;* and (*expanding* by frost) bursts the ewers to make room for its increased volume.

Q. *Why does it not expand* UPWARDS (*like boiling water*), *and* RUN OVER?

A. Because the *surface* is frozen first; and the frozen surface acts as a *plug*, which is more difficult to burst than the earthen ewer itself.

Q. *Why do* TILES, STONES, *and* ROCKS *often* SPLIT *in winter?*

A. Because the moisture in them *freezes;* and (expanding by frost) *splits the solid mass.*

Q. *In winter-time,* FOOT-MARKS *and* WHEEL-RUTS *are often covered with an icy* NET-WORK, *through the interstices of which the soil is clearly seen:*—WHY *does the water freeze in* NET-WORK?

A. Because it freezes first at the *sides* of the foot-prints: other crystals gradually shoot across, and would cover the whole surface, if the earth did not *absorb* the water before it had time to freeze.

Q. *In winter-time, these* FOOT-MARKS *and* WHEEL-RUTS *are sometimes covered with a perfect* SHEET *of ice, and not an icy net-work:—Why is* THIS?

A. Because the *air is colder* and the *earth harder* than in the former case, in consequence of which, the *entire surface* of the foot-print is frozen over before the earth has had time to absorb the water.

Q. *Why is not the ice* SOLID *in these ruts?*—WHY *is there only a very thin* FILM *or* NET-WORK *of ice?*

A. Because the earth *absorbs most of the water,* and leaves only the icy *film behind.*

Q. *Why do* WATER-PIPES *frequently* BURST *in* FROSTY *weather?*

A. Because the water in them *freezes;* and (*expanding by frost*) bursts the pipes to make room for its increased volume.

Q. *Does not water expand by* HEAT *as well as by* COLD?

A. Yes; it expands as soon as it is more than 42 degrees, *till it boils;* after which time, it flies off in steam.

Freezing water, 32°. 212°, Boiling water.

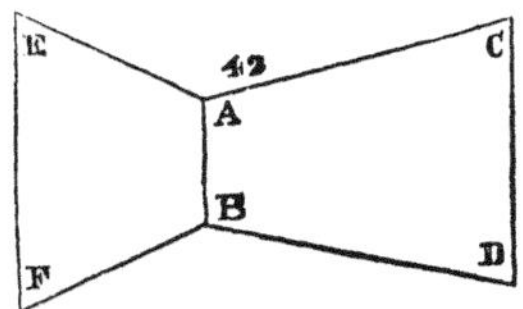

Here A B measures the bulk of a portion of water at 42 degrees.

It goes on increasing in bulk to C D, when it boils.

It also goes on increasing in bulk to E F, when it freezes.

Q. WHEN *does* WATER *begin to* EXPAND *from cold?*

A. When it is reduced to 42 degrees. Water is wisely ordained by God to be an *exception* to a very general rule—it *contracts* till it is reduced to 42 degrees, and then it *expands till it freezes.*

The general rule is this—That cold *condenses* and *contracts* the volume of nearly everything; but water is *not contracted* by cold after it freezes, (which it does at 32°).

Q. WHY *does water expand when it freezes?*

A. Because it is converted into *solid crystals* which *do not fit so closely* as particles of water do.

Q. *Why is the* BOTTOM *of a river* NEVER FROZEN?

A. Because water *ascends* to the surface, so soon as it becomes colder than 42 degrees; and (if it freezes) *floats there* till it is melted.

Q. *Show the* WISDOM *of* GOD *in this wonderful exception to a general law.*

A. If ice were *heavier than water*, it would *sink;* and a river would soon become a *solid block of ice*, which could never be dissolved.

The general rule is—that all substances become *heavier* from condensation; but ice is *lighter* than water.

Q. *Why does not the* ICE *on the* SURFACE *of a river* CHILL *the water* BENEATH *and make it freeze?*

A. 1st—Because water is a *very bad conductor*, and is heated or chilled by CONVECTION only:

2dly—If the ice on the surface were to communicate its *coldness* to the water beneath, the water beneath would communicate its *heat to the ice*, and the ice would instantly *melt:* and

3dly—The ice on the surface acts as a *shield*, to prevent the cold air from *penetrating through the river*, to freeze the water below the surface.

Q. *Why does* WATER FREEZE *at the* SURFACE *first?*

A. Because the surface is in *contact with the air*, and the air *carries away its heat.*

Q. *Why does the coat of ice grow* THICKER *and* THICKER *if the frost* CONTINUES?

A. Because the *heat* of the water (immediately below the frozen surface) *passes through the pores of the ice* into the *cold air.*

Q. *Why are not* WHOLE RIVERS FROZEN (*layer by layer*), *till they become solid ice*

A. Because water is so *slow* a conductor, that our frosts never continue *long enough* to convert a whole river into a solid mass of ice.

Q. *Why does not* RUNNING *water freeze so* FAST *as* STILL *water?*

A. 1st—Because the motion of the current *disturbs the crystals*, and prevents their forming into a continuous surface: and

2dly—The heat of the *under* surface is communicated to the *upper* surface by the *rolling of the water.*

Q. *When* RUNNING *water is* FROZEN *why is the* ICE *generally very* ROUGH?

A. Because little flakes of ice are first formed and *carried down* the stream, till they meet some *obstacle* to *stop* them; *other* flakes of ice (impinging against them) are arrested in like manner; and the *edges* of the different flakes *overlapping* each other, *make the surface rough.*

Q. *Why do* SOME *parts of a* RIVER FREEZE LESS *than* OTHERS?

A. Because *springs* issue from the bottom; and (as they bubble upwards) *thaw the ice,* or make it thin.

Q. *When persons* FALL *into a* RIVER *in winter-time why does the* WATER *feel remarkably* WARM?

A. Because the *frosty air* is at least 10 or 12 degrees *colder* than the water is.

The water below the surface is at least 42°; but the air 32°, or even less.

Q. *Why is* SHALLOW *water* FROZEN *more* QUICKLY *than* DEEP *water?*

A. Because the *whole volume* of water must be cooled to 42 degrees, before the *surface can be frozen:* and it takes a longer time to cool down a *deep* bed of water than a *shallow* one.

Q. *Why is* SEA-WATER RARELY FROZEN?

A. 1st—Because the *mass of water is so great,* that it requires a very long time to cool the whole volume down to 42 degrees:

2dly—The *ebb and flow* of the sea interfere with the cooling influence of the air : and

3dly—*Salt* water never freezes till the surface is cooled down 25 degrees *below freezing point.*

Q. *Why do some* LAKES RARELY (*if ever*) FREEZE?

A. 1st—Because they are *very deep:* and

2dly—Because their water is supplied by *springs*, which bubble from the bottom.

Q. *Why does the* DEPTH *of water* RETARD *its* FREEZING?

A. Because the *whole volume of water* must be reduced to 42 degrees, before the *surface will freeze:* and the *deeper* the water, the *longer* it will be before the whole volume is thus reduced.

Q. *Why do* SPRINGS *at the bottom of a lake* PREVENT *its* FREEZING?

A. Because they keep continually sending forth *fresh* water, which prevents the lake from being reduced to the necessary degree of coldness.

Q. *It is* COLDER *in a* THAW, *than in a* FROST. *Explain the reason of this.*

A. When frozen water is *thawed,* it *absorbs* heat from the *air*, &c., to melt the ice; in consequence of which, the heat of the air is greatly reduced.

Q. *It is* WARMER *in a* FROST *than in a* THAW. *Explain the reason of this.*

A. When water *freezes*, it gives out *latent heat*, in order that it may be converted into *solid ice;* and, as much heat is liberated from the water to the atmosphere, the air feels *warmer*.

Q. SALT DISSOLVES ICE. *Explain the reason of this.*

A. Water freezes at 32°, but *salt* and water will not freeze till the *air* is 25 degrees *colder;* if, therefore, salt be added to frozen water, it dissolves it.

Unless the thermometer stands below 7°.

Q. *Will any thing* DISSOLVE ICE *besides* SALT?

A. Yes; any *acid*, such as sulphuric acid, nitric acid, &c.

Q. *Why is a mixture of* SALT *and* SNOW *colder than* SNOW *itself?*

A. Because *salt dissolves the crystals* of snow into a fluid: And whenever a solid is converted into a fluid, *heat is absorbed*, and the cold made more intense.

Q. *Why does* FROST *make the* EARTH CRACK?

A. Because the water absorbed by the earth in warm weather, expanding by the frost, thrusts the particles of earth apart from each other, and leaves a chink or crack between.

Q. *Show the* WISDOM *of* GOD *in this arrangement.*

A. These *cracks* in the earth let in air, dew, rain, and many gases favorable to vegetation.

Q. *Why does the* EARTH CRUMBLE *in* SPRING?

A. Because the *ice* of the clods *dissolves;* and the particles of earth (which had been thrust apart by the frost) being left *unsupported,* tumble into minute parts, because their *cement of ice is dissolved.*

Q. *Why does* MORTAR CRUMBLE *away in* FROST?

A. Because it was not *dried in the warm weather;* therefore its moisture *freezes, expands,* and thrusts the particles of the mortar away from each other; but as soon as the frost goes the *water condenses,* and leaves the mortar full of cracks and chinks.

Q. *Why does* STUCCO PEEL *from a* WALL *in* FROSTY *weather?*

A. Because the stucco was not *dried in the warm weather;* therefore its moisture *freezes, expands,* and thrusts its particles away from the wall; but, as soon as the water condenses again by the thaw, the stucco (being unsupported) *falls by its own weight.*

Q. *Why cannot* BRICKLAYERS *and* PLASTERERS *work in* FROSTY *weather?*

A. Because *frost* expands mortar, and causes the bricks and plaster to *start from their position.*

Q. *Why do* BRICKLAYERS COVER *their work with* STRAW *in spring and autumn?*

A. Because straw is a non-conductor; and prevents the mortar of their new work from *freezing*, during the cold nights of spring and autumn.

Q. *Why are* WATER PIPES *often covered with* STRAW *in winter-time?*

A. Because straw (being a non-conductor) prevents the *water of the pipes from freezing*, and the *pipes from bursting.*

Q. *Why are delicate* TREES *covered with* STRAW *in* WINTER?

A. Because straw (being a non-conductor) prevents the *sap of the tree* from being frozen.

Q. *Can* WATER *be* FROZEN *in any way* BESIDES *by frosty weather?*

A. Yes; in very many ways. For example—a bottle of water wrapped in *cotton*, and frequently *wetted with ether*, will soon freeze.

Q. *Why would* WATER FREEZE *if the bottle were kept constantly wetted with* ETHER?

A. Because *evaporation* would carry off the heat of the water, and reduce it to the *freezing point.*

Q. *Why does* ETHER *freeze under the* RECEIVER *of an* AIR-PUMP, *when the air is exhausted?*

A. Because *evaporation* is very greatly increased by the *diminution of atmospheric pressure;* and the ether freezes by evaporation.

FREEZING MIXTURES.

1. If nitre be dissolved in water, the heat of the liquid will be reduced 16 degrees.
2. If 5 oz. of nitre, and 5 of sal-ammoniac (both finely powdered) be dissolved in 19 oz. of water, the heat of the liquid will be reduced 40 degrees.
3. If 3lbs. of snow be added to 1lb. of salt, the mixture will fall to 0° (or 32 degrees below freezing point).

The two following are the coldest mixtures yet known—

1. Mix 3lbs. of muriate of lime with 1lb. of snow.
2. Mix 5lbs. of diluted sulphuric acid with 4lbs. of snow.

Q. *Why is it more easy to* SWIM *in the* SEA *than in a* RIVER?

A. Because the *specific gravity* of salt water is *greater* than that of fresh; and, therefore, it *buoys* up the swimmer better.

Q. *How do cooks ascertain if their* BRINE *be* SALT ENOUGH *for pickling?*

A. They put an *egg into their brine.* If the egg *sinks,* the brine is *not strong enough;* if the egg *floats,* it *is.*

Q. *Why will an* EGG SINK, *if the brine be* NOT STRONG *enough for pickling?*

A. Because an egg will be the *heavier:* but if as much *salt* be added as the water can dissolve, an egg will be lighter than the strong brine, and consequently float on the surface.

Q. WHY *will an* EGG FLOAT *in strong* BRINE *and not in water?*

A. Because the specific gravity of *salt and water* is greater than that of water *only.*

Q. *Why do persons* SINK *in water when they are* UNSKILFUL SWIMMERS?

A. Because they struggle to keep their *head out of water.*

Q. *Explain how this is.*

A. When the head is thrown back boldly into the water, the mouth is kept *above the surface,* and the swimmer is able to breathe:

But when the head is kept *above the surface* of the water, the chin and mouth sink *beneath* it, and the swimmer is suffocated.

This may be illustrated thus:—If a piece of wood be of such specific gravity, that only *two square inches* can float out of water; it is manifest, that if two *other* inches are raised out, the two *former* inches must be plunged *in.* The body (in floating) resembles this piece of wood— If two square inches of the *face* float out of the water, the swimmer can breathe; but if part of the *back* and *crown* of the head be forcibly raised above the surface, a proportional quantity of the face must be plunged *in;* and the mouth becomes covered.

Q. *Why can* QUADRUPEDS *swim* MORE EASILY *than* MAN?

A. 1st—Because the *trunk* of quadrupeds is *lighter* than water; and this is the greatest part of them: and

2dly—The *position* of a beast (when swimming) is a *natural* one.

Q. *Why is it* MORE DIFFICULT *for a* MAN *to swim than for a* BEAST?

A. 1st—Because his body is more *heavy* in proportion than that of a beast: and

2dly—The *position* and muscular action of a *man* (when swimming) differ greatly from his ordinary habits; but beasts swim in their *ordinary* position.

Q. *Why can* FAT *men* SWIM *more* EASILY *than* SPARE *men?*

A. Because *fat is lighter than water;* and the *fatter* a man is, the more *buoyant* will he be.

Q. *How are* FISHES *able to* ASCEND *to the* SURFACE *of water?*

A. Fishes have an *air-bladder* near the abdomen; when this bladder is *filled with air* the fish increases in size, and (being lighter) ascends through the water to its surface.

Q. *How are fishes able to* DIVE *in a minute to the* BOTTOM *of a stream?*

A. They *expel the air* from their air-bladder; in consequence of which, their *size is diminished*, and they sink instantly.

LIGHT.

CHAPTER XXIX.

Q. *What is* LIGHT?

A. Rapid undulations of a fluid called ether, made sensible to the eye by striking on the optic nerve.

See p. 51.

Q. *How* FAST *does* LIGHT TRAVEL?

A. Light travels so fast, that it would go eight times round the earth while a person counts "ONE."

Q. *Does* ALL *light travel equally fast?*

A. Yes; the light of the sun—the light of a candle—or the light from houses, trees, and fields.

Q. *Where does the* LIGHT *of* HOUSES, TREES, *and* FIELDS, *come from?*

A. The light of the *sun* (or of some lamp or candle) is *reflected* from their *surfaces*.

Q. *Why are* SOME *surfaces* BRILLIANT (*like glass and steel*), *and* OTHERS DULL, *like lead?*

A. Those surfaces which *reflect the most light*, are the most *brilliant;* and those which *absorb* light are *dull.*

Q. *What is meant by* REFLECTING LIGHT?

A. Throwing the rays of light *back again* from the surface on which they fall.

Q. *What is meant by* ABSORBING LIGHT?

A. Retaining the rays of light on the surface on which they fall; in consequence of which, their presence is not made sensible by *reflection.*

Q. *Why can a* THOUSAND *persons* SEE *the* SAME OBJECT *at the same time?*

A. Because it throws off from its surface an infinite number of rays in all directions; and one person sees *one* portion of these rays, and another person *another.*

Q. *Why is the* EYE PAINED *by a* SUDDEN *light?*

A. Because the nerve of the eye is *burdened with rays* before the pupil has had time to contract.

Q. *Why does it give us* PAIN, *if a* CANDLE *be brought suddenly towards our* BED *at night-time?*

A. Because the *pupil* of the eye *dilates* very much in the dark, in order to *admit more rays.* When, therefore, a candle is brought suddenly before us, the enlarged pupils *overload* the optic nerves *with rays*, which causes pain.

Q. *Why* CAN *we* BEAR *the candle-light after a few moments?*

A. Because the pupils *contract again* almost instantly; and adjust themselves to the quantity of light which falls upon them.

Q. *Why can we* SEE NOTHING, *when we leave a* WELL-LIGHTED *room, and go into the* DARKER ROAD *or* STREET?

A. Because the pupil (which *contracted* in the bright room) does not *dilate instantaneously;* and the contracted pupil is not able to collect rays enough from the darker road or street to enable us to see objects before us.

Q. *Why do we* SEE BETTER, *when we get* USED *to the* DARK?

A. Because the pupil *dilates* again, and allows more rays to pass through its aperture; in consequence of which, we see more distinctly.

Q. *If we look at the* SUN *for a few moments, why do all* OTHER *things appear* DARK?

A. Because the pupil of the eye becomes so much *contracted* by looking at the sun, that it is *too small* to collect sufficient rays from *other objects* to enable us to distinguish their colors. (*See* "Accidental colors;" pp. 375, 376.)

Q. *If we watch a bright* FIRE *for a few moments, why does the* ROOM *seem* DARK?

A. Because the pupil of the eye becomes so much *contracted* by looking at the fire, that it is *too small* to collect sufficient rays from the objects around to enable us to distinguish their colors.

Q. *Why can we see the* PROPER COLORS *of every object again, after a few minutes?*

A. Because the pupil dilates again and accommodates itself to the light around.

Q. *Why can* TIGERS, CATS, *and* OWLS, *see in the* DARK?

A. Because they have the power of *enlarging the pupil of their eyes* so as to collect several scattered rays of light; in consequence of which, they can *see distinctly* when it is not light enough for us to see *any thing at all.*

Q. *Why do* CATS *and* OWLS SLEEP *almost all* DAY?

A. Because the pupil of their eyes is *very broad*, and daylight *fatigues* them; so they close their eyes for relief.

Q. *Why do* CATS *keep* WINKING, *when they sit before a* FIRE?

A. Because the pupil of their eye is

very broad, and the light of the fire is painful; so they keep shutting their eyes to relieve the sensation of too much light.

Q. *Why do* TIGERS, CATS, OWLS, *&c.*, PROWL *by* NIGHT *for prey?*

A. Because they *sleep* all *day* when the strong light would be painful to them; and as they can see clearly in the *dark*, they prowl then for prey.

Q. *Why do* GLOW-WORMS *glisten by* NIGHT *only?*

A. Because the light of day is *so strong* that it *eclipses* the feeble light of a glow-worm; in consequence of which, glow-worms are *invisible by day.*

Q. *Why can we* NOT *see the* STARS *in the* DAY-TIME?

A. Because the light of day is so powerful that it *eclipses the feeble light of the stars:* in consequence of which, they are invisible by day.

Q. *Why can we see the* STARS *even at* MID-DAY, *from the bottom of a deep* WELL?

A. Because the light of the stars is not overpowered by the rays of the sun, which are lost in the numerous reflections which they undergo in the well.

The rays of the *sun* will enter the well very *obliquely*: whereas, many *stars* will shine *directly over the well.* See pp. 348, 349.

Q. *What is the* USE *of* TWO EYES, *since they present only one image of any object?*

A. To *increase the light*—or to take in *more rays of light* from the object looked at, in order that it may appear *more distinct.*

Q. *Why do we* NOT *see things* DOUBLE, *with* TWO EYES?

A. 1st—Because the *axis of both eyes is turned to one object;* and, therefore, the *same impression* is made on the retina of *each eye:* and

2dly—Because the nerves (which receive the impression) have *one point of union* before they reach the brain.

This is not altogether satisfactory, although it is the explanation generally given. The phenomenon probably is rather psychological than material.

Q. *Why do we* SEE OURSELVES *in a* GLASS?

A. Because the rays of light from our face *strike against the surface of the glass,* and (instead of being absorbed) *are reflected,* or sent back again to our eye.

Q. *Why are the rays of light* REFLECTED *by a* MIRROR?

A. Because they cannot *pass through the impenetrable metal* with which the back of the glass is covered; so they *rebound back,* just as a *marble* would do, if it were thrown against a wall.

Q. *When a marble is rolled towards a wall, what is the path* THROUGH WHICH IT RUNS *called?*

A. The line of INCIDENCE.

Q. *When a marble* REBOUNDS *back again, what is the path it* THEN *describes called?*

A. The line of REFLECTION.

See figure below. If AB be the line of incidence, then BC is the line of reflection; and *vice versa.*

Q. *When the light of our face goes* TO *the* GLASS, *what is the path through which it goes* CALLED?

A. The line of *incidence.*

Q. *When the light of our face is reflected* BACK *again from the mirror, what is this* RETURNING *path called?*

A. The line of *reflection.*

Q. *What is the* ANGLE *of incidence?*

A. The angle between the line of *incidence* and the *perpendicular.*

Q. *What is the* ANGLE *of reflection?*

A. The angle between the line of *reflection* and the perpendicular. (*See Fig.*)

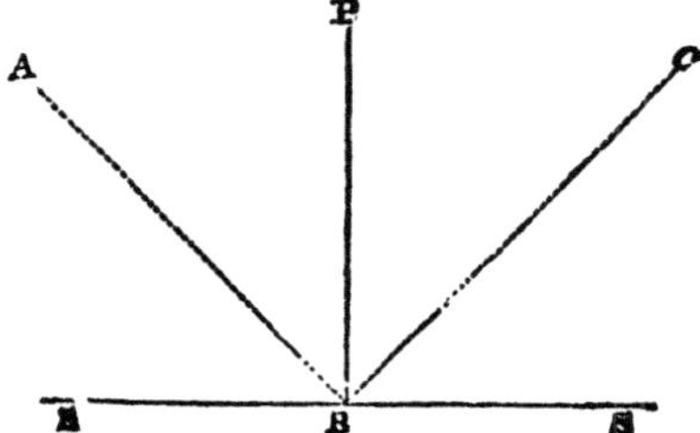

Let SS be any surface, PB a perpendicular to it.—If a marble were thrown from A to B, and bounded back to C; then ABP would be called the angle of *incidence*, and CBP the angle of *reflection*.

Q. *Why does our reflection in a mirror seem to* APPROACH *us, as we walk* TOWARDS *it; and to* RETIRE FROM *us, as* WE *retire?*

A. Because the lines and *angles of incidence* are always *equal* to the *lines* and *angles of reflection;* in consequence of which, the *image* will always seem to be as far *behind* the mirror as the *real object* is *before* it.

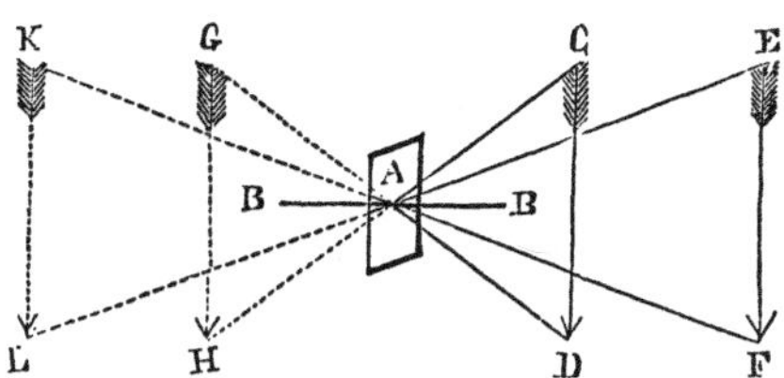

Suppose A to be a mirror—CA, EA and DA, FA, the lines of incidence; then GA, KA and HA, LA, are the lines of reflection. When the arrow is at CD, its image will appear at GH, because line CA=GA, and line DA=HA; and also the angle CAB=angle GAB, and angle DAB=HAB. For a similar reason, if the arrow were at EF, the image would seem to be at KL.

Q. *Why can a man see his* WHOLE PERSON *reflected in a* LITTLE MIRROR, *not* 6 *inches in length?*

A. Because the *lines and angles of incidence* are always equal to the *lines and angles of reflection;* in consequence of which, his image will seem to be as far *behind* the mirror as his person is *before* it.

Take the last figure—CD is much larger than the mirror A; but the head of the arrow C is reflected obliquely behind the mirror to G; and the barb D appears at H.—Why? Because line CA=GA, and line DA=HA; also the angle CAB=angle GAB, and angle DAB=HAB.

Q. *Why does the* IMAGE *of any object in* WATER *always appear* INVERTED?

A. Because the *angles of incidence* are always equal to the *angles of reflection.*

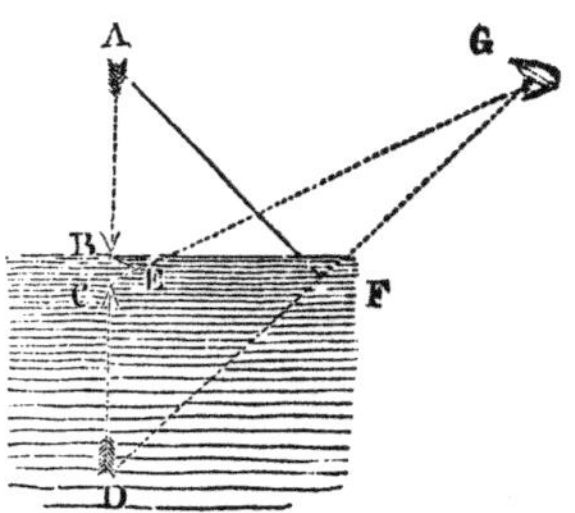

Here the arrow-head A strikes the water at F, and is reflected to D; and the barb B strikes the water at E, and is reflected to C.

If a spectator stands at G, he will see the reflected lines CE and DF produced as far as G.

It is very plain, that A (the more *elevated* object) will strike the water, and be projected from it more perpendicularly than the point B; and, therefore, the image will seem inverted. *See p.* 345.

Q. *When we see our* REFLECTION *in* WATER, *why do we seem to* STAND *on our* HEAD?

A. Because the *angles of incidence*

are always equal to the *angles of reflection.*

Suppose our head to be at A, and our feet at B; then the shadow of our head will be seen at D, and the shadow of our feet at C. (*See figure on p.* 346.)

Q. *Why do* WINDOWS *seem to* BLAZE *at* SUN-RISE *and* SUN-SET?

A. Because glass is a good *reflector of light;* and the rays of the sun (striking against the window-glass) are *reflected*, or thrown back.

Q. *Why do* NOT *windows reflect the* NOON-DAY *rays also?*

A. They do, but the reflection is *not seen.*

Q. *Why is the reflection of the* RISING *and* SETTING *sun seen in the window, and* NOT *that of the* NOON-DAY *sun?*

A. Because the rays of the noon-day sun enter the glass *too obliquely* for their reflection to be seen.

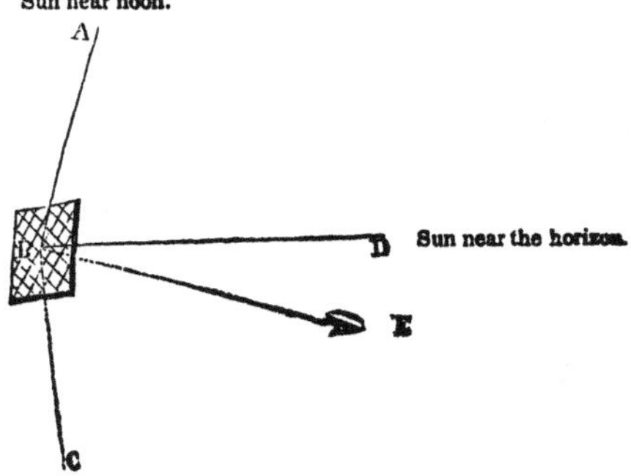

In the preceding cut, AB represents a ray of the noon-day sun striking the window at B; its reflection will be at C.

But DB (a ray of the rising or setting sun) will be reflected to E (the eye of the spectator.)

Q. *Why can we not see the* REFLECTION *of the* SUN *in a* WELL, *during the day-time?*

A. Because the rays of the SUN *fall so obliquely* that they *never reach* the surface of the water at all, but strike against the brick sides.

THE SUN.

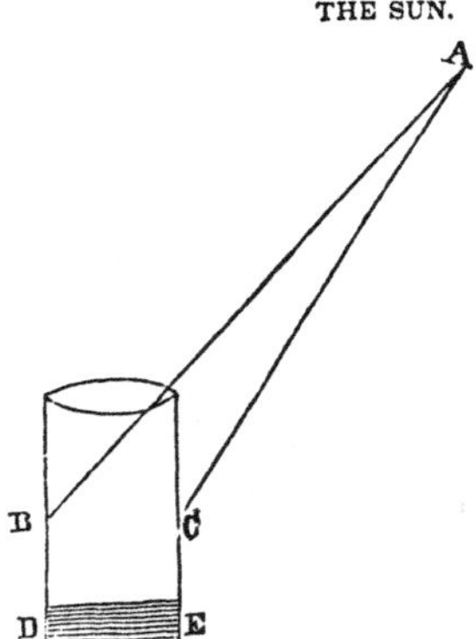

Let BDEC be the well, and DE the water.

The ray AB strikes against the brick-work *inside* the wall; and

The ray AC strikes against the brick-work *outside* the well.

None will ever touch the water DE.

Q. *Why are* STARS REFLECTED *in a* WELL *although the* SUN *is* NOT?

A. Because the rays of those STARS, which pass nearly *over-head*, will not fall so obliquely into the well as the rays of the sun.

THE MOON OR A STAR.

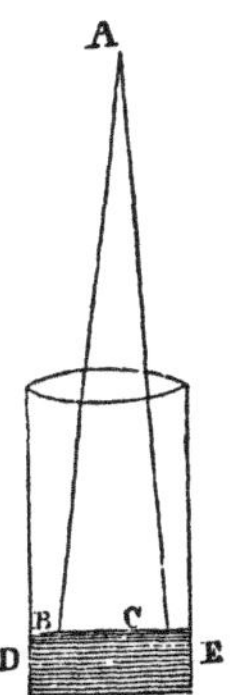

Here the star's rays AB, AC, both strike the water DE, and are reflected by it.

Q. *On a lake of water, the* MOON *seems to make a* PATH *of light towards the eye of the spectator, while all the* REST *of the lake seems* DARK—WHY *is this?*

A. Because the lake is in deep *shadow;* and many rays which would be eclipsed by the broad light of day become visible.

The same *path* of light may be discerned in the day-time, when a *cloud* passes over the sun.

Q. *In a sheet of water at noon, the sun appears to shine upon only* ONE *spot, and all the* REST *of the water seems* DARK—WHY *is this?*

A. Because the rays fall at various degrees of obliquity on the water, and are reflected at *similar angles;* but as only those which *meet the eye of the spectator* are visible, all the water will appear dark except *that one spot.*

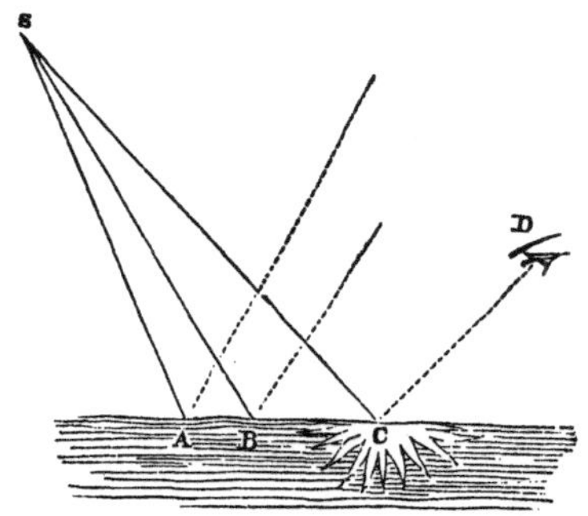

Here, of the rays SA, SB, and SC, only the ray SC meets the eye of the spectator D.
The spot C, therefore, will appear luminous to the spectator D, but no other spot of the water ABC.

Q. *Why are* MORE STARS *visible from a* MOUNTAIN *than from a* PLAIN?

A. Because they have less *air* to pass through. As air *absorbs* and *diminishes* light; therefore, the *higher* we ascend, the *less light* will be absorbed.

Q. *Why do the* SUN *and* MOON *seem* LARGER *at their* RISING *and* SETTING, *than at any other time?*

A. Because the arch of the sky (in which the sun and moon are seen) is further distant at the horizon than it is over-head.

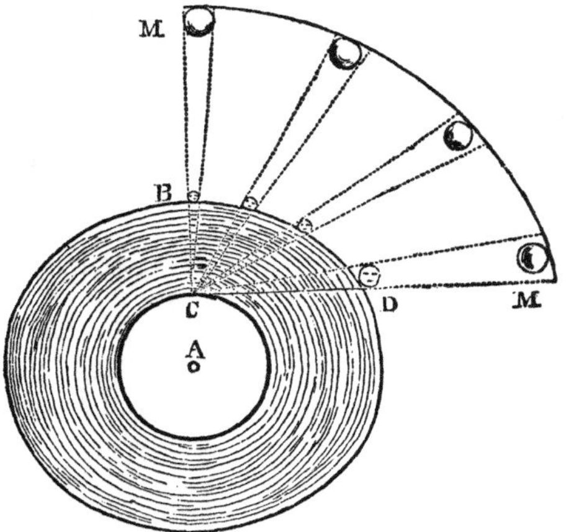

Let MM be the orbit of the sun or moon.

Let BD be the arch of the sky, in which the sun and moon are seen by us.

It will be seen from the figure, that the sun or moon at the horizon will appear much larger, because CD is longer than CB.

The Phenomenon referred to on p. 350, (called the horizontal Sun and Moon), has perplexed philosophers to the present hour. The solution given is not altogether satisfactory—Sir J. Herschell says, "The dilated size of the sun or moon, when seen near the horizon, has nothing to do with *refraction*. It is an illusion of the *judgment*, arising from the terrestrial objects interposed, or placed in comparison with them. Actual measurement with a proper instrument corrects our error, without, however, dispelling our illusion—the whole is owing to the effect of *parallax*."

Q. *Why can we* NOT SEE *into the* STREET *or road, when* CANDLES *are* LIGHTED ?

A. 1st—Because glass is a reflector, and throws the candle-light *back into the room* again : and

2dly—The pupil of the eye (having become *contracted* by the light of the room) is *too small* to collect rays enough from the dark street to enable us to *see into it.*

Q. *Why do we often see the* FIRE REFLECTED *in our parlor* WINDOW *in winter-time ?*

A. Because glass is a *good reflector ;* and the rays of the fire (striking against the window-glass) *are reflected back into the room again.*

Q. *Why do we often see the image of our* CANDLES *in the window, while we are sitting in our parlor ?*

A. Because the rays of the candle (striking against the glass) are *reflected back into the room ;* and the *darker* the night, the *clearer* the reflection.

Q. WHY *is this reflection more clear, if the external* AIR *be* DARK ?

A. Because the reflection is not *eclipsed* by the brighter rays of the sun *striking on the other side of the window.*

Q. *If the* SHADOW *of an object be thrown on a wall—the* CLOSER *the object is held to the* CANDLE, *the* LARGER *will be its* SHADOW. *Why is this ?*

A. Because the rays of light *diverge* (from the flame of a candle) *in straight lines* like lines drawn from the centre of a circle.

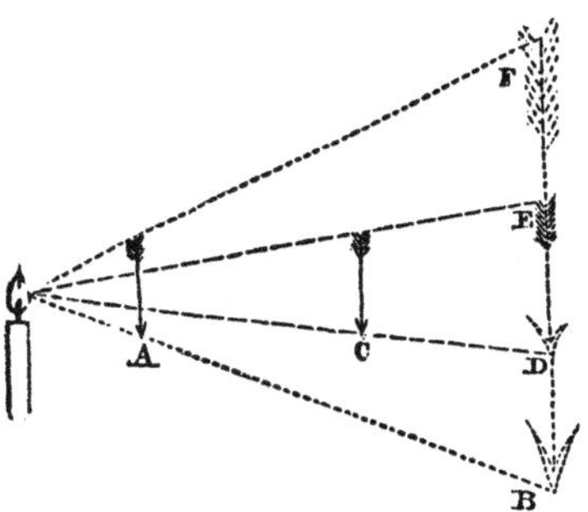

Here the arrow A held close to the candle, will cast the shadow BF on a wall; while the same arrow held at C would cast only the little shadow DE.

Q. *When we enter a long* AVENUE *of* TREES, WHY *does the avenue seem to get* NARROWER *and narrower till the two sides appear to* MEET?

A. Because the *further the trees are off*, the more *acute will be the angle* that any opposite two make with our eye.

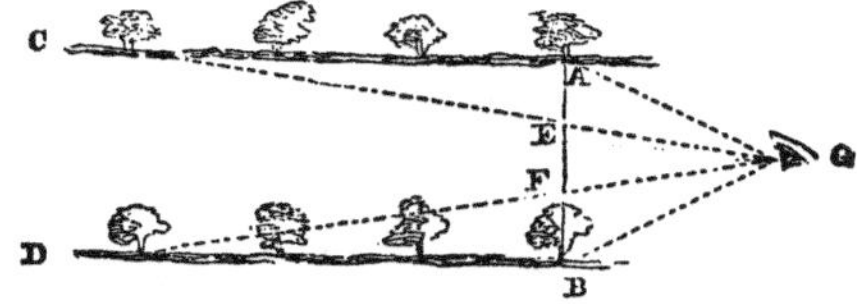

Here the width between the trees A and B will seem to be as great as the line AB:

But the width between the trees C and D will seem to be no more than EF.

Q. *In a long, straight* STREET, WHY *do the houses on the opposite sides seem to* APPROACH NEARER *together as they are more* DISTANT?

A. Because the more *distant the houses* are the more *acute will be the angle* which any opposite two make with our eye.

Thus in the last figure,

If A and B were two houses at the *top* of the street, the street would seem to be as wide as the line AB:

And if C and D were two houses at the *bottom* of the street, the street there would seem to be no wider than EF.

Q. *In an* AVENUE, WHY *do the* TREES *seem to be* SMALLER *as their distance increases?*

A. Because the *further the trees are off*, the more *acute will be the angle* made by their perpendicular height with our eye.

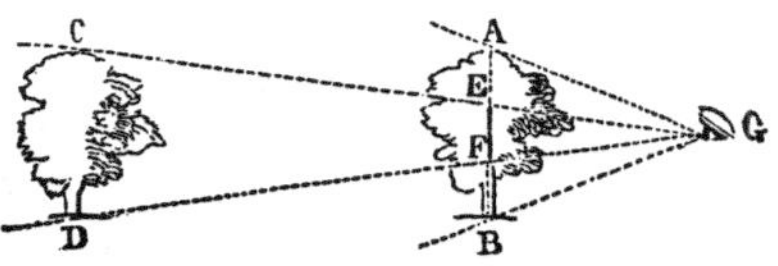

Here the first tree AB will appear the height of the line AB; but the last tree CD will appear only as high as the line EF.

Q. *In a long, straight* STREET, WHY *do the houses seem to be* SMALLER *and smaller, the* FURTHER *they are* OFF?

A. Because the *further any house is off*, the more *acute will be the angle* made by its perpendicular height with our eye.

Thus in the last figure,

If AB be a house at the top of the street, its perpendicular height will be that of the line AB.

If CD be a house at the bottom of the street, its perpendicular height will appear to be that of EF.

Q. *Why does a man on the* TOP *of a* MOUNTAIN, *or church spire, seem to be no* BIGGER *than a* CROW?

A. Because the angle made in our eye by the *perpendicular height of the man* at that distance, is no bigger than that made by a *crow close by.*

Let AB be a man on a distant mountain, or spire, and CD a crow close by:

The man will appear only as high as the line CD, which is the height of the crow.

Q. *Why does the* MOON *appear to us so much* LARGER *than the* STARS, *though, in fact, it is a great deal* SMALLER?

A. Because the moon is *very much nearer to us* than any of the stars.

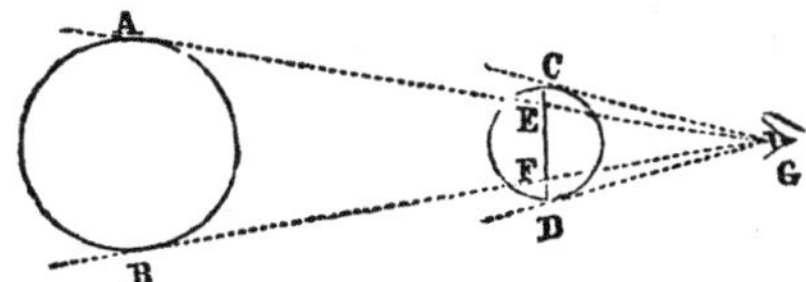

Let AB represent a fixed star, and CD the moon.

AB, though much the larger body, will appear no bigger than EF; whereas the moon (CD) will appear as large as the line CD to the spectator G.

The moon is 240,000 miles from the earth, not quite a quarter of a *million* of miles. The nearest fixed stars are 20,000,000,000,000. (i. e., 20 billions.)

If a ball went 500 miles an hour, it would reach the moon in twenty days: but it would not reach the nearest fixed star in 4,500,000 years. Had it begun, therefore, when Adam was created, it would be no further on its journey than a coach (which has to go from the Land's End, Cornwall, to the most northern parts of Scotland) after it has passed about three-quarters of a mile.

Q. *Why does the* MOON *(which is a sphere)* APPEAR *to be a* FLAT *surface?*

A. Because it is *so far off* that we cannot distinguish any difference between the *length of the rays* issuing from the *edge* and those which issue from the *centre.*

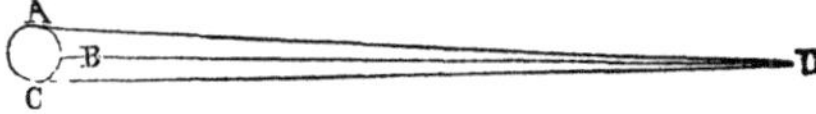

The rays AD and CD appear to be no longer than the ray BD; but if all the rays seem of the same length, the part B will not seem to be *nearer* to us than A and C; and therefore ABC will look like a flat or straight line.

The rays AD and CD are 240,000 miles long.

The ray BD is 238,910 miles long.

Q. *Why do the* SUN *and* STARS *(which are spheres) appear to be* FLAT *surfaces?*

A. Because they are such an *immense way off*, that we can discern *no difference of length* between the rays which issue from the *edge* and those which issue from the *centre* of these bodies.

The rays AD and CD appear no longer than BD; and as B appears to be no nearer than A or C, therefore A, B, C, must all seem equally distant; and ABC will seem a flat or straight line. (*See last figure, p.* 356.)

Q. *Why does* DISTANCE *make an object* INVISIBLE?

A. Because no visible perpendicular can be inserted between the lines which form the angle; or because the lines actually cross before they meet our eye.

Here the tree AD would not be visible to the spectator C, even if he were to approach as far as B; because no visible perpendicular can be inserted between the two lines AC, DC, at the point B, and after B the lines would cross: Therefore, the tree would be invisible from C, till after the spectator had passed B.

Q. *Why do* TELESCOPES *enable us to* SEE *objects* INVISIBLE *to the naked eye?*

A. Because they gather together more luminous rays from obscure objects than the *eye* can; and form a bright image of them in the tube of the telescope where they are magnified.

As many times as the dimensions of the *object-glass* exceed the dimensions of the *pupil of the eye*, so many times the penetrating *powers* of the telescope will exceed that of the naked eye.

Q. *When a* SHIP *(out at sea) is approaching the shore, why do we* SEE *the small* MASTS *before we see the bulky* HULL ?

A. Because the *earth is round;* and the *curve* of the sea *hides the hull* from our eyes after the tall *masts* have become visible.

Here, only that part of the ship above the line AG can be seen by the spectator A; the rest of the ship is hidden by the swell of the curve DE.

Q. *What is meant by* REFRACTION ?

A. *Bending* a *ray of light*, as it passes from one medium to another.

Q. How *is a ray of light* BENT, *as it passes from one medium to another ?*

A. When a ray of light passes into a *denser* medium it is bent *towards* the perpendicular. When it passes into a *rarer* medium it is bent *from* the perpendicular.

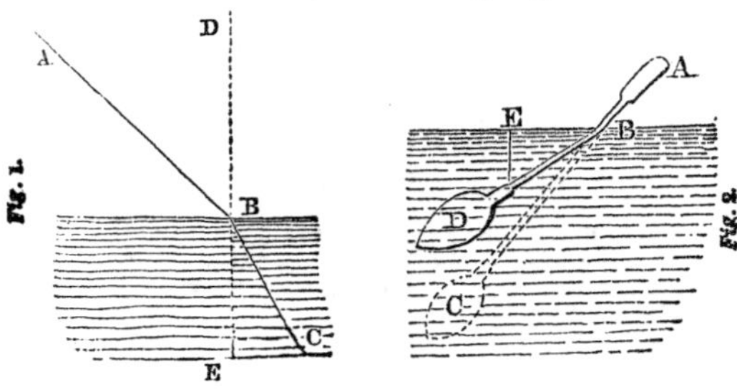

Suppose DE to be a perpendicular line.

If AB (a ray of light) enters the water, it will be bent *towards* the perpendicular to C.

If (on the other hand) CB (a ray of light) emerges *from* the water, it would be bent *away from* the perpendicular towards A.

Q. *Why does a* SPOON *(in a glass of water) always appear* BENT?

A. Because the light (reflected from the spoon) is *refracted* as it *emerges from the water.*

See Fig. 2, *p.* 358. The spoon ABC will appear bent, like ABD.

Q. *Why does a river always appear more shallow than it really is?*

A. Because the light of the bottom of the river is REFRACTED, as it emerges out of the water.

See Fig. 2, *p.* 358. The bottom of the river will appear elevated like the bowl of the spoon D.

Q. *How much deeper is a river than it seems to be?*

A. About one-third. If, therefore, a river seems only 4 feet deep, it is really 6 feet deep.

The exact apparent depth would be 4½. To find the real depth, multiply by 4 and divide by 3—thus $4\frac{1}{2} \times 4 \div 3 = 6$, real depth.

N. B. Many boys get out of their depth in bathing, in consequence of this deception. Remember, a river is always one-third deeper than it appears to be:—thus, if a river seems to be 4 feet deep, it is in reality nearly 6 feet deep, and so on.

Q. *Why do fishes seem to be nearer the surface of a river than they really are?*

A. Because the rays of light from the fish are *refracted*, as they emerge from the eye: and (as a bent stick is not so far from end to end, as a straight one) so the fishes appear nearer to our eye than they really are.

See Fig. 2, *p.* 358.

Q. *Why are some persons* NEAR-SIGHTED?

A. Because the COR'NEA of their eye is so *prominent*, that the image of distant objects is formed *before it reaches the* RET'INA; and, therefore, is not distinctly seen.

Q. *What is meant by the* "COR'NEA *of the* EYE?"

A. All the *outside* of the visible part of the *eye-ball.*

The curve ABC is called the COR'-NEA.

If this curve be too prominent (or convex), the eye is near-sighted.

If too flat (or concave), the eye is far-sighted.

Q. *What is meant by the* "RET'INA *of the* EYE?"

A. The net-work, which lines the *back of the eye*, is called the ret'ina.

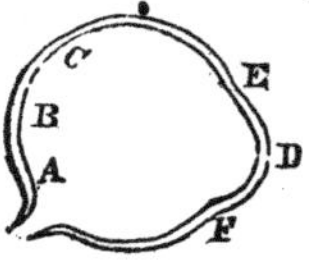

The net-work ABC is called the ret'-ina, and the projecting part DEF is called the cor'nea.

N. B. This net-work is composed of a spreading out of the fibres of the nerve of vision.

Q. *What sort of* GLASSES *do* NEAR-SIGHTED *persons wear?*

A. If the cornea be *too convex* (or projecting), the person must wear double *concave glasses*, to counteract it.

Q. *What is meant by* "DOUBLE CONCAVE GLASSES?"

A. Glasses hollowed-in *on both sides.*

A The figure A is double concave, or concave on both sides.

Q. *Where is the* IMAGE *of objects formed, if the cornea be too convex?*

A. If the cor'nea be *too convex*, the image of a distant object is formed in the *vitreous humors* of the eye, and not on the *ret'ina.*

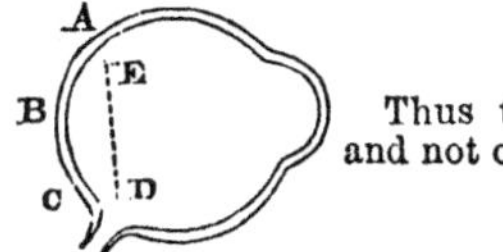

Thus the image is formed at DE, and not on ABC (the retina).

Q. *What is the use of* DOUBLE CONVEX SPECTACLE *glasses?*

A. To *cast the image further back*, in order that it may be thrown upon the ret'ina and become visible.

Q. *Why are* OLD *people* FAR-SIGHTED?

A. Because the humors of their eyes are *dried up by age;* in consequence of which, the COR'NEA *sinks in*, or becomes flattened.

Q. *Why does the* FLATTENING *of the* COR'NEA *prevent persons seeing objects which are* NEAR?

A. Because the cor'nea is *too flat*, and the image of near objects is not *completely* formed, when their rays reach the RET'INA; in consequence of which, the image is imperfect and confused.

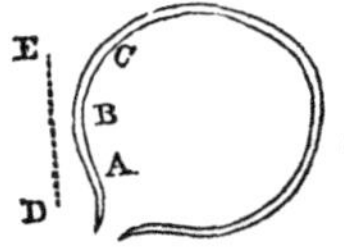

The perfect image is made at DE; and not on ABC (the retina).

Q. *What sort of* GLASSES *do* OLD *people* WEAR?

A. As their cor'nea is *not sufficiently convex*, they must use *double convex glasses*, to enable them to see objects near at hand.

Q. *What sort of glasses are* "DOUBLE CONVEX SPECTACLE-GLASSES?"

A. Glasses which *curve outwards* on both sides.

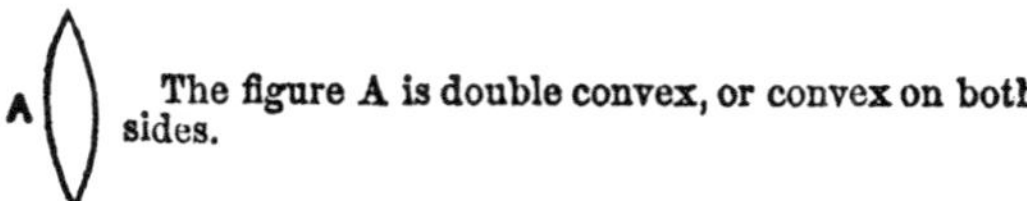

The figure A is double convex, or convex on both sides.

Q. *What is the use of* DOUBLE CONVEX *spectacle-glasses?*

A. To *shorten the focus of the eye,*

and bring the image of distant objects upon the ret'ina.

Q. *Why do* NEAR-SIGHTED *persons bring objects* CLOSE *to the eye, in order to* SEE THEM?

A. Because the distance between the *front and back of the eye is so great*, that the image of distant objects is formed in *front* of the *ret'ina;* but when objects are brought *near to the eye*, their image is thrown *further back*, and made to fall on the ret'ina.

Q. *Why do* OLD *people* HOLD *objects* FAR OFF, *in order to see them better?*

A. Because the distance between the *front and back of their eyes is not great enough:* when, however, objects are held further off, it compensates for this defect; and a perfect image is formed on the ret'ina.

Q. *Why are* HAWKS *able to see such an* IMMENSE *way off?*

A. Because they have a muscle in the eye which enables them to *flatten their cor'nea*, by drawing back the crystalline lens. *See p.* 362.

This muscle is called the Marsupium.

Q. *Why can* HAWKS *see objects within half-an-inch of their eye, as well as those a long way off?*

A. Because their eyes are furnished with a flexible bony rim, which throws the *cornea forward*, and makes the hawk *near-sighted.* *See p.* 360.

Q. *Into how many* PARTS *may a* RAY *of* LIGHT *be* DIVIDED?

A. Into three parts: BLUE, YELLOW, and RED.

N. B. These three colors, by combination, make seven. 1.—RED. 2.—ORANGE (or red and yellow). 3.—YELLOW. 4.—GREEN (or yellow and blue). 5.—BLUE. 6.—INDIGO (a shade of blue); and 7.—VIOLET (or blue and red).

Q. *How is it known, that a ray of light consists of several different colors?*

A. Because, if a ray of light be cast upon a triangular piece of glass (called a prism), it will be distinctly divided into seven colors: 1.—Red; 2.—Orange; 3.—Yellow; 4.—Green; 5.—Blue; 6.—Indigo; and 7.—Violet.

Q. *Why does a* PRISM DIVIDE *a ray of light into* VARIOUS COLORS?

A. Because all these colors have *different refractive susceptibilities.* Red is refracted *least*, and blue the *most;* therefore, the *blue* color of the ray will be bent to the *top* of the prism, and the *red* will remain at the *bottom.*

Here the ray AB (received on a prism at B), would

have the blue part bent up to C; the yellow part to D: and the red part no further than E.

Q. *What is meant by the* REFRACTION *of a ray?*

A. *Bending it* from its straight line.

Thus the ray AB of the last figure is refracted at B into three courses, C, D, and E.

Q. *What is the cause of a* RAINBOW?

A. When the clouds opposite the sun *are very dark,* and rain is *still falling* from them, the rays of the bright sun *are divided by the rain-drops,* as they would be by a prism.

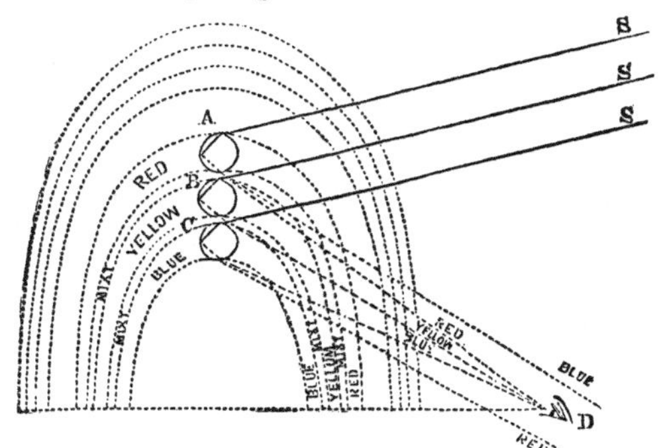

Let A, B, and C, be three drops of rain; SA, SB, and SC, three rays of the sun. SA is divided into three colors; the blue and yellow are bent *above* the eye D, and the *red* enters it.

The ray SB is divided into the three colors; the blue is bent *above* the eye, and the red falls *below* the eye D; but the *yellow* enters it.

The ray SC is also divided into the three colors. The blue (which is bent most) enters the eye; and the other two fall below it. Thus the eye sees the blue of C, and of all drops in the position of C; the yellow of B, and of all drops in the position of B; and the red of A, and of all drops in the position of A; and thus it sees a rainbow.

Q. *Does* EVERY *person see the* SAME *colors from the* SAME DROPS?

A. No; *no two persons* see the *same rainbow.*

To another spectator, the rays from SB might be *red* instead of yellow; the ray from SC yellow; and the blue might be reflected from some drop below C. To a *third* person, the red may issue from a drop above A, and then A would reflect the yellow, and B the blue, and so on.

Q. *Why are there often* TWO RAINBOWS *at one and the same time?*

A. In *one* rainbow we see the rays of the sun *entering the rain-drops at the top,* and reflected to the eye *from the bottom.*

In the *other* rainbow, we see the rays of the sun *entering the rain-drops at the bottom,* and reflected to the top, whence they reach the eye.

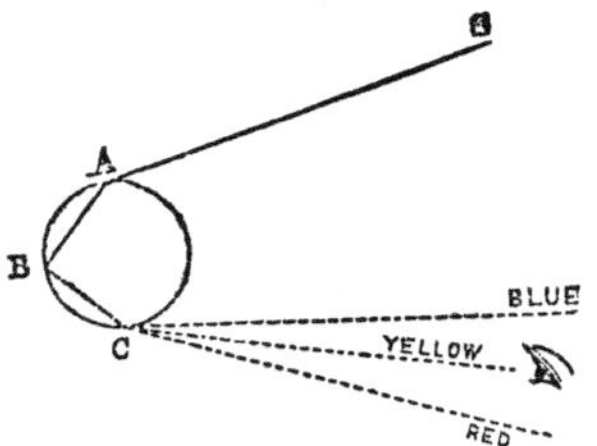

Here the ray SA (of the primary rainbow) strikes the drop at A—is refracted or bent to B—is then reflected

to C, where it is refracted again, and reaches the eye **of the** spectator. (*See below.*)

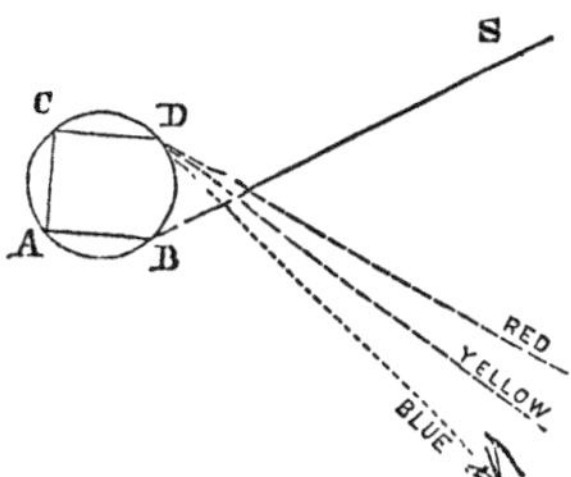

Here the ray of SB (of the secondary rainbow) strikes the drop at B—is refracted to A—is then reflected to C—is again reflected to D, when it is again refracted or bent, till it reaches the eye of the spectator.

Q. *Why are the* COLORS *of the* SECOND *bow all* REVERSED?

A. Because in *one* bow we see the rays, which enter at the *top* of the rain-drops, *refracted from the bottom:*

But in the *other* bow we see the rays which enter at the *bottom* of the rain-drops (after two reflections), *refracted from the top.*

See figure on next page.

Here ABC represent three drops of rain in the SECONDARY (or upper) RAINBOW.

The *least* refracted line is RED, and BLUE the *most.*

So the RED (or *least* refracted rays) of all the drops in the position of A—the YELLOW of those in the position of B—and the BLUE (or the *most* refracted rays) of the lowest drops, all meet the eye D, and form a rainbow to the spectator.

The reason why the primary bow exhibits the stronger colors is this—because the colors are seen after *one* reflec-

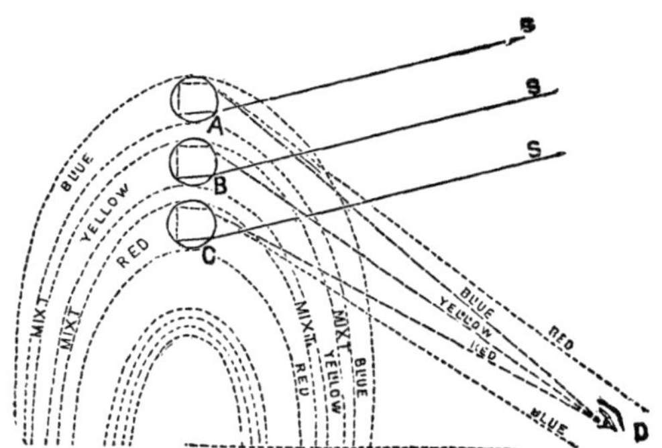

tion and *two* refractions; but the colors of the secondary (or upper) rainbow, undergo *two* reflections and *two* refractions.

(*See figure on p.* 365.) Here also the *least* refracted ray is RED, and the *most* refracted BLUE (as in the former case); but the position of each is reversed.

Q. *Why does a* SOAP BUBBLE *exhibit such a* VARIETY *of* COLORS?

A. Because the *thickness of the film* through which the rays pass, is constantly varying.

Q. *How does the* THICKNESS *of the* FILM *affect the* COLOR *of the soap bubble?*

A. Because different *degrees of thickness* in the film produce different *powers of refraction;* and, therefore, as the *thickness* of the film varies, different colors reach the eye.

Q. *Why is a* SOAP BUBBLE *so constantly* CHANGING *its* THICKNESS?

A. Because the water *runs down from the top* to the bottom of the bubble, till the crown becomes so *thin* as to burst.

Q. *Why are the late* EVENING CLOUDS RED?

A. Because RED rays, being the *least refrangible*, are the *last* to disappear.

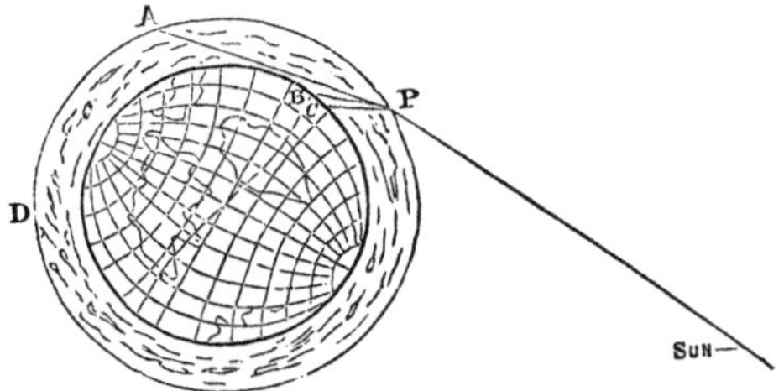

Suppose PA to be a red ray, PB yellow, and PC blue—if the earth turns in the direction of CBD, it is quite manifest that a spectator standing at C or B (carried round in the same direction), would lose sight of the red rays (A) last of all.

Q. *Why are the early* MORNING *clouds* RED?

A. Because RED rays being the *least refrangible* are the *first* to appear.

See last figure.—We must suppose the sun to be on the left side of the diagram—or (what will answer the same purpose) suppose the earth to be turning in the direction of DAP, then it is quite clear, that every person on the earth's surface will pass under A (the red rays) before he passes under B or C, (and therefore his early morning rays will be red.)

Q. *Why are the* EDGES *of* CLOUDS *more* LUMINOUS *than their* CENTRES?

A. Because the *body of vapor* is *thinnest* at the edges of the clouds.

Q. *What is the cause of morning and evening* TWILIGHT?

A. When the sun is below the horizon, the rays which strike upon the atmosphere or clouds are *bent down towards the earth*, and produce a little light called twilight.

See figure on p. 369.—Here the rays of PA will give *some* light.

Q. WHY *is a ray of* LIGHT *composed of* VARIOUS COLORS?

A. To vary the color of different objects. If solar light were of *one color only*, all objects would appear of *that one color*, or else black.

Q. *Some things are of* ONE COLOR, *and some of* ANOTHER. *Explain the cause of this.*

A. As every ray of light is composed of all the colors of the rainbow; *some* things reflect *one of these colors* and some *another*.

Q. WHY *do some things reflect* ONE COLOR, *and some* ANOTHER?

A. Because the *surface* of things is so *differently constructed*, both physically and chemically.

Q. *Why is a* ROSE RED?

A. Because the surface of a rose *ab-*

sorbs the *blue* and *yellow* rays of light, and *reflects* only the *red.*

Q. *Why is a* VIOLET BLUE?

A. Because the surface of the violet *absorbs* the *red* and *yellow* rays of the sun, and *reflects* the *blue* only.

Q. *Why is a* PRIMROSE YELLOW?

A. Because the surface of the primrose *absorbs* the *blue* and *red* rays of solar light, and *reflects* the *yellow.*

The chief reason why some rays are *absorbed* and others *reflected* is, because the *corpuscles* which compose the colored substance vary in magnitude:—thus, for example, if the diameter of a corpuscle of equal density with air be 21 millionth of an inch, it will reflect purple; if, on the other hand, it be 29 millionth of an inch, it will reflect red, and so on.

Q. *Why are some things* BLACK?

A. Because they *absorb all the rays* of light and reflect *none.*

Q. *Why are some things* WHITE?

A. Because they *absorb none of the rays* of light, but reflect them all.

Q. *Why are* COALS BLACK?

A. Because they *absorb all the rays of the sun* which impinge upon them.

Q. *Why are* FROTH, *and* SPRAY, *and many* CLOUDS, WHITE?

A. Because they consist of an infinite number of small bubbles or vesicles, which act like *prisms* in dividing the rays of light; which, by *uniting* again before they meet the eye, give the appearance of white.

Q. *Why are* SNOW, SUGAR, *and* SALT WHITE?

A. (See page 312.)

N. B. The combination of *all* colors makes WHITE.

Q. *Why are the* LEAVES *of plants* GREEN?

A. Because a peculiar chemical principle, called chlo'rophyll, is formed within their *cells;* which has the property of absorbing the *red* rays and of reflecting the blue and yellow; which mixture produces *green.*

Chlorophyll (χλωρον φυλλον, a green leaf) is the green matter of vegetable substances. *Pronounce* klo-ro-fill.

Q. *Why are leaves a* LIGHT *green in* SPRING?

A. Because the chlo'rophyll is not fully formed.

Q. *Why do leaves turn* BROWN *in* AUTUMN?

A. Because the chlo'rophyll undergoes *decay,* and is not replaced as it is in spring.

Q. *Why are plants a* PALE YELLOW, *when kept in the* DARK?

A. Because chlo'rophyll can be formed only by the agency of the *sun's rays.*

Q. *Why are* POTATOES YELLOW?

A. Because they are grown *underground;* and, therefore, can form no chlo rophyll in their tubers.

Q. *Why are potatoes which grow* EXPOSED *to the air and light* GREEN?

A. Because chlo'rophyll is formed in them under the influence of the sun's light.

Q. *Why are* SOME *things* TRANSPARENT?

A. Because every part between the two surfaces has a *uniform refracting* power, or (in other words) has in every place the same density.

And, therefore, the rays of light *emerge* on the opposite side.

Q. *Why are some things* NOT TRANSPARENT?

A. Because the particles which compose them are separated by minute *pores* or *spaces,* which have a different density from the particles themselves.

Therefore, the rays of light are reflected and refracted too often to emerge.

Q. *Why are* DRY PAPER *and calico* (*which are* OPAQUE) *made transparent by being* OILED?

A. Because the pores are filled by the oil, which has nearly the same density as the substance of the paper itself —by which means a uniform density is effected, and the substance becomes transparent.

Q. *Why is* GLASS (*which is transparent*) *rendered* OPAQUE *by being ground or pulverized?*

A. Because the whole substance

from surface to surface is no longer of one uniform density.

Q. *Why are* SOME *things* SHINING, *and others* DULL?

A. Because some things *reflect* rays, and are *bright;* but others *absorb* them.

Q. *Why do* DESERTS DAZZLE *from sunshine?*

A. Because each grain of sand *reflects the rays of the sun* like a mirror.

Q. *If you move a stick (burnt at one end) pretty briskly* AROUND, *it seems to make a* CIRCLE OF FIRE—WHY *is this?*

A. Because the eye *retains the image* of any bright object, *after the object itself is withdrawn;* and as the spark of the stick returns *before the image has faded* from the eye, it seems to form a *complete circle.*

Q. *If separate figures (as a man and a horse) be drawn on separate sides of a card, and the card* TWISTED *quickly, the man will seem to be seated on the horse*—WHY *is this?*

A. Because the image of the horse *remains upon the eye* till the *man* appears.

The Thaumatrope is constructed on this principle.

Q. *Why do the* STARS TWINKLE?

A. Because the inequalities and undulations in the atmosphere produce *unequal refractions of light;* and these unequal refractions cause the *twinkling* or irregular brilliancy of the stars.

Q. *If we look at a* RED-HOT FIRE *for a few minutes,* WHY *does every thing seem* TINGED *with a* BLUISH GREEN *color?*

A. Because bluish green is the "ACCIDENTAL COLOR" of red; and if we fix our eye upon *any color whatsoever*, we see every object tinged with its *accidental color* when we turn aside.

The *accidental color* is the color which would be required to be added, in order to make up *white* light. *See p.* 360.

Q. *Why does the eye perceive the* ACCIDENTAL COLOR *when the fundamental one is removed?*

A. Because the nerve of the eye has become tired of the one, but still remains fresh for the perception of the *other*.

Q. *If we wear* BLUE GLASSES, *why does every thing appear tinged with* ORANGE *when we take them off?*

A. Because *orange* is the "*accidental color*" of blue; and if we look through *blue glasses*, we shall see its "*accidental color*" when we lay our glasses aside.

Q. *If we look at the* SUN *for a few moments, every thing seems tinged with a* VIOLET *color*—WHY *is this?*

A. Because *violet* is the "accidental color" of *yellow;* and as the sun is *yellow*, we shall see its "accidental color" *violet* when we turn from gazing at it.

Q. *Does not the* DARK SHADOW (*which seems to hang over every thing after we turn from looking at the sun*) *arise from our eyes being* DAZZLED ?

A. Partly so: the pupil of the eye is *very much contracted* by the brilliant light of the sun, and does not adjust itself immediately to the feebler light of terrestrial objects; but, independent of this, the "ACCIDENTAL COLOR" of the sun being *dark violet*, would tend to throw a shadow upon all things. (*See p.* 340.)

Q. *Why is* BLACK *glass for spectacles the* BEST *for wear in this respect?*

A. Because *white* is the accidental color of *black;* and if we wear *black glasses*, every thing will appear *in white light* when we take them off.

Q. *Why does every thing seem shadowed with a* BLACK MIST *when we take off our common* SPECTACLES ?

A. Because the glasses are *white;* and black being its "accidental color," every thing appears in a *black shade* when we lay our glasses down.

The accidental color of red is bluish green.
" " " of orange " blue.
" " " of violet " yellow.
" " " of black " white.

And the converse of this is true:—

The accidental color of bluish green is red.
" " " of blue " orange.
" " " of yellow " violet.
" " " of white " black.

(The law of an accidental color is this—The accidental color is always half the spectrum. Thus, if we take half the length of the spectrum by a pair of compasses, and fix one leg in any color, the other leg will hit upon its accidental color.)

N. B. The spectrum means the seven colors (red, orange, yellow, green, blue, indigo, and violet), divided into seven *equal* bands, and placed side by side in the order just mentioned.

SOUND.

CHAPTER XXX.

Q. *How is* SOUND *produced?*

A. The vibration of some sonorous substance produces motion in the air, called SOUND-WAVES, which strike upon the *drum of the ear* and give the sensation of sound.

Q. *What are* MUSICAL SOUNDS?

A. Regular and uniform successions of vibrations.

Q. *How* FAST *does* SOUND TRAVEL?

A. About 13 miles in a minute, or 1142 feet in a second of time.

Light would go 480 times round the whole earth, while sound is going its 13 miles.

Q. *Why are* SOME *things* SONOROUS *and others* NOT?

A. The sonorous quality of any substance depends upon its *hardness and elasticity*.

Q. *Why are* COPPER *and* IRON SONOROUS *and not* LEAD?

A. Copper and iron are *hard and elastic;* but as lead is neither hard nor yet elastic, it is *not sonorous.*

Q. *Of what is* BELL-METAL *made?*

A. Of *copper and tin* in the following proportions:—In every 5 pounds of bell-metal there should be 1 pound of tin, and 4 pounds of copper.

Q. *Why is this mixture of tin and copper used for* BELL-METAL?

A. Because it is much *harder* and more *elastic* than any of the pure metals.

Q. *Why is the* SOUND *of a bell* STOPPED *by* TOUCHING *the bell with our finger?*

A. Because the weight of our finger *stops the vibrations* of the bell; and as soon as the bell *ceases to vibrate*, it ceases to make sound-waves in the air.

Q. *Why does a* SPLIT BELL *make a hoarse, disagreeable sound?*

A. Because the *split* of the bell causes a *double vibration:* And as the sound-waves *clash and jar*, they impede each other's motion, and produce discordant sounds.

Q. *Why does a* FIDDLE-STRING *give a musical sound?*

A. Because the bow drawn across the string *causes it to vibrate;* and this vibration of the string *sets in motion the sound-waves of the air*, and produces musical notes.

Q. *Why does a* DRUM *sound?*

A. Because the parchment head of the drum *vibrates* from the blow of the drum-stick, and sets in motion the sound-waves of the air.

Q. *Why do* MUSICAL GLASSES *give sounds?*

A. Because the glasses *vibrate* as soon as they are struck, and set in motion the sound-waves of the air.

Q. *Why do* FLUTES, *&c., produce musical sounds?*

A. Because the breath of the performer causes the *air in the flute* to *vibrate;* and this vibration sets in motion the sound-waves of the air.

Q. *Why do* PIANO-FORTES *produce musical sounds?*

A. Because each *key of the piano* (being struck with the finger) lifts up a little hammer which *knocks against a string;* and the vibration thus produced sets in motion the sound-waves of the air

Q. *Why are* SOME *notes* BASS, *and some* TREBLE?

A. Because *slow* vibrations produce *bass or deep sounds;* but *quick* vibrations produce *shrill or treble ones.*

Q. *Why is an instrument* FLAT *when the* STRINGS *are* UNSTRUNG?

A. Because the vibrations are *too slow;* in consequence of which, the sounds produced are not *shrill* or *sharp* enough.

Q. *Why can persons, living a mile or two from a town,* HEAR *the* BELLS *of the town churches* SOMETIMES *and not at* OTHERS?

A. Because fogs, rain, and snow, obstruct the passage of sound; but when the air is *cold and clear*, sound is propagated more easily.

Q. WHY *can we* NOT *hear sounds (as those of distant church bells) in* RAINY *weather so well as in* FINE *weather?*

A. Because the falling rain *interferes with the undulations of the sound-waves*, and breaks them up.

Q. *Why can we not hear sounds (as those of distant church bells) in* SNOWY *weather so well as in* FINE *weather?*

A. Because the falling snow *interferes with the undulations of the sound-waves*, and stops their progress.

Q. *Why can we* HEAR *distant clocks* MOST *distinctly in* CLEAR COLD *weather?*

A. Because the air is of more *uniform density*, and there are fewer *currents of air* of unequal temperature to interrupt the sound-waves.

Besides, dense air can propagate sound-waves more readily than rarer air.

Q. *Why can persons (near the* POLES*) hear the* VOICES *of men in conversation for a* MILE *distant in winter-time?*

A. Because the air is very *cold, clear,* and *still;* in consequence of which, there are but few *currents of air* of unequal temperature to interrupt the sound-waves.

Captain Ross heard the voices of his men in conversation a mile and a half from the spot where they stood.

Q. *Why are not* SOUNDS *(such as those of distant church bells) heard so distinctly on a* HOT DAY *as in* FROSTY *weather?*

A. 1st—Because the density of the air is *less uniform* in very hot weather:

2dly—It is *more rarefied;* and, consequently, a worse conductor of sound: and

3dly—It is more liable to *accidental currents,* which impede the progress of sound.

Q. *Why can we not hear* SOUNDS *(such as those of distant clocks) so distinctly in a thick* MIST *or* HAZE *as in a* CLEAR *night?*

A. Because the air is not of uniform density when it is laden with mist; in consequence of which, the sound-waves are obstructed in their progress.

Q. *Why do we hear* SOUNDS *better by* NIGHT *than by* DAY?

A. 1st—Because night air is of *more*

uniform density and less liable to *accidental currents:* and

2dly—Night is more *still* from the suspension of business and hum of men.

Q. *Why is the air of more* UNIFORM DENSITY *by* NIGHT *than it is by day?*

A. Because it is less liable to accidental currents; inasmuch as the breezes (created by the action of the sun's rays) generally *cease* during the night.

Q. *How should* PARTITION WALLS *be made, to* PREVENT *the voices in adjoining rooms from being* HEARD?

A. The space between the laths should be filled with *shavings* or *saw-dust;* and then no sound would ever pass from one room to another.

Q. *Why would* SHAVINGS, *or saw-dust,* PREVENT *the transmission of sound from room to room?*

A. Because there would be *several different media* for the sound to pass through: 1st—the air; 2dly—the laths and paper; 3dly—the saw-dust or shavings; 4thly—lath and paper again; 5thly—the air again: And every change of medium diminishes the *strength of the sound-waves.*

Q. *Why can* DEAF *people hear through an* EAR-TRUMPET?

A. Because the ear-trumpet restrains

the spread of the voice and limits the *diameter of the sound-waves:* in consequence of which, their *strength* is increased.

Q. *Why are* MOUNTAINS NOISELESS *and quiet?*

A. Because the air of mountains is *very rarefied;* and, as the air becomes *rarefied*, sound becomes less *intense.*

Q. *How do you know that the* RARITY *of air* DIMINISHES *the intensity of* SOUND ?

A. If a bell be rung in the receiver of an air-pump, the sound becomes *fainter and fainter* as the air is exhausted; till at last it is almost *inaudible.*

Q. *What is the cause of* ECHO ?

A. Whenever a sound-wave strikes against any *obstacle* (such as a wall or hill), *it is reflected* (or thrown back); and this *reflected sound* is called an ECHO.

The same laws govern echo as light. (*See p.* 338.)

Q. *What places are most famous for* ECHO ?

A. Caverns, grottoes, and ruined abbeys; the areas of halls; the windings of long passages; the aisles of cathedral churches; mountains and icebergs.

Q. *Why are caverns, grottoes, and ruins,* FAMOUS *for* ECHOES ?

A. 1st—Because the sound-waves cannot pass *beyond* the cavern or grotto, and, therefore, *must flow back:* and

2dly—The *return-waves* (being entangled by the cavern) are *detained* for a short time, and come *deliberately* to the ear.

Q. *Why are halls, winding passages, and cathedral aisles,* FAMOUS *for* ECHOES?

A. Because the sound-waves *cannot flow freely forward;* but perpetually strike against the winding walls, and are beaten *back.*

Q. *Why are* MOUNTAINS *and icebergs* FAMOUS *for* ECHOES?

A. Because they present a *barrier* to the sound-waves, *which they cannot pass,* and are sufficiently elastic to *throw them back.*

Q. *Why do not the* WALLS *of a* ROOM *or church produce* ECHO?

A. Because sound travels with such *velocity* that the echo is *blended with the original sound;* and the two produce but *one impression* on the ear.

Sound travels 13 miles in a minute; and no echo is heard, unless the surface (against which the sound strikes) is 65 feet from the place whence the sound originally proceeded.

Q. *Why do very* LARGE *buildings (as cathedrals) often* REVERBERATE *the voice of the speaker?*

A. Because the walls are *so far off from the speaker* that the echo does not *get back in time* to blend with the original sound ; and, therefore, *each* is heard separately.

Q. *Why do* SOME *echoes repeat only* ONE *syllable?*

A. Because the echoing body is very *near*. The *further* the echoing body is off, the *more sound* it will *reflect:* If, therefore, it be very *near*, it will repeat but one syllable.

Q. *Why does an* ECHO *sometimes repeat* TWO *or more syllables?*

A. Because the echoing body is *far off;* and, therefore, there is time for one reflection *to pass away* before *another* reaches the ear.

N. B. All the syllables must be *uttered*, before the echo of the first syllable reaches the ear—If, therefore, a person repeats 7 syllables in 2 seconds of time, and hears them *all* echoed, the reflecting object is 1142 feet distant; (because sound travels 1142 feet in a second, and the words take one second to *go to* the reflecting object, and one second to *return.*)

Q. *Why are* TWO *or more* ECHOES *sometimes heard?*

A. Because separate reverberating surfaces receive the sound and reflect it in succession.

17 miles above Glasgow (Scotland) near a mansion called Rosneath, is a very remarkable echo. If a trumpeter plays a tune and stops, the echo will begin the same tune and repeat it all accurately:—as soon as this echo has ceased, *another* will echo the same tune in a lower tone; and after the second echo has ceased, a *third* will succeed with equal fidelity, though in a much feebler tone.

At the Lake of Kilkarney in IRELAND, there is an echo which plays an excellent "*second*" to any simple tune played on a bugle.

Q. *Why do* WINDOWS RATTLE *when* CARTS *pass by a house?*

A. 1st—Because glass is *sonorous;* and the air communicates its vibrations to the glass, which echoes the same sound: and

2dly—The *window-frame* being *shaken,* contributes to the noise.

Window frames are shaken, 1.—By sound-waves impinging against them; 2.—By a vibratory motion communicated to them by the walls of the house.

PART III.

MISCELLANEOUS.

*** This part is little else than a collection of various questions propounded by different correspondents, pupils, and private friends, set down, without regard to arrangement, in the order in which they were proposed; together with a few leading questions to break up some which would have been otherwise too intricate, and others which naturally arose out of the subject under consideration.

Q. *Why do the* BUBBLES *in a* CUP *of* TEA *range round the* SIDES *of the* CUP?

A. Because the cup *attracts them.*

Q. *Why do all the* LITTLE BUBBLES *tend towards the* LARGE *ones?*

A. Because the large bubbles (being the superior masses) *attract them.*

Q. *Why do the* BUBBLES *of a* CUP OF TEA FOLLOW *a* TEA-SPOON?

A. Because the tea-spoon *attracts them.*

Q. *Why are the* SIDES *of a pond covered with* LEAVES, *while the* MIDDLE *of the pond is quite* CLEAR?

A. Because the shore *attracts* the leaves to itself.

Q. *Why do all fruits, &c., (when severed from the tree,)* FALL *to the* EARTH?

A. Because the earth *attracts them.*

Q. *Why do persons who water* PLANTS *very often pour the water into the* SAUCER, *and not over the* PLANTS?

A. Because the water in the saucer is *drawn up* by the mould (through the hole at the bottom of the flower-pot) and is transferred to the stem and leaves of the plant by CAPILLARY ATTRACTION. (*See p.* 75.)

Q. *Why is vegetation on the* MARGIN *of a* RIVER *more* LUXURIANT *than in an open* FIELD?

A. Because the porous earth on the bank *draws up water* to the roots of the plants by CAPILLARY ATTRACTION.

Q. *Why is a* LUMP *of* SUGAR *(left at the bottom of a cup) so* LONG *in* MELTING?

A. Because (as it melts) it makes the tea above it *heavier;* and (so long as it remains at the bottom) is surrounded by tea fully *saturated* with sugar; in consequence of which, the *same* portions of liquid will hold *no more sugar in solution.*

Q. *Why does the* LUMP *of* SUGAR MELT *more* QUICKLY *when* STIRRED ABOUT?

A. Because *fresh portions of unsatu-*

rated tea come in contact with the lump, and soon dissolve it.

Q. *Why does a* PIECE OF SUGAR *(held in a spoon at the* TOP *of our tea) melt very* RAPIDLY?

A. Because, as the tea becomes *sweetened*, it *descends to the bottom of the cup* by its own gravity; and *fresh* portions of unsweetened tea are brought constantly into contact with the sugar till the lump is entirely dissolved.

Q. *How can a* SICK ROOM *be kept* FREE *from unhealthy* EFFLUVIA?

A. By sprinkling it with vinegar boiled with myrrh or camphor.

Q. *Why does* LIME *destroy the offensive smells of* BINS, SEWERS, *&c.?*

A. Because it decomposes the offensive gases upon which the smell depends, and destroys them.

Q. *Why does* CHLORIDE *of* LIME *fumigate a sick room?*

A. Because the chlorine absorbs the *hydrogen of the stale air;* and by this means removes both the *offensive smell* and the *infection* of a sick room.

Q. *How can the* TAINT *of* MEAT *be removed?*

A. Either by washing with PYROLIGNEOUS ACID—or by covering it for a few hours with common CHARCOAL—or by putting a *few lumps of charcoal* into the *water in which it is boiled.*

Q. *Why do these things* DESTROY *the* TAINT *of meat?*

A. Because they *combine* with the *putrescent particles*, and neutralize their offensive taste and smell.

Q. *Why should* BED-ROOMS, COTTAGES, HOSPITALS, *and* STABLES, *be washed occasionally with* LIME WHITE?

A. Because the lime *is very caustic*, and removes all organic matters adhering to the walls,

Q. *Why will strong* SOUCHONG TEA POISON FLIES?

A. Because it contains *prussic acid*, which destroys their *nervous system.*

Q. *Why is strong* GREEN TEA UNWHOLESOME?

A. Because it contains *prussic acid*, which destroys the *nervous system.*

Q. *Why is a* DEAD *man* TALLER *than a living one?*

A. Because at death the CARTILAGES are *relaxed.* So, also, after a night's rest, a man is *taller* than when he went to bed.

Q. *What is* SLEEP?

A. Sleep is the *rest of the brain* and *nervous system.*

Q. *Why can we not* SEE, *when we are asleep with our* EYES OPEN?

A. Because the "RET INA of the eye" is *inactive* and at rest.

Q. *Why can we not* HEAR *in sleep?*

A. Because the nerve of hearing (seated within the TYMPANUM of the ear) is at rest.

Q. *Why can we not* TASTE *when we are asleep?*

A. Because the nerves *at the end of the tongue* (called papillæ) are inactive and at rest.

Q. *Why can we not* FEEL *when we are asleep?*

A. Because the *ends of the nerves* (called papillæ) situated in the skin, are inactive and at rest.

Q. *Why have persons in sleep no* WILL *of their own, but may be moved at the will of* ANY *one?*

A. Because the "CEREBELLUM" (or *posterior* part of the brain) is inactive and at rest.

Q. *Why have* DREAMERS *no power of* JUDGMENT *or* REASON?

A. Because the "CEREBRUM" (or *front* of the brain) is inactive and at rest.

Q. *Why do some persons* LOSE *all* POWER *of* SENSATION?

A. Because the "CEREBRUM" (or *front* of their brain) *has been injured.*

Q. *Why does a person* FEEL *when he is* TOUCHED?

A. Because the ends of certain

nerves (called "PAPILLÆ") situated in the skin, are *excited;* and produce a nervous sensation called FEELING.

Q. *Why are persons able to* TASTE DIFFERENT FLAVORS?

A. Because the "PAPILLÆ" of the tongue and palate are *excited* when food touches them, and produce a nervous sensation called TASTE.

Q. *Why are* OLD *people* UNABLE *to* WALK?

A. Because their *muscles become rigid.*

Q. *Why does* ABUNDANCE *of* DEW *in the morning indicate, that the day will be* FINE? p. 189.

A. Because dew is never deposited in *dull, cloudy* weather, but only in very *clear, calm* nights; when the cold currents of air are not mixed with those of a warmer temperature.

Q. *Why does an* OAR *in water appear bent?* p. 358.

A. Because the part *out* of the water is seen in a different medium to the part *in* the water; and the rays of these two parts, meeting together at the surface of the river, *form an angle*- -or, in other words, make the oar look as if it were bent.

As all the rays of light are refracted (or bent) more in their passage through *water* than in their passage through *air*, they will tend to cross each other at the surface of the water, and, of course, form an elbow or angle.

Q. *If a piece of* BROWN PAPER *be submitted to the action of a* BURNING GLASS, *it will catch fire much* SOONER *than a piece of white paper would; Explain the reason.* p. 175.

A. Because *white* paper *reflects* the rays of the sun, or throws them back; in consequence of which, it appears more luminous, but is not so much heated, as dark *brown* paper, which *absorbs* the rays and readily becomes heated to ignition.

Besides, brown paper is of a looser and more combustible fabric than white paper.

Q. *Why does a lady's* BLUE DRESS *appear* GREEN *by* CANDLE LIGHT? *pp.* 76, 364.

A. Because the light of a candle is tinged with *yellow;* and this *yellow* tinge, mixing with the *blue* dye of the dress, produces *green.*

Q. *Why does the* SUN *look red in a* FOG? *p.* 127.

A. Because *red* rays have a greater momentum than any other rays; and this superior momentum enables them to penetrate the dense atmosphere more readily than either blue or yellow rays, which are either *absorbed* or *reflected* by the fog.

"Momentum" means, the impetus or *power of penetrating the fog.*

Q. *Why is an* INK-SPOT *on linen* BLACK *when first made?*

A. Because the ink produces a chemical change in the internal condition of the fibres of the linen, by which it loses its power of *reflecting* light; and, as it *absorbs* the rays of the sun, the spot seems *black.*

The *black* color of ink is composed of a compound of Tannic acid, sesqui-oxide of iron, and water.

"Tannic acid" is an acid which exists in oak trees, especially in the bark, but is abundant in nutgalls. It derives its name from its property of combining with the skins of animals and converting them into leather, which is called *tanning* them.

"Sesqui-oxide of iron" means, that *one atom and a half* of oxygen is mixed with one atom of iron.—The amount of oxygen in an oxide is always expressed by some similar affix, thus

Protoxide—1 atom of oxygen
Binoxide—2 atoms of oxygen
Teroxide—3 atoms of oxygen
&c.
} and one of the substance oxidized called the *base.*

Per-oxide—the highest possible degree of oxidation, &c.

Sesqui-oxide—1½ atom of oxygen and 1 of base.

Q. *Why does the black ink-spot on linen turn* YELLOW *after a few days?*

A. Because the compound, which composes the blackness of ink, is destroyed by exposure to air; and the linen partially recovers its power of reflecting colors, but with a preference to *yellow* rays.

The tannic acid and water are in a measure taken up by the air, and the oxide of iron leaves a yellow iron mould behind.

Q. *Why does* BRUSHING *the* HAIR *much make the head itch? p.* 142.

A. 1st—Because the friction of the hair-brush excites *electricity* in the hair, which thus becomes overcharged and irritates the skin: and

2dly—The hair-brush excites increased action in the vessels and nerves of the scalp, producing a slight degree of inflammation, which is indicated by a sensation of itching.

Q. *Why does a* CANDLE FLICKER, *especially just previous to its being* BURNT OUT? *pp.* 76, 80.

A. Because it is *unequally* supplied with combustible gases.—When a candle is nearly burnt out, there is not sufficient tallow or wax to keep up the regular supply of combustible gas; in consequence of which, the flame flickers, i. e *blazes*, when it is supplied with gas, and *goes out* for a moment, when the supply is defective.

Q. *If the* "COPPER" (*or boiler*) *attached to a kitchen range, be filled with cold water* AFTER *the fire has been some time lighted, it will very often* CRACK (*or burst*). *Why is this? p.* 118.

A. Because the heat of the fire has caused the "copper" to *expand;* but the cold water very suddenly *condenses* again those parts with which it comes in contact: and, as one part is *larger* than the other, the copper cracks or bursts.

Q. *What is color?*

A. An inherent property in *light.*—The reason why different things appear of different colors, is owing to their power of *reflecting* some rays and *absorbing* others.

N. B. It must not be forgotten, that color is not an inherent property of the *flower, carpet, rainbow,* &c., but an inherent property of the *light,* which falls upon them.

The reason why one thing reflects one ray, and another thing reflects another ray, is owing to the different thickness of the corpuscules which compose them—the acid or alkaline properties of their juices or dyes—the uniformity and texture of their parts—and so on; in consequence of which, some ray or rays are reflected in preference to others.

Q. *Why, do all things appear* BLACK *in the* DARK? *p.* 371.

A. Because there is no *light;* and as color is the inherent property of *light,* therefore, in the dark all things are *without* color.

Of course, in certain degrees of darkness, objects are actually *invisible.* The question refers to that peculiar degree of darkness, when the *forms* of objects may be seen, but not their *hues.*

Q. *Why are the* FLAG-STONES *of our streets frequently* LOOSENED *after a* FROST? *p.* 326.

A. Because the moisture beneath them, *expanded* during the frost and raised the flag-stones from their beds; but afterwards, the moisture thawed and condensed again, leaving the flag-stones loose.

Q. *Why is a* ROOM WARMER, *when the window* CURTAINS *are* DRAWN? *p.* 165.

A. Because air is a bad conductor; and the air, confined between the curtains and the window, opposes both the escape of *warm* air *out* of the room, and of *cold* air into the room.

Q. *Why are rooms much* WARMER, *for being furnished with* DOUBLE DOORS *and* WINDOWS? *p.* 165.

A. Because air is a *bad conductor;* and the air confined between the double doors and windows, opposes both the escape of *warm* air *out* of the room and of *cold* air *into* the room.

Q. *Why is* LOOSE *clothing* WARMER *than that which fits closely? p.* 165.

A. Because air is a bad conductor; and the quantity of air, confined between our body and clothing, prevents; 1st—the heat of our body from escaping; and 2dly—The external air from coming into contact with our body.

Q. *Why does* WETTING *a* CORNELIAN *make it more* TRANSPARENT? *p.* 373.

A. Because the pores of the cornelian are then filled with *water;* and as the density of the mass is rendered somewhat more uniform than when those pores were filled with air, the stone becomes more transparent.

The water on the surface of the stone acts also as a varnish, to make the external coating more lustrous.

N. B. Transparency depends on the uniformity of parts. If the parts of any substance are not pretty uniform, the rays of light are refracted and absorbed so frequently, that no part of them can emerge on the opposite side.

Q. *Why does* IRON *rust?*

A. Because water is decomposed, when it comes in contact with the surface of iron; and the oxygen of the water combining with iron produces an oxide, which is generally called rust.

N. B. Water is a compound of Oxygen and Hydrogen, in the following proportions: 8 lbs. of oxygen, and 1 lb. of hydrogen=9 lbs. of water.

Q. *Why does* PAINTING *iron prevent it from* RUSTING? *p.* 232.

A. Because paint prevents the moist air from coming in contact with the iron.

Q. *Why is a dull* FIRE REVIVED *by sweeping clean the hobs, bars, ash-grate, &c. of the stove?* *pp.* 52, 53.

A. Because the air, which was arrested by the loose dust and coals, finds its way *freely* to the fire, so soon as these obstacles are swept away.

N. B. The brightness of a fire depends on its supply of oxygen, derived from the air.

Q. *Why does* STIRRING *a dull* FIRE *serve to quicken it?* *pp.* 52, 53.

A. Because it breaks up the clotted

cinders and coals, making a passage for the air into the very heart of the fire.

A fire should be stirred from the bottom, and not from the top.

Q. *Why does* SOAPY WATER *"lather?"* p. 324.

A. Because soap makes the water *tenacious*, and prevents its bubbles from bursting; "Lather" is only an accumulation of bubbles.

Q. *Why is well-made* BREAD *full of holes or eyes?* p. 257.

A. Because the fermentation of the dough throws up little bubbles filled with carbonic acid gas; and when the dough is baked, these bubbles are made *permanent* in the bread.

Q. *Why do the* SAILS *of a* WIND-MILL *turn round?* p. 108.

A. Because the wind, blowing against the oblique surface of the sails, pushes them out of the way, driving them from place to place in a restless round.

Q. *After striking a finger-glass, why is the* SOUND SILENCED, *upon touching the glass with your finger?* p. 378.

A. Because the pressure of your finger stops the *vibrations* of the finger-glass; and, so soon as the finger-glass *ceases to vibrate*, it ceases to make sound-waves in the air.

Q. *Why does a* WET SPONGE CLEAN *a* SLATE? *p.* 321.

A. Because the water of the wet sponge *dissolves* the pencil marks made upon the slate.

Something is due to the mechanical action of the mere friction.

Q. *Why do* STARS TWINKLE *more than usual, just previous to* RAIN? *p.* 374.

A. 1st—Because the air is unequally filled with vapor, which offers constant obstructions to the passage of the rays: and

2dly—Because clouds and other opaque vapors passing through the air, veil for a little time the light of the stars, which again becomes apparent after the clouds have passed:—This constant *shutting* off the light for very brief intervals, produces what is called *twinkling.*

The answers are not altogether satisfactory: probably difraction and the interference of different rays with each other, will be found, at some future time, to explain the phenomenon better.

Q. *Why does* MILK BOIL OVER *more readily than water?* *p.* 324.

A. Because the bubbles of milk, produced by the process of boiling, are more tenacious than the bubbles of water; and these bubbles, accumulating and climbing one above another, soon overtop the rim of the saucepan and run over.

Q. *If a* PICTURE *be* GLAZED, *you cannot see the "print" in certain positions; why not?* p. 352.

A. 1st—Because glass is a reflector; and, whenever the strong light of the sun is reflected from the glass to the eye of the spectator, the glass becomes intensely luminous, and the picture remains in comparative darkness: and

2dly—When the spectator is so placed, as to catch the rays of light reflected from the glass, his eye is *dazzled* with the strong light, and cannot see the more faintly illuminated picture behind it.

Q. DUST *very* RARELY *flies by* NIGHT: *why is this?* p. 188.

A. 1st—Because the dews of night moisten the dust, and prevent its rising into the air: and

2dly—As the surface of the earth is *colder* than the air after sunset, the current of the wind will incline *downward;* and tend rather to press the dust down than to buoy it up.

Q. *When the cork of a* SODA-WATER *bottle is drawn, why is a loud* REPORT *made?* p. 102

A. Because soda-water contains eight

times its own bulk of carbonic acid gas; which, being suddenly liberated, strikes against the air, and produces a report.

In the same way, as when we strike our hand upon the table.

Q. *Why does the* CORK *of a* SODA-WATER *bottle* FLY OFF, *the instant it has been released from the bond which held it in?* p. 102.

A. Because the vast quantity of carbonic acid gas forced into the soda-water can no longer be confined; and seeking to escape, drives out the cork with great violence.

Q. *Why do our* HANDS *and* LIPS CHAP *in frosty and windy weather?* p. 295.

A. 1st—Because the wind or frost absorbs the moisture from the surface of the skin: and

2dly—The action of wind or frost produces a kind of inflammation on the skin.

Cold acts very readily upon the skin, exciting a kind of erysipelas, of a *red* color; if the cold is continued, the skin becomes pale and languid, and the patient suffers from chaps, chilblains, &c. The question, however, is one belonging to the physician, rather than the natural philosopher.

Q. *When a* BLACK SUBSOIL *is dug or ploughed up, it turns of a reddish* BROWN *color after a short time; why is this?* p. 233.

A. Because the soil contained a certain compound of iron, called the "*pro-*

toxide," which is black: This protoxide of iron, absorbing more oxygen from the moist air, is converted into another compound, called the "per-oxide of iron," which is of a reddish rusty color.

There are two oxides of iron, the one containing more oxygen than the other. The protoxide, which contains the least oxygen, is *black*; the peroxide, which contains the most oxygen, is *red*. p. 394.

Q. *Why are* DECAYING VEGETABLES *always* WET? p. 253.

A. Because the *hydrogen* and *oxygen* of the vegetables are given up by decay, and form into *water*.

Water is composed of the two gases oxygen and hydrogen in the following proportions: 8 lbs. of oxygen and 1 lb. of hydrogen = 9 lbs. of water.

N. B. Decaying vegetables combine into the following new forms: 1st, The oxygen and hydrogen form into water: and 2dly, The carbon unites with the oxygen of the air, and produces carbonic acid gas.

Q. *If a house be faced with* STUCCO *to resemble stone, why does the facing very often* FLAKE OFF *in winter, and leave the house unsightly?* p. 333.

A. Because the stucco was not quite dry; therefore, its moisture freezing and expanding, thrusts the stucco away from the wall; and when the thaw sets in, the stucco being unsupported, will fall by its own weight.

Q. *Why do the* LUSTRES *of a* CHANDELIER *seem tinted with* VARIOUS *brilliant colors?* p. 364.

A. Because each "drop" of the chandelier is so cut, as to act like a prism: It decomposes the light, and reflects the different rays thereof from its different points or angles.

Q. HORN *is* TRANSPARENT, *why are* NOT ***horn*** SHAVINGS *transparent also? p.* 373.

A. Because the surface of the shaving has been torn and rendered rough; and the rays of light are too much reflected and refracted by the rough surface to be transmitted through the shaving, so as to produce transparency.

Q. *When a glazier is mending a window,* ***and*** *cleans the pane with his brush, why do the loose pieces of putty (on the* OPPOSITE *side of the window-pane)* DANCE *up and down? p.* 142.

A. When glass is rubbed, electricity is excited in the parts submitted to the friction, and on the part *opposite* also; the electricity attracts light substances, such as loose fragments of putty: As soon as these fragments have touched the excited part of the glass they become charged, and fall back again; the ledge on which they fall deprives them of their burden, and they then fly up again to receive a fresh charge: This process being repeated often, makes the commotion in the loose fragments of putty, referred to in the question.

A very pretty experiment of a similar kind may be made thus: Take a common window glass, wipe it quite dry and warm, and support it on two wine glasses like the slab of a table: Place *underneath* the window glass, at the distance of about two inches, some bran, sand, small pieces of paper, Dutch gold, pith, &c.: If you now rub the *upper* surface of the window glass with a silk rubber, the light substances beneath will dance up and down.

N. B. The rubber may be made thus: Take a common cork cut evenly and flat, cover it with a piece of silk, and run a skewer into the upper surface for a handle. A little amalgam applied to the rubber will greatly improve the experiment.

Q. *When you rub a piece of paper with* INDIAN RUBBER, *why is the paper sticky? p.* 34.

A. Because the friction of the Indian rubber against the surface of the paper develops electricity, to which this stickiness is mainly to be attributed.

Q. *If you dry a piece of common* BROWN PAPER *by the fire and draw it once or twice between your two* KNEES, *why will it* STICK *fast to the wall? p.* 34.

A. Because the friction develops electricity on the paper, which manifests itself by this property of adhesion.

Q. *Why can noises be* HEARD (*in a calm day*) *at a* GREATER DISTANCE *on the sea than on land? p.* 381.

A. 1st—Because the air over the sea is generally denser and more laden with moisture, than the air over the land is: *p.* 139.

2dly—The density is more *uniform*; *p.* 380, and

3dly,—Water being more *elastic* than and, is a better propagator of sound.

Q. *The height of* MOUNTAINS *may be ascertained by a* BAROMETER : *Explain the reason of this?* p. 383.

A. As we ascend a high mountain, the quantity of air above us becomes less and less every step we ascend, and requires less mercury to balance it; in consequence of which the mercury in the tube of the barometer *falls.*

If a pile of books be placed on a table, the bottom book will sustain the *most* weight, and every book will sustain less and less, as we get nearer and nearer to the top: The air somewhat resembles this pile. That on the surface *of the earth* resembles the *bottom* book of the pile; and, as we ascend a mountain, the quantity of air above keeps diminishing, and the weight to be sustained is in proportion less.

For general practical purposes we may take this for a rule: for every 100 feet of perpendicular height, the barometer will fall $\frac{1}{10}$ of an inch. If, therefore, the barometer has fallen $1\frac{1}{2}$ inch, you know the mountain is 1500 feet high.

Q. *How does* STARCH *assist in giving a smooth* GLAZED SURFACE *to* LINEN? p. 373.

A. It fills up the interstices between the threads; and makes the fabric of more uniform density.

"Interstices between the threads."—Put your fingers close, and lay your open hand on the table—a little *groove* may be seen, where the fingers divide; these grooves may be called *interstices;* and, when we speak of the "interstices of linen," we mean the groove or space between thread and thread.

Q. *If a* DROP *of* WATER *be spilt on a table-cloth why will it* SPREAD *in all directions?* p. 75.

A. Because the threads of the cloth absorb the water by capillary attraction.

Q. *Why does* SALT PRESERVE *meat?*

A. Because it removes the *water* contained in the animal fibre; absorbing it, and leaving the meat dry.

The reason stated above is not the *sole* reason, though it is certainly the chief one. The following have some influence also:

2. Salt is composed of chlorine and sodium; the chlorine of the salt takes up the hydrogen of the meat as it is given off, and prevents the offensive taste and smell of decay:

3. Brine draws away the *albu'men* from between the muscular fibres, which is very subject to putrefaction.

4. The salt *unites* with the muscular fibre, and makes a new chemical compound, much less subject to decay: and

5. It keeps the *air* from the meat, the flies, &c.

Q. *Is* SALTED *meat equally nutritious as fresh meat?*

A. No: Because the *albu'men* of the meat is separated from the flesh by the brine; as well as the alkaline phosphates and some other substances of great value.

"Phosphates" *pronounce* fos'-fates.—Phosphates are alkaline, and mineral.—ALKALINE PHOSPHATES are *phosphoric acid* combined with some *alkali*, such as soda, potash, magnesia, &c.

"Albu'men of the meat"—a substance like the *white of an egg*, which lies between the muscular fibres of all flesh, and makes the meat *tender*.

"The alkaline phosphates of meat" are such as these: the phosphate of soda, the phosphate of potash, and the phosphate of magnesia, which are extracted from the meat by the *acid* re-action of the brine.

Q. *Why is the* FLESH *of* OLD *animals very* TOUGH?

A. Because it contains very little *al-bu'men*, and much muscular fibre.

Q. *Why is* MEAT *always* TOUGH, *if it be put into the boiler before the water boils?*

A. Because the water is not hot enough to coagulate the albumen between the muscular fibres of the meat, which therefore runs into the water, and rises to the surface as a scum.

Q. *Why is* MEAT TOUGH, *which has been* BOILED TOO LONG?

A. Because the albumen becomes hard, like the white of a hard boiled egg.

The best way of boiling meat to make it tender is this. Put your joint in very brisk boiling water; after a few minutes, add a little cold water. The boiling water will fix the albu'men, which will prevent the water from soaking into the meat—keep all the juices in—and prevent the muscular fibre from contracting. The addition of cold water will secure the cooking of the *inside* of the joint, as well as of the surface.

Q. *Why should* VEGETABLES *be* ALWAYS *eaten with salted meat?*

A. Because they are all rich in POTASH, which the brine has deprived the meat of.

Q. *Why are* LAMB *and* VEAL *more* TENDER *than beef and mutton?*

A. Because they contain more albu'-men, and less muscular fibre.

Albu'men is a substance like the white of an egg.

Q. *Why do* LAMB *and* VEAL TAINT *more quickly than beef and mutton?*

A. Because they contain a large quantity of albu'men, which is very liable to undergo putrefaction.

Q. *Why are small birds, such as quails, larks, partridges, &c., covered with lard, when they are roasted?*

A. To make them tender and savory. The covering of lard prevents the savory constituents of the bird from evaporating with the water: in consequence of which, the flesh is more tender and sapid.

"Sapid" i. e. full of flavor.

Q. *Why does melted* WAX *become* HARD, *when cold?* *p.* 109.

A. Because the particles collapse; and, being packed more closely together, form a solid.

The sole difference between a liquid and a solid is this—In a SOLID the particles are packed more closely together, than they are in a *liquid*. The tendency of heat is, to *drive* the particles *further apart* from each other, and thus to *liquify* solids.

Q. *Why does* PAINT *often* BLISTER *from heat?*

A. Because the heat, penetrating through the paint, extracts some little moisture from the wood, and turns it into vapor or steam. As this vapor requires room, it throws up blisters in the paint, to make room for its expanded bulk.

Q. *Why are* ROTTING LEAVES HOT? *pp.* 60, 253.

A. Because the fermentation of rotting leaves produces *carbonic acid gas*, which production is always attended with heat. In fact *rotting* is a species of slow *combustion.*

N. B.—The carbon of the leaves unites with the oxygen of the air, to produce carbonic acid gas. p. 259.

The new combinations disturb *latent heat*, and make it sensible.

Q. *Why are* ROTTING LEAVES DAMP? *p.* 253.

Answered before, see page 403.

Q. *Why does* BREAD *become* HARD, *after it has been* KEPT *a few days? p.* 153.

A. Because the vapor and gases escape, leaving the solid particles dry; so that they collapse, and become more solid and hard.

Q. *Why is* NEW BREAD INDIGESTIBLE?

A. Because the change called "pan'-ary fermentation," is not completed.

"Panary" from the Latin word *Panis* (bread); "panary fermentation" means, the fermentation that dough undergoes in order to become bread.

The *sugar* of the dough is converted into alcohol and carbonic acid by fermentation; the dough being adhesive, prevents the escape of these products, till the mass is *baked;* when the gas expands, bursts through the mass, leaving a number of holes or bladders, to show where it was confined.

So long as the bread is warm, the process of fermentation is going on; and, therefore, bread should never be eaten, till it is 24 hours old.

Q. *Why are* PLANTS WHITE, *which are kept in the* DARK? *p.* 372.

A. Because chlo'rophyll can be formed only by the agency of the sun's rays; and it is this peculiar chemical principle, which gives the green tinge to healthy leaves and plants.

Chlo'rophyll is the green coloring matter of leaves.

Q. *Why does* OIL *become* THICK *in* WINTER-TIME? *p.* 268.

1st—Because it is condensed by the cold, and rendered more solid: and

2dly—Because the "ste'arine," which is held in solution in warm weather, is separated by the action of the cold; and deposited as a thick white almost-solid matter.

"Stearine" (from the Greek word *στεαρ, suet*) is the *solid* or *hard* ingredient of all fat, suet, oil, &c. The *soft* or *liquid* part is called oleine from the Latin word oleum (*oil.*)

Q. *Why is mutton* FAT, *&c., solid, and* OIL *liquid?*

A. Because fat contains a predominance of solid ste'arine; and only a very small quantity of the liquid oily substance, called oleine. On the other hand, oil contains more of the liquid oleine, and less of the solid matter, called ste'arine.

Q. *Why is* BUTTER HARD *in winter, and* SOFT *in* SUMMER-*time ?*

A. Because in winter-time the weather is too cold to melt the ste'arine, and the butter is solid; but the heat of summer dissolves it, or holds it in solution in the oily substance called oleine, and the butter is soft and liquid.

Q. *Why does a* POP-GUN *make a loud* REPORT, *when the paper bullet is discharged from it ?* *p.* 102.

A. Because the air confined between the paper bullet and the discharging rod, is suddenly liberated, and strikes against the surrounding air; this makes a report in the same way, as when any two *solids* (such as your hand and the table) come into collision.

Q. *How does* STEAM *make the whistle of a locomotive engine sound ?* *p.* 110.

A. The whistle is so constructed, as very frequently to obstruct the free passage of the steam through the jet; in consequence of which, very rapid vibrations are caused in the air, producing the sharp shrill sound of the locomotive whistle.

No sound is ever produced in any sounding body, unless there are 12½ vibrations in a second of time; if there are

7680 vibrations, the sound is sharp and shrill; the shrillness increasing, as the vibrations increase in number.

Q. *Why will* BRIGHT IRON LOSE *its* POLISH *by being put into a* FIRE? *p.* 231.

A. Because the oxygen of the air very readily unites with the surface of *hot iron*, and forms a metallic oxide; which displays itself, in this case, by a *dull leaden* color, instead of a red *rust*.

Q. *Why does* SOUND SEEM LOUDER *in* CAVES, *than on a plain?* *p.* 381.

A. Because the sides of the cave confine the sound-waves, and prevent their spreading; in consequence of which their *strength* is greatly increased.

Q. *Why does* PAINT PRESERVE *wood?*

A. 1st—Because it covers the surface of the wood, and prevents both air and damp from penetrating into the pores:

2dly—Because paint (especially of a white color) being a bad conductor, preserves the wood of a more uniform temperature: and

3dly—Because it fills up the pores of the wood, prevents insects and vermin from harboring therein and eating up the fibre.

Q. *Why does* UNSEASONED WOOD DECAY *much more rapidly than wood well seasoned?*

A. Because the albu'men which the

sap contains, produces a species of fermentation; during which, the cell'ulin and ligneous matter of the wood are turned into carbonic acid and water.

"Albu'men," a substance resembling the *white* of an egg.
"Cellulin," the substance which composes the *cells* of wood, as wax composes the cells of a honey-comb in a bee-hive.
"Ligneous matter," or vegetable fibre, is the hard or woody part of wood.

Q. *Why is* WOOD *placed in a stream of running* WATER *to* SEASON *it?*

A. Because the running water washes away the sap; and thus prevents fermentation and decay.

Q. *Why will solutions of salts* PREVENT *the* DECAY *of wood steeped therein?*

A. Because the salts unite with the albu'men of the sap, coagulate it, and prevent fermentation.

Q. *Why does* MOTHER *of* PEARL *show so many colors? pp.* 364, 370.

A. Mother of pearl consists of a vast number of very thin half-transparent layers of unequal thickness, over-lapping each other like the scales of a fish.

Where these layers terminate are very small grooves or streaks running in all directions, which act like prisms.

It is these *streakings* or grooves, which

cause the various and changing colors of mother of pearl.

The same thing may very easily be imitated, and is frequently done in what are called "iris ornaments," first invented by John Barton, Esq., of the Royal Mint. These iris ornaments are made of steel, and have about 30,000 grooves per inch; they are used in court dresses, for buttons, sword handles, &c., and are very brilliant indeed.

Mother of pearl may be also imitated by taking impressions of it in wax, balsam of tolu, isinglass, or gum; these impressions will exhibit all the shades and colors of mother of pearl, merely because the impression will be streaked or grooved in a similar way.

Q. *Why can you fill a* DRY GLASS BEYOND *the level of the brim? p.* 206.

A. Because the mass of water in the glass holds the overplus back, by the power of attraction.

Q. *Why will the overplus instantly flow over, if the edges of the glass are wet?*

A. Because the water on the edge of the glass has an affinity to the water towering above it, no less than the water in the body of the glass has; and in this state of equilibrium the force of gravity, acting on the elevated particles of water, causes them at once to fall over.

Q. *If you leave a little tea in your cup, and rest your spoon on the bottom of the cup, why does the* TEA RUSH *to the* SPOON? *p.* 387.

A. Because the spoon attracts it, by what is called capillary attraction.

The sloping spoon makes with the sides or bottom of the cup a space in the shape of a very small wedge; where the aperture is small, the cup and spoon draw the tea up by the force of attraction; and the *narrower* the opening, the *stronger* the attraction.

Q. *When* LIQUOR *is decanted or poured from a bottle, why does it* GURGLE? *p.* 256.

A. This bubbling noise is made by the air bursting *into* the bottle, and the liquor bursting *out.*

The liquor, filling the neck of the bottle, prevents the air from getting freely in; and the air, pressing against the mouth of the bottle, prevents the liquor from getting freely out: in consequence of which, the air bursts into the neck of the bottle, and the liquor runs from the same, by fits and starts, as either is able to prevail: as this process is repeated, the noise produced is called a gurgle.

Q. *Why will* LUCIFER MATCHES IGNITE *by merely drawing them across any rough surface? pp.* 99, 221.

There are two sorts of lucifer matches; those that ignite *silently*, and those that ignite with an *explosion.*

A. SILENT LUCIFERS are made of *phosphorus*, which has an affinity to oxygen at the lowest temperature; insomuch that the little additional heat, caused by the friction of the match across the bottom of the lucifer-box, is sufficient to ignite it; and, at the same time, to ignite the sulphur with which the match is tipped.

EXPLOSIVE LUCIFERS are made of *chlorate of potash*, which will *explode* by very slight friction, and produce combustion.

"Chlorate of potash" is a compound of chloric acid and potash. Chloric acid is a compound of two gases, chlorine and oxygen.

Q. *Why will not lucifer matches ignite, if they are* DAMP? *p.* 48.

A. 1st—Because the cold, produced by the *evaporation* of the water, neutralises the heat produced by the friction of the match across the bottom of the lucifer-box: and

2dly—Because the damp prevents the free accession of oxygen to the match, without which it cannot burn.

Q. *When our likeness is reflected in a looking-glass, the entire image is* REVERSED; *so that our* RIGHT *cheek is the* LEFT *cheek of the reflection, &c.; why is this? p.* 345.

If a person stands *opposite* to us, his position in regard to the cardinal points of the compass is altogether reversed.

As in a mirror all the lines and angles of *incidence* equal the lines and angles of *reflection*, it is manifest that those parts of the person which are *nearest* the mirror, will *seem* to be nearer than those more remote; but, if our right cheek were to cross over to the right cheek of the reflection, then this law would be broken.

Our right cheek would cross over to the right cheek in the mirror, and our left to the left, ${}^{B}_{A}\times{}^{A}_{B}$ in which (without doubt) the extreme points of the diagonals **A A, and B B**, are further apart than A is from B.

Q. *A* SILVER *tea-spoon becomes* MORE HEATED *by hot tea, than one of* INFERIOR *metal (as German silver, Nickel, &c.); why is this?* *p.* 156.

A. Because silver is a better *conductor* than German silver or Nickel.

The three best conductors of heat are, 1. Gold, 2. Silver, 3. Copper.

Q. *If you scrape a slip of paper with a knife, why will the* PAPER CURL?

A. Because the *under* surface of the paper is *contracted* by the scraping, which brings the particles closer together; this contraction of the under surface bends the slip of paper into a curl or arch.

Q. *Why does the* STOPPLE *of a decanter* STICK *fast, if it be put in damp?*

A. If the stopple be damp, it fits the decanter *air-tight;* and if the decanter was last used in a heated room, as soon as the hot air inclosed in the inside has been condensed by the cold, the weight of the external air will be sufficient to press the stopple down, and make it stick fast.

Q. *Why does the* STOPPLE *of a* SMELLING-BOTTLE *very often* STICK *fast?*

A. Because the contents of a smelling-bottle are very volatile, and leave the neck of the bottle, and the stopple, damp.

If the smelling-bottle was last used in

a hot room, as soon as the hot air and volatile essence, inside the bottle, have been condensed by the cold, the weight of the external air will be sufficient to press the stopple down and make it stick.

In the last two instances, the pressure of air forces the stopple down too far, so that it is like a cork which has been forced into a bottle: Hence there are two mechanical forces to contend against; 1st, The weight of air on the stopple which holds it down, as an exhausted receiver is held tight on the plate of an air-pump: and 2dly, The neck of the bottle, (expanded by heat when the stopple was put in,) will girt it with great pressure, so soon as it is contracted again by cold.

Q. *Decaying vegetables are first of a brownish tint, why do they afterwards turn of a* DEEP BLACK?

A. Because the hydrogen of the decaying vegetables is separated from the mass by the process of decay, and leaves a larger proportion of carbon behind.

Vegetable fibre contains	52½	per cent. of carbon.
When partially decayed	54	" " " "
When black with decay	56	" " " "

Q. *Why is an* OAK STRUCK *by* LIGHTNING *more frequently than any other tree?*

A. Because the *grain* of the oak, being *closer* than that of any other tree of equal bulk, renders it a better conductor.

It is said, that the sap of the oak contains a large quantity of *iron* in solution, which impregnates the wood and bark, thus increasing its conducting power.

Q. *Why does a* LOBSTER, *which is black while alive, turn* RED *by being* BOILED?

A. The *blackness* is due to a peculiar

coloring matter secreted by the lobster; which, however, turns *red* when exposed to the heat of boiling water.

Q. *Why does a* SHRIMP, *which is nearly* WHITE *while alive, turn* RED *by being* BOILED ?

A. The delicate pinky whiteness is due to a peculiar coloring matter secreted by the shrimp; which, however, turns *red* when exposed to the heat of boiling water.

Many coloring matters pass into each other under very slight changes of condition. *g. e.*

Blue indigo changes to *white* indigo, if only one atom more of hydrogen be added. So also, the green chlorophyll of leaves changes into the infinite hues of the petals of flowers.

The science of colors is not at present sufficiently understood to give very lucid explanations of these changes; the *facts* are known, and little else besides.

Q. *Why is the* SHADOW *of the* MOON *stronger than the shadow of the sun?*

A. Because the *light* of the moon is not so *strong* as the light of the sun; in consequence of which, the dispersed and reflected rays of the moon cannot reduce the opacity of shadows so much, as the more intense rays of dispersed and reflected daylight.

" The opa'city of shadows," i. e. the darkness of shadows.

Q. *Why does* HARTSHORN *take out the red spot in cloth, produced by any* ACID ?

A. Because hartshorn is an *alkali*

and the peculiar property of every alkali s to neutralize acids.

"Alkali" pronounce Al′-ka-li. Soda, potash, magnesia, &c., are alkalies.

Upon this principle effervescing drinks are made of a carbonate of soda (an alkali), and citric or tartaric acid. Effervescence is produced, by the giving off of carbonic acid during the process of neutralization.

N. B.—The carbonic acid is made from the *carbon* (of the carbonate of soda) combining with the oxygen of the acid. *p.* 43.

Q. *Why will* POWDERED SULPHUR QUENCH FIRE *more readily than water ?*

A. 1st—Because powdered sulphur has a very strong affinity for oxygen, and converts it into *sulphurous acid;* as this is the case, the fire is deprived of its essential food (oxygen), and is, in fact, *starved* out: and

2dly—Because sulphurous acid throws off dense white *fumes*, and surrounds the fire with an extinguishing atmosphere.

The difference between sulphurous acid and sulphuric acid is this: sulphurons acid contains less oxygen than sulphuric acid. When we burn sulphur in air, it throws off suffocating white fumes, called sulphurous acid.

Q. *How does* STARCH STIFFEN *linen ?*

A. By filling the interstices of the fabric with a solution of starch, by which means the linen is made more rigid.

Q. *Why should* LIGHTNING-CONDUCTORS *be* POINTED ?

A. Because points conduct electricity

away *silently* and *imperceptibly:* but knobs produce an *explosion*, which would endanger the building.

Points empty the clouds of electricity, acting at a much greater distance than knobs; thus a Leyden jar of considerable size may be safely and silently discharged, by holding the point of a needle an inch or two off.

Blades of grass, the ears of corn, and other pointed objects, serve to empty the clouds of their electricity.

Q. *Why do* BRICKS *turn* GREEN, *after they have been exposed to the weather?*

A. The "green" is a moss or lichen, which grows on the bricks; the seeds of which were carried to the surface by the winds.

Q. *When* POTATOES *are boiled, why are those at the* TOP *of the boiler* COOKED SOONER *than those nearer the fire?*

A. 1st—Because the *hottest* particles of the water rise to the *top* of the boiler, and the *coldest* particles sink to the bottom: and

2dly—Because the top of the boiler is always enveloped with very hot escaping steam; in consequence of which, the potatoes on the top are subjected to more intense heat, than those at the bottom of the boiler are.

Q. *If a* SILVER SPOON, *which has been tarnished by an* EGG, *be rubbed with a little* SALT, *why will the tarnish disappear?*

A. The tarnish in this case is *sulphu-*

ret of silver, produced by the sulphur of the egg combining with the silver spoon. Salt acts upon this sulphuret of silver thus—

The sodium of the salt combines with the sulphur, and produces sulphate of soda. The sulphur being thus taken away from the silver, the tarnish disappears.

"Sulphuret of silver," i. e. sulphur in combination with silver.

Salt is a compound of the metal called sodium, and the gas called chlorine.

"Sulphate of soda" is a combination of sulphuric acid and soda.

Q. *Why are* BOOKS *discolored by* AGE *or* DAMP?

A. Because the fibre of the paper becomes partially decomposed, and various impurities from the atmosphere (or other sources) become mixed with it.

Q. *Why does* SOUR MILK CURDLE?

A. Milk consists of five ingredients: 1, Ca'sein or curd; 2, Butter; 3, Sugar; 4, Water; 5, Certain Salts.

The Ca'sein or curd of *sweet* milk is like the white of an egg before it is boiled; but the casein or curd of sour milk is like the white of an egg after it is boiled.

This casein or curd of milk is coagulated by acids:—When milk is sour, the *lactic acid* of the sour milk, mixing with the casein, *coagulates* it; in consequence of which, it separates from the water and becomes an insoluble mass; or (in other words) the milk curdles.

"Lactic acid" (from the Latin word Lac, *milk*) is the acid of sour milk. But it is found in several other substances also, as in the fermented juice of beet-root, turnips, carrots, rice-water, tanning bark, &c.

Q. *Why does* MILK *turn* SOUR *by* KEEPING?

A. Because it undergoes a fermentation; during which "lactic acid" is formed, which turns the milk sour.

The lactic acid is formed from the sugar of milk by fermentation.

Q. *Why does* MILK *turn* SOUR *in* HOT *weather, much sooner than in cold?*

A. Because heat very greatly accelerates the process of fermentation; during which lactic acid is formed, which turns the milk sour.

Q. *Why can you* NEVER BOIL STALE MILK *without curdling it?*

A. Because stale milk is in an incipient state of fermentation, which the heat of the fire greatly accelerates: The lactic acid which is formed during fermentation, mixing with the casein of the milk, coagulates it.

Casein (*pronounce* cas'-e-in) is the curd of milk coagulated by *acids* only.

Q. *Why does* RENNET CURDLE MILK?

A. Because it converts the sugar of milk into lactic acid, which mixes with the casein and coagulates it.

Milk contains soda and potash; so long as these alkalies are combined with the casein of the milk, the compound is soluble in water, and the milk sweet: but when the acid deprives the casein of the alkalies by combining with them itself, then the casein is no longer soluble in water, but is precipitated or curdled.

Rennet is the prepared inner membrane of the stomach of a calf· so called from the German word *rinnen* (to curdle.)

Q. *Why does* CHURNING *cream convert it into* BUTTER?

A. Cream is the *fat* or butter of milk, contained in little globular cases of albu men:

By churning, this film or envelop of albu'men is broken, and the butter or fat set free.

The globules are invisible to the naked eye, but may be distinctly seen floating about milk, by a tolerable microscope.

Albu'men is a substance resembling the white of an egg.

Q. *Why does the* SUN *or fire* WARP WOOD?

A. Because heat draws out the moisture from that part of the wood which faces it, and causes the heated surface to shrink; as, therefore, the heated surface of the wood *shrinks*, and is smaller than the *other* surface, it draws it into a curve, and the wood is warped.

Q. *Why does the* SUN, *for the most part*, FADE *artificial* COLORS?

A. Generally, the loss of color arises from the oxidation of the substances used in dyeing; as tarnish and rust are an oxidation of metals.

Sometimes, however, the ingredients of the dye are otherwise decomposed by the sun; and the color (which is due to a *combination* of ingredients) undergoes a change, as soon as the sun deranges or destroys that combination.

Q. *When a* KNIFE *is sharpened on a* GRINDSTONE, *why is* OIL *or water used?*

A. To make the contact more perfect. The oil or water fills up the interstices of the rough stone, and makes a more uniform surface: In consequence of which, the *entire edge* of the blade is submitted to an equal portion of friction, which would otherwise be rough and uneven.

Q *Why does* BAKING *dough convert it into* BREAD?

A. When flour is baked in an oven its starch is changed into a gum called dextrin: and

A similar change is produced upon the farinaceous portion of the dough. The *yeast* (added to the dough) converts part of the starch and sugar into alcohol and carbonic acid: Of these, the alcohol evaporates in the oven, and the carbonic acid forces the dough into bubbles, in its effort to escape, rendering the bread light and full of eyes.

In 100 lbs. of bread, and 100 lbs. of dough, we have

	STARCH.	SUGAR.	DEXTRIN.
In dough,	68 lbs.	5 lbs.	0=100
In bread,	53½ "	3½ "	18=100

whereby it will be seen that 16½ lbs of starch have been converted into the gum called dextrin by baking.

Dextrin is a gummy matter similar to that which composes the cells of wood (called cellu'lin), only it is soluble in cold water.

Diastase (*pronounce* di-as'-tase) is a peculiar vegetable principle of malt extracted by water, which converts starch into dextrin or sugar.

Q. *Why does* BREAD *become mouldy, after it has been* KEPT *a few days?*

A. Because spores of the mould fungus, floating in the air, fix themselves in the decaying bread and germinate.

Fungi germinate only in *decaying* bodies.

Spores (*one syllable*) or Sporules (*two syls.*) from the Greek word σπορα (*seed*) is a word used by botanists to indicate the seed of cryptogamic or flowerless plants. They differ from seeds in this respect, every part of the spore shoots into a plant, and not one particular point alone, as in common seeds.

Q. *Why does* MEAT PUTREFY *sooner in hot,* DAMP *weather, than in cold?*

Putrefaction is simply the decomposition of the original elements, and their reunion in a new order. The new order is as follows:

1st. Carbon and oxygen unite to form carbonic acid;
2dly. Hydrogen and oxygen " " " water;
3dly. Hydrogen and nitrogen " " ammonia.

N. B.—Carbon unites with oxygen with a readiness pro

portioned to its heat: When *red* hot, the combination is *most* readily effected.

The reason why meat taints more rapidly in *hot* weather than cold, is this; Because the carbon of the meat unites with the oxygen of the air more readily when hot than cold: and

The reason why damp aids putrefaction is this; Because the *damp*, deposited on the surface of the meat, is of itself one of the compounds of putrefaction, and leaves an excess of hydrogen in the meat: and

Thus the original proportions and combinations of the meat are altered and decomposed.

The chief reason why salt *preserves* meat is because it absorbs the water from it, and deprives it of hydrogen.

Q. *Why does* MEAT PUTREFY *most rapidly in very* CHANGEABLE *weather?*

A. Because moisture is more freely deposited on the meat in very changeable weather; and this moisture is a chief compound of putrefaction.

Q. BIRDS, *after they are killed,* KEEP *longer in their* FEATHERS, *than when they are plucked; why is this?*

A. Because the feathers prevent the *air* or *damp* from getting so readily to the bird, to produce fermentation or decay.

Q. *Why do* PLANTS, *which are kept on a window,* BEND *to the* GLASS?

A. Because the side *away* from the light *grows faster*, than the side *facing* the light, and pushes the top of the plant over in a curve.

Wood is *warped* by the fire, because the *under* surface is smaller than the upper.

And paper is made to curl by scraping the under surface with a knife for the same reason.

N. B.—Woody tissue is deposited in the stem most abundantly on the side *nearest the light;* and where *wood* is formed most, *growth* is slowest, because the part is less succulent.

Q. *Why does* INDIAN-RUBBER *erase* PENCIL MARKS *from paper?*

A. Indian-rubber contains a very large quantity of carbon: Black-lead is carbon and iron.

Now, the carbon of the Indian-rubber has so great an attraction for the black-lead, that it takes up the loose traces of it left on paper by a pencil.

Q. *Why does* WATER ROT WOOD? *and why does* AIR *rot* WOOD?

A. Because it converts the solid part of the wood into what is called *humus*, by oxidation; thus—

1st—The *carbon* of the wood is oxidised into carbonic acid; and

2dly—The *hydrogen* of the wood is oxidised into water—the residue becomes humus or mould.

"Humus," *pronounce* U'-mus. The black mould of our gardens is called humus, and is produced by the decay of vegetable matter by the action of air and water.

Q. *Why does* WATER *make a* HISSING *noise, when it is poured on* FIRE ?

A. Because the part which comes in contact with the hot coals is immediately converted into *steam;* and, as it flies upward, meets other particles of water not yet vaporised; the collision produces very rapid vibrations in the air, and a hissing noise is the result.

Q. *Why does* HOT IRON *make a hissing noise, when plunged into* WATER ?

A. Because the hot iron converts into steam the particles of water, which come in immediate contact with it; and, as the steam flies upwards, it passes by other particles of water not yet vaporised: the collision produces very rapid vibrations in the air, and a *hissing* noise is the result.

Q. *Why will* HOT IRON BEND *more easily than cold ?*

A. Because it is not so *solid.* The particles are driven further apart by heat, and the attraction of cohesion weakened; in consequence of which, the particles can be made to move on each other more readily.

By a still further application of heat, the particles wil

be driven so far asunder from each other, that the solid iron will liquefy: in which state the particles will move on each other almost without resistance.

Q. *Why does* IRON *turn first* RED *and then* WHITE *from* HEAT ?

A. Light and heat depend upon vibrations; the more rapid the vibrations, the more intense the light and heat; *White* heat is a more intense degree of heat than red, and occurs only when the vibrations are most rapid.

Candescence occurs when bodies are heated to 800° It begins with a dull red color, passes to an orange tint and ultimately to a shining white.

The more perfect the combustion of carbon the whiter its color.

Probably these varying colors depend upon some variety in the thickness of the molecules of the heated substance, caused by the influence of heat; whereby it is made to reflect different colors according to the varying thickness of the molecules. But the subject is not well understood at present.

Molecules (*pronounce* mo -le-cules) are very small particles of matter in a *mass.* ATOMS have no regard to aggregation.

Q. *Why does* WATER FREEZE *more quickly than* MILK ?

A. Because milk contains *salts* in solution; in consequence of which, it requires a greater degree of cold to congeal it than water.

Water freezes at 32°, but *salt* and water will not freeze unless the thermometer sinks below 7°.

Q. *Why does* HOT WATER FREEZE *more quickly than cold ?*

A. Because there is a slight *agitation*

on the surface of hot water, which promotes congelation; by assisting the crystals to change their positions, till they take up that which is most favorable to their solidification.

Other causes may have a minor influence, as for example: In hot water, the particles are subdivided into smaller globules by the heat, and offer less resistance to the action of cold than larger ones. 2dly. The *air* has been expelled from the water by the process of boiling—hence the Indians always used *boiled* water in their ice-pits.

N. B.—Air must be expelled from water before it can be frozen.

Q. *Why will a little* OIL *on the surface of water prevent its* FREEZING?

A. Because oil is a bad conductor, and prevents heat from leaving the water.

The surface of water never freezes, till the whole mass is cooled down to 42°.

Q. *Why does water in a very* EXPOSED *place freeze more rapidly than that which is under cover, or in places less exposed?*

A. 1st—Because evaporation goes on more rapidly, when water is exposed; and carries away heat from the general mass: and

2dly—Any covering will radiate *heat* into the water below, and prevent the mass from cooling down to 42°.

"Radiate heat" means, to send heat out in rays.

Q. *Why are* GLUE, GUM, STARCH, *and* PASTE, *adhesive?*

A. Because the water used with them rapidly evaporates, and leaves them solid.

They lose their adhesiveness when dissolved in water; and, therefore, must always be suffered to become *dry*, before they will hold with tenacity.

Q. *Why does a rail-way* TRAIN *make more* NOISE, *when it passes over a* BRIDGE *or* MEADOW, *than when it runs over* SOLID GROUND ?

A. Because the bridge (or meadow) is very elastic, and *vibrates* much more from the weight of the train, than the solid earth; in consequence of which, it produces more definite sound-waves.

The bridge acts as a sounding-board; and the water or earth, below the bridge, *repeats* the sound.

Q. *Why does* MILK BOIL *more* QUICKLY *than water ?*

A. Because *less steam* is carried off from the *thick* liquid (milk), than from the *thin* liquid (water); in consequence of which, the heat of the whole mass rises more quickly.

Q. *Why will* MILK BURN *very easily, when boiled, while water will not do so ?*

A. 1st—Because milk contains solid organic substances, capable of burning; which water does not:—and

2dly—Because the heat of the fire coagulates the albu'men of the milk which falls to the bottom, and adheres to the boiler.

Albu'men is a substance resembling the white of an egg.

Q. *Why does* WAX *become* SOFT, *before it turns* LIQUID?

A. Because it absorbs heat sufficient to *loosen* the contact of its particles, before it has absorbed sufficient to *liquefy* the mass.

Q. *If you heat* STEEL RED HOT *in the fire, and then plunge it suddenly into cold water, it becomes* HARD *and* BRITTLE; *why is this?*

A. Because the sudden chill violently expels the latent heat, which would have settled in the steel, had it been allowed to cool slowly.

The malleability and toughness of metals depend upon their power of absorbing heat.

Q. *Why are the* ICE-PITS *of India lined with straw and coarse blanketing—stopped up with* STRAW *at the mouth, instead of a door—and* THATCHED *on the roof, instead of being covered with slates or tiles?*

A. Because straw and coarse blanketing, being very bad conductors indeed, prevent the external heat from getting to the ice-pits to dissolve the ice.

Q. *How do the natives of* INDIA *provide themselves with* ICE, *when the temperature is much higher than the freezing point?*

A. They make a hole in the earth about 2 feet deep, and 30 feet square: They cover the bottom of this hole, to the depth of a foot, with the stalks of Indian corn or sugar-canes:

On this bed they place fleet unglazed earthern pans about an inch and a quarter deep, and pour into them (at sun-set) soft water, which has been *boiled* and suffered to cool. At sun-rise the water is found to be frozen, and is thrown into the ice-pit.

The reason of this is: The vessels being porous, part of the water evaporates through the pans, and reduces the heat of the water sufficient for congelation.

Q. *Why is it customary, in very* HOT COUNTRIES, *to sit in rooms separated by* CURTAINS, *instead of walls; and to keep these curtains constantly sprinkled with* WATER?

A. Because curtains are bad conductors of heat; and the rapid evaporation of water reduces the temperature of the room 10 or 15 degrees.

Q. *Why is it impossible to* WRITE *on* GREASY PAPER?

A. Because grease has no affinity for water or ink, and, therefore, will not mix with it.

Q. *Why is rain said to "bring down the cold?"*

A. Because the change in the atmosphere, which causes rain to fall, *sets free latent heat*, and makes it sensible.

Frost is broken up by the rains; and the sharp, piercing *wind*, being laden with vapor, is much mitigated.

Q. *Why does* TURPENTINE *take out* GREASE *spots from cloth?*

A. Because it dissolves fixed oils.

The *fixed* oils are all greasy oils, such as sperm oil, olive oil, &c. The other sort of oils, called *volatile* or *essential* oils, are those used in perfumery, &c.

Q. *Why does* OXALIC *acid take out* INK *spots?*

A. Because it dissolves the tannate of iron, of which the black portion of the ink consists.

"Tannate of iron" is tannic acid combined with iron. Tannic acid is the acid of tan, or oak bark.

Q. *When* COPPER *is exposed to moist air, it is incrusted with a green coating, called* VERDIGRIS; *why is this?*

A. Because the oxygen of the moist air combines with the copper, and forms what is called a hydrate of the carbonate of the protoxide of copper.

"Protoxide" (πρωτος-oxide, the lowest or first state of oxidation): The protoxide of copper is a combination of one portion of oxygen, and one of copper. Hydrate (from the Greek word ὑδωρ, *water*) is a compound containing water; but in all hydrates, the substance forms so intimate a union with water, as to solidify it, and render it a component part. A "hydrate of the carbonate of copper," is a compound of water, carbonic acid, and copper; and "A hydrate of the carbonate of the protoxide of copper," is copper in its lowest state of oxidation, in which carbonic acid and water is so united, as to form a solid.

Q. *Why does* ZINC TARNISH *in the air?*

A. Because the oxygen of the moist air combines with the zinc, and forms an oxide of zinc.

An "oxide of zinc" is oxygen in union with zinc.

Q. *Why does* SALT *turn silver* BLACK?

A. Because it precipitates an oxide of silver on the surface of the spoon, the color of which is black.

"Marking ink" is made of soda and the nitrate of silver; the black mark being due to the oxide, precipitated on the cloth.

Q. *How can the* BLACK *stain of* SILVER, *made by salt, be* REMOVED?

A. By washing the silver in hartshorn, or common ammonia; by which means, the oxide will be re-dissolved and the blackness entirely disappear.

Q. *Why does* WAXING *cotton or thread make it* STRONGER?

A. Because it cements the loose filaments to the cord; and makes the strands of the thread more compact.

The "filaments of the cotton," are the loose fibres hanging about it. The "*strands*" are the twists or single yarns twisted into a thread. Sewing cotton contains two, three, and occasionally more than three strands.

Q. *The cromb of walking-sticks is made by* BOILING *the end of the stick, and then bending it into an arch; why is a* STICK *made* FLEXIBLE *by* BOILING?

A. Wood contains many substances soluble in hot water, as starch, sugar, gum, &c., and several other substances which are softened by it: as, therefore, several substances are dissolved, and others softened by boiling water, the stick is rendered flexible.

Cell'ular fibre and woody matter, when boiled in water, become soft and gelatinous.

Q. *Explain how* MANURE *makes* LAND FERTILE.

A. As plants extract a certain amount of *salts* from the soil, which are entirely removed at harvest, it is obvious that the soil will become gradually impoverished, unless these matters are restored; this restoration is made by *manuring* the soil.

Q. *Why is* GUANO *valuable as a* MANURE?

A. Because it contains nitrogen and ammonia, both of which are essential to plants.

Q. *What is the use of* LIME, MARL, *&c., as* MANURE?

A. 1st—They decompose vegetable substances: and

2dly—They liberate the alkalies in union with the silica of the soil.

Silica (*pronounce* Sil'-i-cah), from the Latin word Silex, *flint*—one of the most common substances on the earth—containing the following varieties—white chuckystone—violet amethysts—red quartz—yellow cairngorum—Brazil pebbles for spectacle glasses—rock crystal—chalcedony—agate—blood-stones—cornelian—flint, &c.

Q. *Why do you see the reflection of* TWO *candles, or two fires, in a looking-glass or window-pane, though there is only* ONE *candle or fire in the room?*

A. Because each surface of the looking-glass or window-pane makes a reflection.

N. B.—In order to see these two reflections, you must not stand directly before the glass, but a little on one side.

Q. *Why is the* SKY BLUE *on a fine day, and not red or orange?*

A. Because the momentum of red and orange rays (being greater than that of blue) causes them to penetrate *beyond* the clouds; but the blue rays are stopped on their passage, and reflected.

Q. *Why is it* LIGHT *when the heavens are covered with thick* CLOUDS?

A. Because the multiplied reflections of the sun in the atmosphere are sufficient to give light upon the earth, even when thick clouds are passing over the disc of the sun.

Q. *Why are putrefying* FISH LUMINOUS? *p.* 266.

A. Because the carbon of the fish, uniting with oxygen, forms carbonic acid; and the *phosphoric acid* of the fish (being thus deprived of oxygen) is converted into *phosphorus:* as soon as this is the case, the phosphorus begins to unite with the oxygen of the air, and becomes luminous.

Carbonic acid is a compound of carbon and oxygen.

Phosphoric acid is a compound of phosphorus and oxygen. If you take the oxygen away from phosphoric acid, the residue, of course, is phosphorus.

The luminousness spoken of is due to the *slow combustion* of the phosphorus, while it is uniting with the **oxygen** of the air.

Q. *Why is the* SEA *often* LUMINOUS *in summer-time? p.* 266.

A. Because the small jelly fish decay; the phosphoric acid which they contain (being deprived of oxygen) is converted into *phosphorus*, unites with the oxygen of the air, and becomes luminous.

Q. *What causes the disease commonly called the itch?*

A. It is produced by an *insect* called the "itch insect," which burrows in the skin, and is greatly encouraged by filth. Sulphur, corrosive sublimate, &c., will destroy the insect, and cure the disease.

Corrosive sublimate is made of 200 parts of mercury with 72 of chlorine. It is plain to see how the disease is contagious.

Q. *Why does the use of* SALT BEEF *produce scurvy?*

A. Because the soluble salts are removed from the beef by brine: in consequence of which, it cannot restore to the human system those salts, which are essential to preserve the blood in a healthy state.

Q. *Why is* LIME-JUICE *a perfect* CURE *for* SCURVY?

A. Because it contains the very salts,

removed from the beef by the action of brine.

Namely—alkaline phosphate—and sulphate, chloride and phosphate of lime.

"Alkaline phosphates" are such as these—phosphate of soda, phosphate of potash and phosphate of magnesia; i. e. soda, potash, or magnesia, in combination with phosphoric acid.

"Sulphate of lime," a compound of sulphuric acid and lime.

"Chloride of lime," a compound of chlorine gas and lime.

"Phosphate of lime," a compound of phosphoric acid and lime.

Q. *Why does the use of* VEGETABLES *generally* PREVENT SCURVY?

A. Because they contain the soluble salts removed from the beef by brine; which being restored by the vegetables, preserve the blood in a healthy state.

Q. *Why does* WOOD DECAY?

A. Because the oxygen of the air unites with the carbon and hydrogen of the wood, and forms carbonic acid and water.

Q. *When* WINE *is spilt on a* TABLE-CLOTH, *napkin, or handkerchief, how can the* STAIN *be* REMOVED?

A. By dipping it in a weak solution of chlorine.

Bleaching powder is only lime impregnated with chlorine.

Q. *When* WINE *is spilt on a table-cloth, &c.,*

why do persons generally cover the part immediately with SALT?

A. Because salt is a compound of chlorine and sodium; and the chlorine of the salts acts as a bleaching powder.

Q. *When* INFECTIOUS DISEASES *prevail, how can the contagious matter be removed from bed-rooms, hospitals, houses, &c.?*

A. By using a solution of chlorine, or of sulphurous acid; which will not only remove the contagious matter, but also the offensive smell of a sick room.

Q. *What is an excellent remedy against* RATS *and* MICE?

A. Sulphuretted hydrogen. All that is necessary is to introduce the beak of a retort into a rat-hole, while sulphuretted hydrogen is being given off.

It will destroy the rats and make the hole unfit for others to frequent.

Sulphuretted hydrogen is made thus. Put into a retort or glass bottle a quantity of sulphuret of iron, prepared by *heating a rod of iron red hot;* bring it in contact with a roll of sulphur—allow the sulphuret of iron formed to drop into water; pour over it a small portion of water, and then add an equal quantity of sulphuric acid; sulphuretted hydrogen will be given off most copiously.

Q. *Why does* GUNPOWDER EXPLODE?

A. Because of the instantaneous production and expansion of carbonic acid, sulphurous acid, and nitrogen.

Gunpowder consists of 76 parts of nitre, 13 charcoal and 11 sulphur.

Q. *An object in the* SHADE *is not so bright and apparent, as an object in the sun; why is it not?*

A. Because objects in the shade are seen by reflected light *reflected*, i. e. the light is *twice* reflected: and, as the rays of light are always absorbed in some measure by every substance on which they fall, therefore, some light is lost; 1st—Before the *second* reflection is made, and 2dly—In the object that *makes* the second reflection:

Part of the rays are absorbed, and part are scattered in all directions by irregular reflections; so that rarely more than *half* is reflected, even from the most polished metals.

Q. *Why are* GREEN GOOSEBERRIES, CURRANTS, *&c.*, HARD; *and* RIPE *ones* SOFT?

A. Because they contain an infinite number of little cells, with thick walls; these become thinner from day to day, as the fruit ripens, until they break; when the fruit becomes soft.

Q. *Why is* PORTER *much* DARKER *than ale or beer?*

A. Because the malt of which porter is made is dried at a higher temperature and slightly *charred.*

Small beer is a weak wort fermented, and contains 1½ per cent. of alcohol.

Ale is a stronger wort, and contains 7 per cent. of alcohol.

Porter contains 4½ per cent. of alcohol.

Brown stout contains 6½ per cent. of alcohol.

Burton ale contains 8½ per cent. of alcohol.

Q. *If* WINE *or* BEER *be imperfectly corked, why does it rapidly turn sour?*

A. Because *air* gets into the liquor; and the oxygen of the air, combining with the alcohol of the liquor, produces ace'tic acid.

1 alcohol and 4 oxygen, become 1 hydrous acetic acid and 2 water.

Q. *Why does pyroligneous acid* PRESERVE MEAT *and remove its taint?*

(Pyroligneous acid, is vinegar extracted from wood.)

A. Because it contains a small quantity of creasote, which is a great preservative of all animal substances.

Creasote, *pronounce* Cre-a-sote (from two Greek words, *κρεας*, *flesh*, and *σωζω*, *I save*), an extract from the oil of tar, and a powerful antiseptic.

Q. *Why are* HAMS *preserved by* SMOKING *them?*

A. Because the smoke of a wood fire contains creasote, which is a great preservative of all animal substances.

Q. *Is* TEA *a* NUTRITIOUS *beverage?*

A. Yes; the tea-leaf contains the largest amount of nutritive matter of any plant used as human food; though only a portion is extracted by our common method of making tea. When soda is added, the *casein* of the leaves is dissolved, and the nutritive quality of the tea is much increased.

Casein *pronounce* Cas'-e-in, from the Latin word caseus, *cheese;* because cheese consists chiefly of the casein of milk. It is found in many vegetable substances, as peas, beans, lentils, &c., and is the same as the substance called legu'mine.

Q. *How do the Tartar tribes make a most nutritious food from tea?*

A. They boil the leaves with soda, and eat them with salt and butter.

Q. SOAP *is made of oil or fat. How is it that oil and fat make water greasy, whereas* SOAP *destroys grease?*

A. Oil contains two parts; the solid part called *stearine*, and the liquid part called oleine.

Stearine of oil is not soluble in water; but when soda or potash is boiled with it, the oily principle flies off, and the stearine is converted into an oxide of potassium, which is quite soluble in water.

Stearine (*pronounce* Ste'-a-rine), from the Greek word στεαρ, *suet;* the *acid* of stearine unites with the soda or potash, and the oily principle called *glycerine* flies off.

Oxide of potassium is the fundamental part of potash; it is what chemists call a metallic oxide.

Q. *What is the difference in composition between* HARD *soap and* SOFT SOAP?

A. The *hard* soaps are made of soda, and the soft soaps are made of potash.

Q. *Why is sorrel sour?*

A. Because it contains oxalic acid.

Oxalic, from the Greek word οξαλις, sorrel. Oxalic acid is sometimes erroneously called "*salt of lemons.*"

Q. *Why are unripe* APPLES, GOOSEBERRIES, *and* RHUBARB, SOUR.

A. Because they contain malic acid.

Ma'lic, from the Latin word malum, *an apple.*

Q. *Why are tamarinds and unripe* GRAPES *sour?*

A. Because they contain tartaric acid.

Tartaric acid is the acid of tartar. Tartar is a substance deposited by wine; adhering, like a hard crust, to the sides of the casks.

Q. *Why does* TANNING *hides convert them into* LEATHER?

A. Because oak bark contains tannic acid; and, on evaporation, this acid precipitates a solution of *glue* upon the hides, which converts them into leather.

Q. *Why are citrons, limes,* LEMONS, *and unripe* ORANGES, SOUR?

A. Because they contain citric acid.

Citric, from the Latin word citrus, *a lemon* or *citron.*

Q. *Why is* VINEGAR SOUR?

A. Because it contains ace'tic acid.

Ace'tic, from the Saxon word æced, *vinegar;* whence also *acid*, i. e. *like vinegar.*

Q. *Why do old* WINE CASKS SMELL OFFENSIVELY?

A. Because wine (and whiskey) contain an acid called œnanthic acid; which unites with the alcohol of the wine, and forms a salt of an offensive smell.

This salt is called the œnanthate of ethyle, i. e. the winey acid of ether.

Œnanthate, from the Greek word οινος, wine; and "ethyle," from the two Greek words, αιθηρ-υλη, the basis or fundamental principle of ether.

Q. *When a* CANDLE *is* BLOWN OUT, *whence arises the* OFFENSIVE ODOR ?

A. The tallow distills a substance in the smoke, called acryle, which has a very offensive smell.

"Acryle" (*pronounce* ac-ryle) from two Greek words, ακρη-υλη, the basis or principle of a wick or end, i. e. the odor which issues from a wick-end, after it has been blown out.

Q. *What causes the decay of teeth ?*

A. After the enamel is worn off, the dentine or ivory of the tooth is left bare: This dentine or ivory is full of little tubes, filled with *lime ;* Now, the acids of saliva, mucus, and food, dissolve this lime, and fill the tubes with foreign matters ; after which, the tubes *dissolve* or crumble away, leave the *nerve* exposed, and the pain of tooth-ache ensues.

Dentine (from the Latin word dens, *a tooth*) is the main part of the tooth.

Q. *Why does* CREASOTE CURE TOOTH-ACHE ?

A. Creasote acts as a caustic, and burns away the mortified bone, or ulcer formed upon it, which produced the pain.

Tooth-ache arises from numerous causes, as cold, stomach, caries, or decay, &c. Creasote is a remedy for tooth-ache only when the pain arises from caries.

Ca'-ri-es is a Latin word which signifies, mortification or ulcer of the bone.

Q. *What is Indian rubber?*

A. The oil or resin from various species of ficus, oxidised in contact with air.

"Fi'-cus," the fig-tribe.

Q. *What is gutta percha?*

A. The oil or resin of a tree which grows in Malacca (Asia), called Isonandra gutta, oxidised in contact with air.

Q. *What wines contain the* MOST *spirit, and what the least?*

A. *Champagne* is one of the weakest wines, then *hock*, then *claret*, then *sherry*, and *port* is one of the most potent. Four glasses of port being nearly equal to five glasses of sherry.

Champagne	contains	about	12	per cent.	of alcohol.
Hock	"	"	13	"	"
Claret	"	"	16	"	"
Sherry	"	"	19	"	"
Port	"	"	23½	"	"

Q. *What is the origin of the term* PROOF *spirit?*

A. It is derived from the old method of testing spirit, which was thus: the spirit to be tested was poured over *gunpowder*, and ignited; if the powder exploded, the spirit was said to be *above proof;* if it did *not* explode, it was said to be *below* proof.

Q. *What do we mean, at the present day, by spirit above and below* PROOF ?

A. If we say that spirit is 10 over proof, we mean this—that 100 gallons of it will require 10 *gallons of water* to reduce the spirit *to* proof strength. So on the converse, if we say that spirit is 10 *under* proof, we mean that 10 *gallons of water* must be taken *from* the spirit to raise it to proof strength.

Proof spirit has .91833 specific gravity; the strength of spirit is now tested by an instrument called an hydrom'eter.

Q. *How is* STEEL *made from* IRON ?

A. The iron is surrounded with charcoal, and placed for six or eight days in a furnace, intensely heated; the carbon unites with the iron, and forms what is called "carburet of iron" (or steel).

Q. *What is meant by* "SHEAR STEEL ?"

A. Steel used for making *shears*, for dressing woollen cloth: Shear steel is broken and welded frequently.

Welded, i. e. hammered together again.

Q. *What is common* MARKING INK ?

A. There are generally *two* bottles—one containing a solution of the carbonate of soda: and another containing a solution of nitrate of silver. The cloth is first moistened with the carbonate of soda, dried, and then written on with a pen dipped in the nitrate of silver. An oxide of silver is thus precipitated, and leaves a black mark behind.

Q. *What is* JEWELLER'S GOLD?

A. An alloy of gold and copper with silver—this gold is liable to tarnish, but its brilliancy can easily be restored, by immersing the metal in ammonia.

Q. *How is* IRON GALVANIZED?

A. By plunging it into melted zinc; when an alloy is formed on the surface, which prevents oxidation.

Q. *What is the difference between* LEAD *and* SOLDER?

A. Solder is a mixture of lead and tin.

Fine solder is 2 tin and 1 lead.
Coarse solder is 1 tin and 4 lead.

Q. *What is* WHITE LEAD, *used for paint?*

A. It is prepared by placing sheets of lead over earthen pots, which contain weak acetic acid, and stand upon tan or dung. The lead, being corroded with the acid, unites with the carbon and oxygen evolved from the dung.

Q. *What is* PEWTER?

A. An alloy of lead (or bismuth) and tin.

In the following proportions: 1 part lead and 20 parts tin.

Q. *What is* BLOCK TIN?

A. Tin purified by heat, and run into moulds, which form blocks of great size.

Some 3 cwt., and some even more.

Q. *How is the* GREEN FIRE *of fireworks produced?*

A. By the nitrate of bary'tes, which burns with a green hue.

(Barytes, *pronounce ba-ry'-tes*) *an earth* so called from a Greek word which signifies *heavy*, (βαρυς.) It is made thus; 100 parts of nitrate of bary'tes well dried, 9 of sulphur, 7 of chlorate of potash, 2 charcoal, 4 sulphuret of antimony, all well dried and mixed in a mortar.

Q. *How is the* RED FIRE *of fireworks produced?*

A. By the *nitrate of stron'tian*, which burns with a red hue.

(Stron'tian is an earth, so called from a village in Argyleshire of the same name, where it was first discovered.) It is made thus; 100 parts of dry nitrate of stron'tian, mixed with 12 parts of chlorate of potash, 30 sulphur, 10 sulphuret of antimony, and 3 charcoal all dried and *rubbed carefully* in a mortar.

N. B.—Unless care be taken the mixture will explode.

ANTIDOTES FOR POISONS.

Q. *If a person has swallowed a* MINERAL *poison, such as* ARSENIC, *what is the best antidote?*

A. A *tea-spoonful of sulphur*—or *half a tea-spoonful of pearl-ash*—or a *wine-glass of soap-suds:*

After a little while, give a table-spoonful of antimonial wine, and plenty of warm water.

Q. *If a person has swallowed a* VEGETABLE *poison, such as* SULPHURIC ACID, AQUA-FORTIS, *or* OXALIC ACID, *what is the best antidote?*

A. Lime, chalk, pearl-ash, magnesia, carbonate of soda, or soap-suds, and a plenty of warm water; a dessert-spoonful of antimonial wine should be added, if at hand.

The chalk or lime, &c., unites with the oxalic acid, and forms oxalate of lime, which is quite innocuous.

Q. *If* LAUDANUM *has been taken, what is the best antidote?*

A. A tea-spoonful of common *mustard;* and to keep the patient walking.

Q. *If* CHLORINE *has been taken, what is the best antidote?*

A. Ammonia, which will neutralize the ill effects of chlorine.

Q. *If* IODINE *has been taken in too large a quantity, what is the best antidote?*

A. *Iron-filings* are the best antidote for an over-dose of iodine.

Q. *If a person feels faint from the fumes of* PRUSSIC ACID, *what is the best antidote?*

A. To *smell the vapors of strong ammonia,* which will soon restore consciousness.

Q. *How can* WARTS, *&c., be* REMOVED?

A. By rubbing them with common solid potash.

Q. *What is the best antidote to* VERDIGRIS?

A. Sugar, or white of egg.

Q. *What is the best antidote to* CORROSIVE SUBLIMATE?

A. White of egg, or milk; which will combine with them, and neutralize their poisonous qualities.

Q. *If a person has eaten too much* FRUIT, *what is the best antidote?*

A. Lime, chalk, pearl-ash, magnesia, carbonate of soda, or soap-suds.

Great relief is often found by eating the hard part of cheese (cut close to the rind) thickly covered with common salt; the reason is plain.

GLOSSARY.

Acetic Acid.		called	Distilled Vinegar.
Citric	"	"	Juice of Lemons.
Nitric	"	"	Aqua Fortis.
Oxalic	"	"	Salt of Lemons.
Sulphuric	"	"	Oil of Vitriol.
Sulph. of Alumina		"	Alum.
"	*Lime*	"	Plaster of Paris.
"	*Iron*	"	Green Copperas.
"	*Copper*	"	Blue Vitriol.
"	*Magnesia*	"	Epsom Salts.
"	*Soda*	"	Glauber Salts.
"	*Zinc*	"	White Vitriol.
Nitrate of Potash		"	Saltpetre.
"	*Silver*	"	Lunar Caustic.
Prussiate of Potash		"	Prussian Blue.
Tartrate of Potash		"	Rochelle Salt.
Acetate of Copper		"	Verdigris.
Muriate of Soda		"	Table Salt.
Oxide of Lead		"	Goulard.
Carb. of Ammonia		"	Smelling Salts.
"	*Lime*	"	Chalk, Marble, &c.
Sup. Acetate of Lead		"	Sugar of Lead.

SUBLIMATES are chemical preparations, the basis of which is quicksilver. In CORROSIVE SUBLIMATES, the quicksilver is *extinguished* either by vitriol, potter's clay, or some other ingredient.

SUBLIMATION is a similar process to distillation; only *solids* (such as metals) are employed, instead of *liquids*.

Thus the fine *blue* used by painters is a sublimate, and made thus:—Take 2 parts of quicksilver, 3 flower of brimstone, 8 sal ammoniac; and (having ground them) put them with the quicksilver into a glass retort, luted at the bottom: place the retort in a sand-heat; and (when the moisture is given off) you will have a splendid blue sublimate for painting.

N. B. It may be profitable to remind the pupil that when the termination "ous" is used, it implies that the substance has less oxygen than when the termination "ic" is added—thus, sulphurous acid contains less oxygen than sulphuric acid, &c

INDEX.

(For Index to Part III, see page 485.)

INDEX TO PART III.

ALWAYS HAPPY;

OR

Anecdotes

OF

FELIX AND HIS SISTER SERENA.

NEW YORK:
PUBLISHED BY JAMES MILLER,
SUCCESSOR TO C. S. FRANCIS & CO.,)
522 BROADWAY.
MDCCCLXIV.

THE CHILD'S OWN

TREASURY OF FAIRY TALES.

Embracing the best and most popular of the old fashioned Fairy Tales, and Illustrated in the highest style of Art.

FAVORITE FAIRY TALES

FOR LITTLE FOLKS.

With 70 Illustrations by THWAITES and others.

POPULAR FAIRY TALES

FOR LITTLE FOLKS.

With 60 Illustrations from original designs.

This series of Fairy Stories has for generations been listened to and read by children with a delight which all others have failed to afford them.

That these editions may be more perfect than ny others extant, they have been embellished with exquisite specimens of high Pictorial Art, from which children may derive those correct ideas that will mature into the beautiful and grand.

AMY DEANE,

And other Tales.

BY VIRGINIA F. TOWNSEND.

ILLUSTRATED.

NEW YORK:
PUBLISHED BY JAMES MILLER,
(SUCCESSOR TO C. S. FRANCIS & CO.,)
522 BROADWAY.
1864

www.ingramcontent.com/pod-product-compliance
Lightning Source LLC
LaVergne TN
LVHW020912110826
845150LV00004B/651

* 9 7 8 1 4 2 5 5 5 6 4 8 8 *